One Nation, Many Faiths

Bloomsbury Advances in Religious Studies

Series Editors: Bettina E. Schmidt, Steven Sutcliffe and Amy Allocco

Founding Editors: James Cox and Peggy Morgan

Bloomsbury Advances in Religious Studies publishes cutting-edge research in the Study of Religion/s. The series draws on anthropological, ethnographical, historical, sociological and textual methods amongst others. Topics are diverse, but each publication integrates theoretical analysis with empirical data. The series aims to refresh the interdisciplinary agenda in new evidence-based studies of 'religion'.

One Nation, Many Faiths

Religious Pluralism and National Identity in an Interfaith Organisation

Liam T. Sutherland

BLOOMSBURY ACADEMIC
LONDON • NEW YORK • OXFORD • NEW DELHI • SYDNEY

BLOOMSBURY ACADEMIC
Bloomsbury Publishing Plc
50 Bedford Square, London, WC1B 3DP, UK
1385 Broadway, New York, NY 10018, USA
29 Earlsfort Terrace, Dublin 2, Ireland

BLOOMSBURY, BLOOMSBURY ACADEMIC and the Diana logo are trademarks of
Bloomsbury Publishing Plc

First published in Great Britain 2025

A catalogue record for this book is available from the British Library.
Names: Sutherland, Liam T., author. Title: One nation, many faiths : religious pluralism and national
identity in an interfaith organisation / Liam T. Sutherland. Description: London ; New York : Bloomsbury
Academic, 2025. | Series: Bloomsbury advances in religious
studies | Revision of the author's thesis (PhD, University of Edinburgh, 2018) under the title: One
nation, many faiths: representations of religious pluralism and national identity in the Scottish interfaith
literature. | Includes bibliographical references and index. |
Summary: "Provides an in-depth, empirical and critical study of a local interfaith organization which is
still lacking in the field of Religious Studies which is then used to
reflect on the global (and 'glocalised') interfaith movement. The book examines how forms of religious
pluralism have been related to nationalism, and the Scottish data is put into dialogue with global studies
of the interfaith movement and studies of other 'national'
contexts such as the wider UK, the US and India" – Provided by publisher.
Identifiers: LCCN 2024030788 (print) | LCCN 2024030789 (ebook) |
ISBN 9781350425866 (hb) | ISBN 9781350425903 (paperback) |
ISBN 9781350425873 (epdf) | ISBN 9781350425880 (ebook)
Subjects: LCSH: Scotland–Religion. | Religious pluralism–Scotland. | Nationalism–Scotland.
Classification: LCC BL980.S63 S98 2025 (print) | LCC BL980.S63 (ebook) |
DDC 201/.509411–dc23/eng/20240909
LC record available at https://lccn.loc.gov/2024030788
LC ebook record available at https://lccn.loc.gov/2024030789

ISBN: HB: 978-1-3504-2586-6
ePDF: 978-1-3504-2587-3
eBook: 978-1-3504-2588-0

Series: Bloomsbury Advances in Religious Studies

Typeset by Newgen KnowledgeWorks Pvt. Ltd., Chennai, India

To find out more about our authors and books visit www.bloomsbury.com
and sign up for our newsletters

For my Mum, Dad and Sister and for my late Grandparents, Aunt and Uncle who'd be gey chuffed that I'd written a book.

Contents

Illustrations

Figure

Table

Acknowledgements

This book would not have been possible without the patience and persistence of my doctoral supervisors in religious studies at the University of Edinburgh, Dr Arkotong Longkumer and Dr Steven Sutcliffe. It is they who first highlighted the interfaith movement as a possible focus for my broad interests in religious pluralism and nationalism in Scotland. Huge thanks are also owed to my examiners Professor Emeritus James L. Cox (Edinburgh) and Professor Emerita Marion Bowman (Open University) who not only immeasurably improved my thesis but have long been supportive senior colleagues and dialogue partners at countless conferences.

Thanks are also owed to Professor Emerita Margaret MacKay of Scottish Studies (Edinburgh) and Professor Emeritus Julian Goodare of history (Edinburgh) for their help in understanding the Scottish historical background and for their reading suggestions. My scholarship would also not be what it is without having such a collegiate environment to work in during my doctorate and hence, thanks to: Dr Chris Cotter, Dr David Robertson, Dr Clement Grene, Dr Stephen Donoho, Dr Krittika Bhattacharjee, Dr Sammy Bishop, Ali Wood, Ylva Thorsén, Dr Anja Pogacnik, Dr Alex Corrigan, Dr Clara Soudan, Dr Áine Warren, Dr Jonathan Tuckett, Dr Tom Breimaier, Dr Ethan Quillen and Andrea Quillen. I have also greatly benefitted from countless collegiate experiences with religion scholars at the British Association for the Study of Religion (BASR) and European Association for the Study of Religion (EASR) conferences. In particular, I would like to thank Dr Paul Tremlett, Professor Emeritus Graham Harvey and Professor Carole Cusack.

I also cannot express enough gratitude to the staff of Interfaith Scotland for their aid in understanding the background and workings of their organization. Special thanks are due to the director Dr Maureen Sier and the founder Sister Isabel Smyth OBE, SND, along with John MacIntyre, former interfaith officer of the Scottish Pagan Federation who allowed me to interview them during my doctoral research. I would also like to thank Else Kek (Finance and Office Manager) and Frances Hume (National Development Officer) and once again Dr Maureen Sier for helping me with my recent queries and for giving permission to use their images. Thanks also to the team at CGL southwest for allowing me to work on this during my downtime. Lastly, I would like to convey my sincerest thanks to the team at Bloomsbury Academic, especially to Emily Wootton, Seb Claas, Lalle Pursglove and to the series editors and the anonymous reviewers.

Edinburgh, 2024

Abbreviations

ACTS	Action of Churches Together Scotland, the leading Christian ecumenical group in Scotland
BJP	Bharatiya Janata Party
BK	Brahma Kumaris
CAIR	Churches Agency for Interfaith Relations
CF	Congregational Federation
CofS	Church of Scotland, the national church of the country known as 'the Kirk' (Scots 'church')
COPFS	Crown Office and Procurator Fiscal Service (the prosecution service in Scots Law)
EIFA	Edinburgh Inter Faith Association
FCS	Free Church of Scotland
FFWPU	Family Federation for World Peace and Unification, formerly known as the Unification Church and popularly known as 'Moonies'
FM	First Minister, title used by heads of devolved governments in Scotland, Wales and Northern Ireland as equivalent to the role of prime minister (PM) at the UK level
GSF	Glasgow Sharing of Faiths.
Guide	IFS *A Guide to the Faith Communities of Scotland* (n.d.)
HMD	Holocaust Memorial Day on 27 January
HSS	Humanist Society Scotland
IC	Iona Community
IFG	Interfaith Group
IG	Interfaith Glasgow
IFM	The Interfaith Movement, the term I use for 'interfaith' as broadly cohesive but not a centralized global movement with shared origins, ethos and practices. Can be qualified by location to refer to multiple interfaith groups (IFGs) in a given national, regional or municipal framework, for example, the Scottish IFM referring to local groups as well as the national one
IFN/IFNUK	The Interfaith Network for the United Kingdom

IFS	Primarily refers to Interfaith Scotland, the national interfaith association of Scotland formerly known as the Scottish Inter Faith Council (SIFC) until 2012 Also the abbreviation for interfaith studies (see IRS)
IFYC	Inter Faith Youth Core
IRS	Interreligious studies, sometimes combined with interfaith studies as IRS/IFS
ISKCON	International Society for Krishna Consciousness, popularly known as 'Hare Krishnas'
LDS	The Church of Jesus Christ of Latter-day Saints, popularly known as the 'Mormons'
MCiS	Methodist Church in Scotland
MP	Member of Parliament, in the UK this refers to the UK Parliament (Westminster)
MSP	Member of Scottish Parliament
NHS	National Health Service
NRM	New Religious Movement
RLF	The Religious Leaders' Forum
Reflections	NHS Scotland *Reflections of Life* (2011)
RSF	Religious Society of Friends, popularly known as 'Quakers'
SAS	Salvation Army – Scotland
SCIO	Scottish Charitable Incorporated Organization
SCoJeC	Scottish Council of Jewish Communities
SEC	Scottish Episcopal Church
SIFC	Scottish Inter Faith Council, founded in 1999 and which become Interfaith Scotland (IFS) in 2012
SIFW	Scottish Interfaith Week, nationwide week of interfaith events running in late November
SNP	Scottish National Party
SPF	Scottish Pagan Federation
SRCC	Scottish Roman Catholic Church
SUA	Scottish Unitarian Association
SWGRBR	Scottish Working Group on Religion and Belief Relations
UFC	United Free Church
URCSS	United Reformed Church – Synod of Scotland
Values	SIFC *Values in Harmony* (2011)
WCC	World Council of Churches
WRP	World Religions Paradigm

Introduction: One nation, many faiths and the need for critical study of interfaith

Arguably the most important developments in the relationship between religions and contemporary societies across the globe have been responses to processes of diversification (Dawson 2016a: 1, 3). In many societies, previously strong links between political regimes, peoples, territories and dominant religions have been undermined (Howard 2021: 14). This has stimulated renegotiations, rejections and attempted revivals of those relationships. One important but understudied expression of religious diversity is the Interfaith Movement (IFM). This movement is made up a plethora of local, national and global interfaith groups (IFGs) as well as the behaviours, norms and models that they have promoted.

It must be acknowledged though that the empirical realities of religious demographics have usually been more complex than broad trends might imply. Even the most seemingly homogenous societies were rarely as homogenous as they were presented to be (Dawson 2016a: 1). Similarly, the promotion of diversity as a core characteristic and norm of contemporary societies should not be understood as produced exclusively by demographic changes themselves but also by the choices and perceptions of elite and grassroots level agents.

While they are sometimes treated as synonymous, it is not uncommon for scholars to differentiate the concepts of diversity from pluralism (Gustafson 2023: 245, Mikva 2023: 5). The former generally refers to the empirical facts rendering a society relatively heterogenous according to given categories (e.g. 'religion', 'ethnicity' etc.) and the latter referring to the ethical-political principle that this should be preserved and even championed. Due to this ambiguity, I will refer throughout this book to 'normative pluralism', that is: pluralism as a moral and political norm espoused by individuals and groups, but also projected onto societies. It entails at minimum, more than mere legal toleration but also the recognition of diverse groups, and the view that the preservation of their identities is a key foundation of civil society.

This normative pluralism is one among many ideological responses to changing political conditions and emerging systems of values which are related to (but do not perfectly mirror) demographic shifts brought about by secularization, immigration and conversion (or deconversion). Labels such as 'homogeneity' and 'diversity' are understood to be somewhat relative, political and ideological or to have an important subjective as well as objective dimension (Dawson 2016a: 18).

However, this should not be taken to imply that there are no empirical, demographic facts which can be established, nor that such claims necessarily have false or manipulative intentions. Indeed, normative pluralism as an ideological position is one to which I am, and no doubt many readers are, sympathetic, but it should be acknowledged that it is normative as much as factual. Normative pluralism reflects the agenda of some actors, and it differs from other ideological responses to global social change such as religious revivalism ('fundamentalism') (Dawson 2016a: 3), anti-immigration sentiment, religious nationalism and so forth.

Some parts of the world, such as the Indian subcontinent (see Chapter 7) and the Balkans, have long been highly religiously diverse. In the case of Scotland though, it could historically be described as almost prototypically religiously homogenous. Scotland is a small constituent country of the UK, consisting of roughly the northern third of Britain and several island chains off its western and northern coast. For all of Scotland's history as a recognizable cultural and political entity, it has been overwhelmingly Christian (Bruce 2014: 1) and since the sixteenth century has been dominated by a specific form of Protestantism: Presbyterianism and its national church – the Church of Scotland (or 'the Kirk' in Scots) (Lynch 1998: 84–5). Nonetheless, this nation has experienced a rapid shift to a highly secular politics and culture from the late twentieth century followed by generational declines in church attendance and Christian identification (Brown 1997: 174). At the same time, a majority of Scots (51.1 per cent) now self-identify as non-religious (National Records of Scotland 2024).

An important part of this process has been the re-conception of Scotland as a nation which is religiously plural, not simply defined by its Christian heritage or even a rejection of it. It is quite conceivable that secularization could have led to a more staunchly secularist identity. Part of the reason is without a doubt because of the growth of non-Christian religious communities formed by immigration and conversion from the nineteenth century and especially the mid-twentieth century on. Overall, though, non-Christian religious minorities even now only make up a small fraction of the national population – just under 4 per cent (National Records of Scotland 2024).

The likely reason is that while a growing number of Scots identify as non-religious, aside from some specific groups such as Humanists, this has not produced a robust collective identity equivalent to Christianity. This has meant that Scotland shifted from a society with formerly a hegemonic religious position to one without anything of the sort. The characteristics of normative pluralism mean that different groups can appeal to it. This facilitates an uneasy compromise between those seeking to maintain influence, those seeking to gain it and those wary of any kind of hegemony.

However, the decline of Scotland's traditional religion has not led to the decline of Scottish national identity; in fact this has become more significant (ibid.). The Church of Scotland was once considered one of the pillars of nationhood especially given that Scotland has not been an independent state for over 300 years (McCrone 1992: 37, 88–9, Lynch 1998: 97). This book is concerned with how religious pluralism relates to national identity, how it has adapted to conditions imposed by national communities and how nations have been transformed by it. It is also more specifically an effort to contribute to the study of the IFM as a distinct social movement and a form of religious activity.

To bring these disparate threads together, this book will use the national interfaith association, Interfaith Scotland (IFS) to analyse how a form of religious pluralism has been constructed and institutionalized. It will also show how IFS and their model of religious pluralism fit into, as well uphold, a certain form of ('civic-cultural') nationalism.[1] I will argue that IFGs are underutilized sources which nonetheless have exemplified and recorded wider societal changes. They offer a unique vantage point which when combined with governmental, mass media or more conventional religious sources can help to flesh out our understanding of these processes. The operation of IFS as an organization and the substantial body of literature that it produces will serve as a single case study within a single country, but, as I will show, a far from unrepresentative one (see Chapters 2, 7).

As briefly introduced earlier, the core argument of the book is that IFS reinforce a structured and limited form of religious pluralism rendered compatible with what I have termed civic-cultural nationalism. IFS construct 'religions' or 'faiths' in a fashion which favours institutionalized leadership and traditionally elite-dominated representations of religions. The category of 'religion' is implicitly understood to be *sui generis* – a unique, self-generated phenomenon, naturally distinct from other aspects of society and culture (see

Pals 1986, 1987, McCutcheon 2003, Segal 2005). It is also held to be intrinsically sacred, of deep importance to both individuals and society (Durkheim 2001).

Furthermore, the religions themselves are represented in ways which conform to what religion scholars call 'the world religions paradigm' (WRP). This means that overarching global traditions or '-isms' are stressed above denominations, sects or specific tangible communities aligned with or classified under them. The transnational and transcultural characteristics of these world religions have encouraged a reliance on scriptural texts and philosophical doctrines, either because they are common resources or because they can be easily transplanted across borders. However, historically they were often the preserve of literate, clerical elites (see Smith 1993, King 1999, Masuzawa 2005, Cox 2007, Owen 2011, Cotter and Robertson 2016).

Alongside this, IFS encourage the diverse communities that they represent to cultivate a sense of national belonging and to actively contribute to the well-being of Scotland. This includes notably 'civic' elements of nationhood: those related to the institutional, legal and political identity of nations, for example, engagement with its democratic processes (Smith 1986: 134, Özkirimli 2005: 22–8, 2010: 35–6, Sutherland 2017a: 11, 2017b: 75–7), a stake in its public sphere and investment in its constitutional future. Due to the particularities of the Scottish context – a widely shared national identity, the lack of a state and division on the question of independence; this has entailed a sense of 'ultimate sovereignty'.

This is just one example of the role of IFGs in a given national context, but it is also suggestive of broader processes which are reshaping religious pluralism and nationalism across the globe. It also highlights the growing influence of IFGs as both active contributors to these processes of change in addition to being important sources through which changes are being documented. In the next section we will explore the key characteristics of the IFM as a response to contemporary religious diversification.

What is the 'Interfaith' movement?

Interfaith is one among several related terms including interreligious, multifaith and multireligious, which are sometimes differentiated and sometimes used interchangeably (Leirvik 2014a: 3, Fahy and Bock 2018: 21, Halafoff 2013: 1, Hedges 2021: 326, Howard 2021: 7, 245, Gustafson 2023: 2). Interfaith has become a predominant term in much of the anglophone world, especially the

UK and the United States, for the more active engagement in these relations (Hedges 2021: 326). Interreligious is more common in continental Europe (Gustafson 2023: 198). Multifaith is sometimes understood to be more passive (Dawson and Prideaux 2018: 364, Gustafson 2023: 202), for example, multifaith spaces (Prideaux 2019), though it is common in Australia for activist groups (Halafoff 2013: 1). Some authors prefer interreligious because of the undeniable Protestant connotations of faith (McCarthy 2018: 10, Allocco, Claussen and Pennington 2018: 38, Mikva 2023: 22). Others argue that interfaith is preferable because it is more inclusive of non-religious commitments (Mosher 2022: 9). Interfaith may be considered more personal, while interreligious has associations with groups and institutions (Leirvik 2014a: 3, Gustafson 2023: 199). Anna Hege Grung has argued in favour of the concept of transreligious because it avoids reinforcing barriers between traditions and includes people with hybrid identities (Grung 2020).

In this book I will rely on the most popular label, interfaith, but I will not be using it in its more general sense to refer to *any* kind of relationship between different religious (or non-religious) populations. My research is concerned with the specific contemporary social movement, one with unavoidably Protestant origin. I simply opt for interfaith because it has arguably become the most popular self-designation for that movement globally, and the one used by the organization under direct empirical study: IFS, as well as its local partners.

Interfaith is a label I apply to a loose, acephalous, decentralized but relatively cohesive global movement (the IFM), along with a plethora of groups, societies, associations (IFGs) and spaces bound by its ethos. When speaking generally of this interfaith ethos or the broader development of interfaith practices I will refer to the interfaith movement (IFM). Nonetheless, the term IFM may also be used in a more qualified sense to refer to multiple IFGs, agents or spaces operating within a given territory, for example, the Scottish IFM, which includes but is not limited to IFS. This will prove useful because both the national and local groups interact with each other and with civic institutions and governments defined by the bounded territory of Scotland.

This movement, the various groups, personnel (activists and participants), spaces and events are those which deliberately and self-consciously include members of different religions (and sometimes non-religious positions). This characteristic is at the very least an important part of their self-understanding or rationale. It is usually their explicit, defining feature and selling point. The interfaith ethos is the sense that harmonious and friendly relations between religions is a fundamental end in itself.

As discussed earlier, religious diversity is a historical-sociological reality, albeit dependent on socially constructed categories, for example, religion, secular, sect and so forth. These categories and the assertions built upon them (e.g. homogeneity/diversity) are often understood in an essentialist way, as reflecting innate or fixed realities because a label has been consistently applied to them (Martin 2014: 37–8, 41–2). Broad categories such as these should not be understood as applying to a *phenomenon* but as classifications of varied and multiple *phenomena*. Nonetheless, the anti-essentialist approach taken here does not conflict with acknowledging that these labels are applied to real people, practices and products; that they have real effects and cannot be ignored. The fact that they shape self-understanding and perceptions of others, as well as relations and experiences of living in a given place and time, make them real enough. This also means that there is also a very real possibility of misrepresenting the people under study and the views, values and conceptions prevalent among them, tied as they are to tangible places, periods and communities.

Nonetheless, these categories are relative to a degree that the same demographic facts can be fed into rival ideological projects. It can be claimed of any society with multiple religious communities that it is religiously diverse, even if that society has a large majority religion and low numbers of other religions. Nonetheless, given that their society does indeed contain members of multiple religions, pluralists can entrench, institutionalize and reinforce this as a societal identity. Once established, broad societal norms and institutions are part of the experience of living in that society. In other words, if multiple groups are tangibly made visible and the idea of pluralism itself is communicated widely, then this may be more influential than the hard facts of demographic statistics. Similarly, agents can stress the existence of a religious majority, no matter how slim that majority might be, especially where they have monopolized the forms of representation, media and governance within that society.

The IFM builds on (1) the fact and perception of religious diversity and (2) the value system and political principle that such diversity is valuable (McCarthy 2007: 3). Nonetheless, the interfaith ethos goes further than this. Its proponents hold that, in addition, religious groups should closely collaborate, relate and engage in dialogue with one another because they have common interests and values as religions (Fahy and Bock 2018: 34, Howard 2021: 6–7). IFGs have also developed increasingly significant roles in relating to civil society and governments. In doing so, they offer an alternative model of the governance of religious diversity than either the establishment of a religion by the state or exclusionary forms of secularism (though, as I will discuss later, they are in a sense also secular, see Hedges 2019). As noted earlier, the growth and institutionalization of the IFM as the primary model of normative *religious* pluralism is how much it differs from models of pluralism which operate in other domains of society. The party-political systems and the market systems which operate in liberal-democratic societies are governed by the norm of competition.

Studying the interfaith movement

Despite forming a distinct, increasingly influential social movement with over a century of history and global reach, the IFM was grossly understudied until quite recently. A definitive history of it was only published a few years ago (Howard 2021). The multilayered characteristics of the IFM still require further empirical research: ethnographies of local groups (e.g. McCarthy 2007, Swamy 2016, Dawson and Prideaux 2018), studies of interfaith media (e.g. Sutherland 2017b, 2018b) and comparative analyses (e.g. Fahy and Bock 2018, Halafoff 2013). The relationship between IFGs and areas outside of the strictly or traditionally 'religious' has been initiated but is still ripe for critical study. These areas and issues include gender[2] (e.g. King 1998, Womack 2020, Grung 2022, Vernon-Yorke 2022), race/ethnicity[3] (e.g. Fahy and Bock 2018: 61, McCarthy 2007: 94–5, 108, Fletcher 2018, Patel 2018, Kujawa-Holbrock 2022, Levine 2022), sexuality (e.g. Womack 2018: 24, Mikva 2023: 39), class[4] (e.g. Swamy 2016, Fahy and Bock 2018: 28–30, Howard 2021: 250) and of course the topic of this monography: nationality (e.g. Leirvik 2005, 2014b, McCarthy 2007, Halafoff 2016, Patel 2018, Widiyanto 2020, Mombo and Iminza 2022).

The aim of this book is to contribute to the critical study of interfaith activism in line with the critical approaches within religious studies (RS) and the wider social sciences. This includes identifying and problematizing prevalent categories and assumptions, reflecting on their ideological role, articulating the power relations underlying naturalized social relations (see Asad 1993, Smith 1982, 1993, Fitzgerald 1997, 2000, McCutcheon 2001, 2003, Lincoln 1996, Martin 2014). Critical studies of IFGs should pose questions such as: who defines what interfaith is or who is included? How does it relate to wider social processes? Who sets the agenda for dialogue? How are the boundaries around acceptable faiths and around faith policed? There are clearly examples of existing scholarship along these lines, but compared to the comprehensive, top-to-bottom scholarship on many religions or social movements, there is much work to be done.

Interfaith dialogue has received quite a bit more attention within theology (see Cohn-Sherbock 2001) but only begun to receive attention relatively recently within RS. Some articles on interfaith dialogue were published in the 1990s (see Morgan 1995, Dunbar 1998, King 1998) and in the mid-2000s a couple of analyses were made of the IFM's growth, characteristics and increasing influence (Brodeour 2005), though as the title one of these studies acknowledged, this was 'an incomplete assessment' (Pederson 2004). In 2007 Kate McCarthy published an exhaustive ethnographic and comparative study of American IFGs: *Interfaith Encounters in America* (see Chapter 7), which highlights the complex internal dilemmas and influences from a sympathetic and critical perspective (McCarthy 2007). Though some of the earliest university-level courses and qualifications were established in the early 2000s in California, England, Indonesia and Norway (Leirvik 2014a: 7), this subject area began to blossom in the 2010s.

In 2013[5] Anna Halafoff published one of the first (likely the first) comparative, global study of the interfaith (or multifaith) movement based on interviews with fifty-six leading interfaith activists: *The Multifaith Movement: Global Risks and Cosmopolitan Solutions* (2013: 5). It provided an invaluable history of the development of the IFM and its shifting priorities and strategies from the late nineteenth to early twenty-first centuries (see Chapter 2). However, it is also a deeply polemical text and in my estimation fails to engage with all but the most surface-level critiques of the movement's assumptions and practices. She did invite her interviewees to reflect on challenges and cited some critics (Halafoff 2013: 27–8). She also acknowledged critiques of the IFM's unrepresentativeness (2013: 102–3) as well as tensions between including conservative practitioners and adherence to progressive values (2013: 121–4, 166), but this left much to be desired. She framed the IFM in terms of highly questionable, neat and moralistic binary between 'cosmopolitans' and 'anti-cosmopolitan' forces (2013: 30, 56–7, 75). This latter category lumps together all manner of fundamentalists, nationalists and even 'free market fundamentalists' (2013: 131) into a single category.

The new field known as interreligious studies or interfaith studies (both names often represented through a slash as IRS/IFS)[6] has begun to flower in the past decade. This is a nascent, rapidly solidifying field but one whose boundaries and relationships to RS, theology and the IFM are hotly debated (see McCarthy 2018, 2020, Patel, Peace and Silverman 2018, Moyaert 2020, Pennington 2022: 17–18). To an external observer it can appear either to be an independent, primarily social scientific field or little more than the academic wing of the IFM depending on what one is exposed to.

One of its foundational texts was *Interreligious Studies: A Relational Approach to Religion* (2014a) by Norwegian theologian Oddbjørn Leirvik. This introduced IRS as a field concerned with the relationships, encounters and spaces between different religious and non-religious positions, a topic which he argued was indebted to both theology and RS (2014a: 9–10). Though Leirvik's book analyses several interfaith initiatives in Norway (2014a: 50–1, see also Leirvik 2005, 2014b), the potential scope of his vision for IRS is indeed much larger.

At the same time, leading interfaith activists such as Eboo Patel, founder of the Chicago-based Inter Faith Youth Core (now Interfaith America), had been cultivating practitioner-based scholarship (see Patel 2018, Patel, Peace and Silverman 2018). Another early promoter of the new field of IRS was Paul Hedges (2012, 2014), who had previously published works on interreligious relations (e.g. 2010). The field has now developed its teaching and research, though primarily in the United States and Europe. It is represented by the European Society for Intercultural Theology (ESITIS) and by the IRS/IFS subunit at the American Academy of Religion (AAR) launched in San Diego in 2014 (Patel, Peace and Silverman 2018: xi, Howard 2021: 241, Mosher 2022: 7, Pennington 2022: 16, Mikva 2023: 21). An independent academic body: the Association for Interreligious/Interfaith Studies was founded in Boston in 2017 (Patel, Peace and Silverman 2018: xiv, Peace 2022: 475). The *Journal of Inter-Religious Dialogue* established in 2009 was renamed to *Journal of Interreligious Studies* in 2014 is its flagship journal (Patel, Peace and Silverman 2018: xv, Pennington 2022: 15–16).

I would argue that one of the most important contributions to the study of the IFM from outside this emerging field was Muthuraj Swamy's *The Problem with Interreligious Dialogue*, a critical ethnography of IFGs in religiously diverse communities in India (see Chapter 7). This study highlights the disconnect between ordinary multireligious populations and the elite, scriptural and prescriptive approach of interfaith activists. It also questions the effectiveness of interfaith dialogue as the best means of quelling religious conflict (Swamy 2016)[7]. Andrew Dawson published a significant study of the Inter Faith Network for the United Kingdom (IFNUK) and its changing relationship with successive governments (Dawson 2016b). Jonathan Fahy and Jan-Jonathan Bock's comparative study of IFGs in London, Doha and Delhi also offered a thorough critical analysis of the core assumptions, operations and characteristics of the IFM (see Chapters 2, 7) (Fahy and Bock 2018).

Several important edited volumes and introductory texts have been published subsequently, which have helped to consolidate the field of IRS/IFS, identify common concerns and also pinpoint its divergent tendencies more clearly. This includes edited volumes such as Patel, Peace and Silverman's *Interreligious/ Interfaith Studies: Defining a New Field* (2018), Hans Gustafson's *Interreligious Studies: Dispatches from an Emerging Field* (2020) and Lucinda Mosher's *Georgetown Companion to Interreligious Studies* (2022). Paul Hedges devoted a chapter of his *Understanding Religion* (2021) to surveying key themes in the study of the IFM, the field of IRS/IFS and its relationship to the broader study of religion. In 2023, two expansive and comprehensive introductions to IRS/ IFS were published: Hans Gustafson's *Everyday Wisdom: Interreligious Studies in a Pluralistic World* (2023) and Rachel S. Mikva's *Interreligious Studies: An Introduction* (2023).

It is absolutely acknowledged that IRS/IFS scholars have increasingly exhibited a capacity to understand and utilize critical scholarship from RS as well as develop their own distinctive critiques. IRS scholars have, for example, recognized the construction of religion categories (Leirvik 2014a: 1) and one of the core analytical concerns of this book – the limitations of the WRP (Mosher 2022: 4, Gustafson 2023: 9–12, Mikva 2023: 7, 19–20). They have even argued that their field's focus on interreligious relationships renders it an alternative *to* the WRP (Minister 2018, Pennington 2022: 20). Many IRS scholars have highlighted the importance of hybridity and multiple forms of belonging (Leirvik 2014a: 53, Mikva 2023: 24–5), disavowed essentialism (Gustafson 2023: 53), remained conscious of issues of representation (Leirvik 2014a: 2), utilized the lived religions approach (Gustafson 2020b, 2023) and even critiqued the assumptions of interfaith dialogue (Hulsether 2018 cited in McCarthy 2020: 173).

Nevertheless, I do not locate my own work within this subfield, and I assert that the IFM should also be studied independently of it, within the broader field of RS and the wider social sciences. This is not to dismiss the utility of IRS/IFS, but I regard it as insufficient for my purposes, just as my approach would be insufficient for many of their aims. There are three key, interlinked reasons why I do not place my work in IRS/IFS: (1) the wide scope of its research focus and (2), its ambivalent relationship to the IFM as well as (3), its unease with the core methodological commitments of the non-confessional, critical study of religion.

While assertions are made about the differences between IRS and IFS (Gustafson 2020a: 3, 2023: 171–2, Leirvik 2020: 18–19, Peace 2022: 473, Pennington 2022: 19), even those are frequently from scholars attempting to reconcile them rather than support one over the other (e.g. Gustafson 2023: 128, 176) and they are still often used interchangeably (Gustafson 2020a: 2, Mosher 2022: 9–10). They appear more like poles of a spectrum rather than two rival approaches. Interreligious Studies (IRS) is depicted as the more RS-orientated of the two, concerned with the critical and empirical study of relations between people of different religions, worldviews or 'lifestances' (Mikva 2023: 28). IFS, on the other hand, is equated with a more confessional or committed stance, close identification with the IFM, the promotion and improvement of interfaith dialogue and training of interfaith leaders (e.g. Patel, Peace and Silverman 2018: xii).

While my approach appears to be aligned with IRS as described here, there are important differences. IRS scholars identify their subject as relations or spaces between religious positions and groups, or all forms of 'religious manyness' (Mosher 2022: 3), which is an exceptionally wide subject matter. Rachel S. Mikva defines the field thus:

> The field of Interreligious Studies (IRS) entails critical analysis of the dynamic encounters – historical and contemporary, intentional and unintentional, embodied and imagined, congenial and conflictual – of individuals and communities who orientate around religion differently. (Mikva 2023: 5–6)

My intention is to focus more clearly on IFGs and the wider movement (the IFM); their practices, norms and relationships with the societies in which they operate. The advantage of this is that the IFM is a distinct historic movement with a specific origin in the nineteenth century and a traceable course of development. It also carries a shared ethos, a set of practices and even shared symbols. The subject matter is locatable within history and is the product of particular social, cultural and (geo)political conditions rather than potentially timeless and universal.

In practice, IRS is far less easy to separate from the IFM than the above-mentioned distinction would suggest, as some scholars admit (Leirvik 2014a: 139, Gustafson 2023: 6). This highlights my second objection: that the relationship between IRS and the IFM is ambivalent at best. It is notable that both Leirvik and Hedges favour the nomenclature IRS and yet argue that it blurs the line between RS and theology as well as interfaith dialogue (Hedges 2014, Leirvik 2014a: 9–10). Though it must be acknowledged that some IRS scholars have called for their field to distance itself from the IFM (see McCarthy 2018: 10–11, Allocco, Claussen and Pennington 2018: 36–7). It is commonly asserted that interfaith activists can also act as conscientious, critical observers and analysts (e.g. Hedges 2021: 326–7, Mosher 2022: 9), which is not disputed in principle or practice. However, this does not address the broader issue that this area has ironically not been more widely opened up to scholars without an interest or background in interfaith dialogue.

Hedges rightly highlights that those involved with the IFM may be less prone to stereotype it than casual observers. However, a division remains between interfaith scholars and wider scholarship, and thus potential for fresh perspectives. The antidote to non-interfaith scholars treating the IFM in a stereotyped fashion is to encourage wider study of the movement among non-interfaith scholars. This requires abandoning any insistence on a common normative agenda, at least as a requirement for all approaches to this subject matter.

Many critiques within this field have the aim of improving interfaith according to predetermined norms, the pursuit of agreed ends by highlighting where practice has fallen short of ideals, or providing a better rationale for the movement (e.g. Halafoff 2013: 27–8, Gustafson 2023: 189–90). Hans Gustafson evocatively compares the relationship between IRS and the IFM as between the characters Micky and Rocky in the 1976 film *Rocky* – between a coach and a boxer (2022, 2023: 176).

As Bruce Lincoln has argued, for scholarship on religion to be historical or social scientific the actors under study cannot *dictate* the parameters and terms through which they are studied and analysed (1996: 10, see also Wiebe 1999: 7). Though, understanding and respecting actors' perspectives is vital too of course, without which there could be no empirical work in the humanities or social sciences. This highlights my third objection to placing my own work within IRS, because there is an apparent unease and even hostility to the methodological restrictions of the non-confessional, critical study of religion.

Even Kate McCarthy, who explicitly called for IRS to place itself within RS, acknowledged that IRS was distinguished by its particular normative agenda (2018: 2–3, 12). She further argues that IRS could promote its normative aims in an RS context, as long as they are framed as civic, for example, promoting tolerance and freedom of religion (2018: 13–14). The problem is that this would seem neither to satisfy the engaged aims of many IRS/IFS scholars nor assuage the concerns of scholars within critical RS (who might take issue with being asked to promote certain values just because they are civic rather than religious).

IRS/IFS scholars often express scepticism about the possibility of non-confessional, outsider'[8] studies of religion (e.g. Moyaert 2020: 38–9, Mosher 2022: 9) and these are not baseless, but they are short-sighted in my view. The basis of this critique of the non-confessional, outsider approach is based on a truism of contemporary scholarship: there is no such thing as *pure* neutrality or objectivity and no one is free from bias; everyone is situated in their social environment (Gustafson 2023: 32, Moyaert 2020: 38–9, Mosher 2022: 9–10).

It does not follow from this that one cannot strive to study religion in a non-confessional, historical and social scientific sense, independent of specific normative agendas. It is rather telling that this truism is often simply repeated without the need for much further discussion, and without quotations of RS scholars demonstrating such blind faith (e.g. Moyaert 2020 38–9, Mosher 2022: 9).

Leirvik presents a more sophisticated version of this argument. Instead of insisting that such a stance is impossible *per se*, he argued merely that it was not possible with regard to this field specifically. This is because according to his understanding of IRS, its subject matter is the relations and spaces between religious and secular identities, worldviews and so forth. It is impossible to be outside of the field of study defined in this way (Leirvik 2014a: 21, 144), which is undeniably true. The problem is that while this might appear profound, it is tantamount to pointing out that all human beings live in societies and are indeed influenced or impacted by religious (and secular) traditions. None of this has rendered the dispassionate study of any of these subjects impossible, so it is unclear why it would be the case with interreligious relations. It also highlights the problem with this expansive definition of the subject under study as any relations or spaces between people with different religious identifications or worldviews rather than participation in a specific social movement.

To claim any scholarly approach as all-inclusive is questionable. IRS/IFS scholars have arguably offered a hyper-reformed version of the WRP. Their efforts to include as many secular, alternative spiritual or hybrid lifestances as possible still assume that the human population could hypothetically all be sheltered under a big enough tent, as long as each was granted a space appropriate to their lifestance. Furthermore, in parallel with the history of the study of specific religions, it can be misleading to focus on the rarefied and sometimes radical perspectives and priorities of a group's intelligentsia. While the proximity of IRS scholars to the IFM is a concern for my approach, so ironically is the limited degree to which they represent it.

Lastly, the implicit assumption of these critiques seems to be that to write from a position of commitment to a religion or specifically non-religious (usually Humanist) stance is authentic while to write from a non-confessional stance is inauthentic. It appears to rest on the notion that the core of one's personhood is one's religious, spiritual or non-religious identities (perhaps also political ideologies, see Swidler 2016 cited in Gustafson 2023: 203). Given the range of positions that IRS attempts to include or relate to though, why is a sincere commitment to the non-confessional social scientific study of religion so difficult to understand? It is itself a tradition with distinct practices, goals and outlooks. IRS/IFS writers are often quite willing to allow theologians to maintain their professional identities, methods and concerns (Moyaert 2020: 36–7, 40), so why not RS scholars?

Lastly, it should be remembered that RS, like other sciences, do in fact have norms: to study religions, empirically and critically as human phenomena; to be transparent and to abide by professional ethics related to researching human subjects and so forth. These are not exciting, world-changing norms of course. They are related to the situational activities of a specific profession, which is perhaps why they are rarely commented on by outsiders, or all that frequently by insiders within that tradition.

Ultimately, my call for more studies within RS should not be understood as an attack on IRS/IFS because I do not hold it to my standards. I do not view my role as having any business in trying to police other disciplines let alone the people under study. In fact, if I am attempting to cajole anyone it is scholars in RS who adhere to the same broad methodological commitments as myself. It is the *lack* of attention paid to interfaith phenomena within these circles which is the problem! Scholars such as myself, who are not interfaith activists, have and will continue to benefit from the input of interfaith scholars. However, it is only by allowing space for those interested in studying IFGs first and foremost as groups of people, as one would study any religious community or social movement without imposing unnecessary normative barriers, that they will have scholarship from a different perspective to draw on.

One reason that further scholarship will be useful is that the IFM has attained a much wider social and political influence than is immediately obvious. The presence of multiple religious representatives at civic events or meetings between religious leaders may seem incidental. It is easy to interpret them as the brief intersection of largely separate milieu, but this is only the tip of the iceberg and it has effects beyond specifically interfaith circles, both reflecting and effecting religious change.

The IFM has begun to shape the understanding and representation of religions in many contemporary societies, having permeated widely within them. Interfaith events have become a routine part of the social engagements of religious, civic and political leaders but also the one way in which many communities relate to wider society. It may be a niche activity for many, but one that interested persons from different walks of life can gain access to with relative ease. In countries such as Scotland, there are many IFGs with ties to religions, universities, hospitals, local governments and schools. Interfaith activities have become part of everyday lived reality, often unnoticed, as links at the bottom of websites, leaflets or posters on campuses, places of worship or community centres.

The study of interfaith along these lines could become a vital subfield of RS following the path of subfields such as the study of new religious movements (NRM) (e.g. Barker 1989) or the study of non-religion (see Chapter 5). It should be rendered into something that non-specialists are made aware of, can utilize but cannot ignore. Like all specialisms, it is too important to be left only to specialists.

Interfaith Scotland: History, role and composition

I have only touched on the case study central to the book so far. It will be necessary to provide a robust profile of IFS, its foundations, development, membership and place in Scottish society. During my doctoral research, I conducted an informal interview with its director – Dr Maureen Sier (Dr Maureen Sier personal communication, 18 November 2015), a formal interview with the IFS' founder, Sister Isabel Smyth OBE, SND (Sister Isabel Smyth personal communication, 20 June 2016) and a correspondence interview with the former interfaith officer of the Scottish Pagan Federation (SPF) John McIntyre (John McIntyre personal communication, 30 October 2016). I also corresponded with Dr Sier again recently (Dr Maureen Sier personal communication, 19 May 2024) and will draw on these discussions periodically throughout the book along with IFS' now voluminous literature.

Interfaith Scotland was founded in 1999 under the name Scottish Inter Faith Council (SIFC), which it held until 2012 when it became a Scottish Charitable Incorporated Organisation (SCIO). It was established with support from the Inter Faith Network of the United Kingdom (IFNUK) by Sister Isabel Smyth OBE SND, a Roman Catholic nun and former RE teacher who had studied RS under Ninian Smart at Lancaster University. SIFC was launched at St Mungo's Museum of Religious Life and Art in Glasgow by the Presiding Officer[9] of the Scottish Parliament, Trisha Goddard MSP (IFNUK 2007: 21, IFS Autumn 2019: 1, IFS n.d.: 2, Sister Isabel Smyth personal communication, 20 June 2016).

It is headed by a director, Dr Maureen Sier, and operates with a small staff from an office in Glasgow.[10] The actual membership of IFS consists entirely of organizations not of individuals, though most of their events are open to the public, and individuals can become 'Friends' of IFS with a small subscription.[11]

All constituent organizations must have a constitution and charitable status (Dr Maureen Sier personal communication, 18 November 2015).

The governing board of IFS is made up of representatives of the Bahá'í Faith, Buddhism, Christianity, Hinduism, Islam, Judaism and Sikhism along with representatives of women of faith, a co-optee, a youth strategy expert and an interfaith expert. The chair of the board is elected among the representatives and the interim chair is currently the Bahá'í representative (Rita Docherty) and a treasurer, currently the Sikh representative (Inderjit Singh). Each board representative is approved by all member-groups classed as part of that tradition[12] (Dr Maureen Sier personal communication, 18 November 2015).

Formerly, the seven religious traditions represented on the board were referred to as 'founding' members with full membership, while other members of the organization were classed as 'associate' members (IFS October 2014–15: 31, ACTS n.d.: 16). This distinction was abolished at their AGM in 2022, and all member-groups are simply classified as full members. Members are now distinguished on equal terms into three categories: 'Abrahamic faiths', 'Dharmic faiths' and 'Other faiths and spiritual traditions' (Dr Maureen Sier personal communication, 19 May 2024).

Associate membership consisted primarily of the other faiths and spiritual traditions such as the Scottish Pagan Federation (SPF), the Druid Network, the Family Federation for World Peace and Unification (FFWPU), the Scottish Unitarian Association (SUA) but also those classed as Abrahamic: the Church of Latter-day Saints (LDS) and as Dharmic: the Brahma Kumaris groups of Edinburgh and Glasgow, respectively.[13] While this two-tier division of the membership is now historic rather than current, it is of considerable interest to this book because it was in place for a formative decade for the organization: from when the SIFC became IFS in 2012 until 2022. It was a solution to several issues with which the SIFC had struggled to resolve: the representation of Christians and of more controversial religions, especially Paganism.

The system introduced in 2012 also further differentiated the representation of world religions as whole traditions from the rank and file member organizations. Until then, because there was a fear of Christian domination, including among Christian interfaith activists; only the Church of Scotland and the Scottish Roman Catholic Church were represented individually. Smaller churches were represented by the ecumenical body Action of Churches Together Scotland (ACTS) (ACTS n.d.: 16). While the two-tier system was abolished in 2022, the distinction between member-organizations and board representation for the founding traditions has continued. The representative system has allowed multiple Christian groups to become members of IFS without overwhelming the representatives of minority religions, the representation of which was a large part of the IFS rationale. The possibility of dialogue with other religions was likely what attracted many Christians to it in the first place.

The issue which motivated the adoption of the division between founding and associate members was the internal tensions within the SIFC over the application for membership of the Scottish Pagan Federation (SPF). While many existing members, especially Hindus and Buddhists supported SPF's application, Catholic and Church of Scotland representatives objected and even threatened to withdraw. Following a protracted period of negotiation, SPF were finally accorded 'observer' status until the adoption of the new system under which they became associate members (ACTS n.d.: 16, John McIntyre personal communication, 30 October 2016). SPF are now full members, classified under the rubric 'other religious and spiritual traditions' and as will become evident, have become much more accepted over time within the Scottish IFM. Nonetheless, the fact that the representative system is still in place means that groups recognized as one of the founding seven world religious traditions continue to possess a more advantageous or privileged position.

IFS can rightly claim to represent almost all religious communities in the country and is the sole national interfaith body,[14] one which has developed a close relationship with the devolved national government. It represents and incorporates many major local IFGs, but it should be noted that they are all independent of it (Dr Maureen Sier personal communication, 18 November 2015), just as IFS is a member of IFNUK and autonomously from it in turn.[15] Those local IFGs and many religious groups which are not members of IFS have often developed friendly informal relations with them[16] and are represented through their literature and events. However, IFS plays a significant role in directing and coordinating the Scottish interfaith scene based on its national remit. On a more practical level, it holds annual networking sessions for local IFGs and offers training courses for their staff and activists (IFS 2016: 4).

Outside of the interfaith sphere, IFS relate to the institutions of civil society, government and the population at large in various ways. They run events for young people across the country: arranging visits to schools and youth conferences (SIFC August 2009: 8, IFS September 2012: 14). In April 2022, they established a National Interfaith Youth Advisory Board, which has since been appointed and met on several occasions (IFS Spring 2023: 3). IFS have played a consultative role for the Scottish National Health Service (NHS) (e.g. SIFC August 2011: 3), the Crown Office Procurator Fiscal Service (COPFS)[17] (SIFC

February 2011: 11), as well as local governments. One of the ways in which they have worked directly with the Scottish Government is by chairing and forming most of the members of the Scottish Working Group on Religion and Belief Relations at the Scottish Parliament (SWGRBR) since 2008 (The Scottish Government 2011: 5). They have also acted as the secretariat for the Scottish Parliament's Cross-Party Group on Freedom of Religion and Belief for six years and report regularly on their proceedings (IFS Autumn 2022: 5).

In addition, they host a plethora of other events, some specifically for their members but most open to the public. IFS performs a vital role for the Scottish IFM in coordinating Scottish Inter Faith Week (SIFW) in late November (in 2023 from 12 to 19) which they founded in 2004.[18] SIFW includes a range of national and local events happening across Scotland, which can be highly varied but based around an annual theme. IFS has proudly reported that SIFW has been an inspiration to similar interfaith weeks in England and Wales (SIFC March 2010: 2). For a long time SIFW was the week of St Andrew's Day on 30 November, a celebration of the country's patron saint but treated as a kind of national day. It is now held earlier in the month, but it is notable that a specific choice was made earlier in the organization's history to maintain the connection to St Andrew's Day and not to shift the dates to coincide with the UN's Interfaith Harmony Week (SIFC February 2011: 9).

The Scottish Government appointed IFS with the responsibility of organizing Holocaust Memorial Day (HMD) in Scotland on 27 January since 2012 until 2022, when it was passed to the Edinburgh Inter Faith Association (EIFA) (IFS Spring 2014: 17, IFS Spring 2022: 18). HMD commemorates the victims of the Holocaust perpetrated by the Nazi regime during the Second World War: European Jews, Roma, homosexuals and the disabled. It also recognizes victims of other genocides, such as the Armenian genocide (1915) in the Ottoman Empire, the 'killing fields' massacres committed by the Khmer Rouge in Cambodia in the 1970s, along with Rwandan, Bosnian and Darfur genocides in the 1990s and 2000s; most recently this included representation of ISIS' genocide against the Yezidis in Iraq (IFS Spring 2019). These events are similarly coordinated at a national and local level, involving IFGs across Scotland. They are devised with the public in mind and usually work closely with schools to include pupils. Events include public lectures, discussions, artistic commemorations, musical concerts and ceremonies. They always invite survivors of these genocides to participate as guests of honour (e.g. IFS Spring 2015: 22). HMD commemorations underscore the importance of normative pluralism, tolerance, harmonious relations and mutual understanding between different communities, as well as the need for governments to respect diversity.

The only other group that can be classed as a national interfaith organization in Scotland is the Religious Leaders Forum (RLF). They are technically distinct from IFS: its board includes leaders from religions which are not formally part of IFS, and they have distinct foundations, but IFS acts as their secretariat (Dr Maureen Sier personal communication, 18 November 2015). The RLF was founded in 2002 by the then leaders of the three major churches in Scotland: the Rt Revd. Finlay MacDonald – moderator of the Church of Scotland, Cardinal Keith O' Brien – head of the Scottish Roman Catholic Church and the Most Revd. Bruce Cameron – primus of the Scottish Episcopal Church. It was established as a response to the terrorist attacks of 11 September 2001 as a means of maintaining regular contact and cordial relations between leadership from different religious communities in Scotland (ACTS n.d.: 17–19).

The other main activity of IFS is producing their substantial body of literature. This includes their regular newsletter published several times a year (which has varied throughout its development) since January 2003 (IFS Autumn 2023: 2), their website, YouTube channel[19] and other social media accounts. They also produce several documents intended to educate the Scottish public about religions and interfaith, or to offer inspiration. They also produced a parliamentary newsletter to reflect on Scottish legislation relevant to religious communities in their early days, which was revived in 2015 along with the role of Parliamentary Officer (IFS 2016: 5). Both their educational documents[20] and newsletter[21] are made available through their website.

They are ultimately intended for public consumption, but they are likely aware that this will have limited circulation. The newsletter is an invaluable source for several reasons. Firstly, because of the sheer volume of content they have produced, the newsletter is currently on its forty-second issue at the time of writing, covering their twenty-five years of operation. I have been unable to access the earliest issues (1–14) which are not on their website, and it was explained that their whereabouts were uncertain. It was also explained that their earlier newsletters were quite sparse (Dr Maureen Sier personal communication, 18 November 2015) but as any perusal of their issues since 2012 will show, they have become substantial documents with a wealth of content and professional production.

The second reason that their newsletter is such an invaluable source is that it offers a snapshot of interfaith and civic events taking place nationwide (see Figure 1.1). This includes IFS' own events of course but also those organized by local groups, government or religious communities which have an interfaith dimension. It provides a rich seam of data, but the very national and interfaith framing imposed by inclusion in its pages is highly significant. The issues always include editorials of some form as well as reportage and commentary on news relevant to the organization or its constituents. It does sometimes include content from outwith Scotland, but this is usually because IFS or Scottish interfaith activists are involved in some way or it speaks clearly to the themes they are addressing. The recording and photography of the events are provided by activists on the ground, who send them to IFS' staff for inclusion (Dr Maureen Sier personal communication, 18 November 2015). It is this relative informality which means that they often include content from Scottish groups who are not members.

The texts which I refer to as 'educational documents', include those which provide knowledge about different religious traditions and compare them according to their values, beliefs, interests and practices. These sources demonstrate the ways in which IFS construct 'religion', just as the newsletter exemplifies their construction of 'Scotland' and 'interfaith'. While I have identified specific patterns within their content, there is little evidence of any marked pressure to conform to these models, let alone censorship. A partial exception to this was SPF, but this relates largely to their quest for membership, not their contributions to IFS' content.[22] These texts have all been written with contributions and consent from these communities.

These documents are sources for the wider inculcation and circulation of interfaith norms in Scottish society and more widely. Implicitly, they further reinforce the harmonious relationship between a structured and limited pluralism with a civic-cultural nationalism, as I will show. All of this reflects wider, *a long durée* influences operating nationally and globally. One of these is the emphasis on the features identified with the WRP which render religions into more closely comparable entities. This is achieved through the choice to select or stress certain characteristics (e.g. doctrines, texts), to adopt similar categories for identification, reproduce compatible quotations and to organize these texts by world religions (as opposed to specific congregations or denominations).

One such document is a slim pamphlet: *A Guide to the Faith Communities of Scotland* (n.d.), which was first produced early in the organization's history but was revised in 2014 in light of changes within IFS and the availability of information from the 2011 census (IFS Spring 2015: 16). The *Guide* includes sections on each of the seven founding traditions: Bahá'í, Buddhism, Christianity, Hinduism, Islam, Judaism and Sikhism along with sections on Paganism, Jainism

Figure 1.1 Front page of Interfaith Scotland *Newsletter Spring 2014* (2014) Interfaith Scotland: Glasgow. Image produced by Interfaith Scotland.

and the Brahma Kumari World Spiritual University. Each tradition is allotted two pages, and comparisons are made through the following categories: basic beliefs, customs and practices, places of worship, main festivals, food and diet and community concerns. The one exception is for the Brahma Kumari section, which is a general description of their institution, the World Spiritual University (IFS n.d.: 22–3). The most notable thing about this document is that in spite of its title, it offers no information about specific communities living in Scotland aside from a discussion of the census results (IFS n.d.: 1–2). Each world religion is described as a singular, undifferentiated phenomenon without alluding to their internal diversity or the broader cultural contexts in which they are found. For example, the fact that Jews are as much an ethnicity as a religion is never alluded to (IFS n.d.: 14–15), and India is not mentioned at all in relation to Hinduism (IFS n.d.: 10–11).

Another significant text is by then Scottish Inter Faith Council (SIFC) *Values in Harmony* (2011), which is much more expansive and includes a foreword by a Scottish Government minister – Fergus Ewing MSP, an introduction and conclusion alongside sections for each tradition. *Values* makes use of authoritative textual sources from each to demonstrate their conformity to a common system of values defined by the 'golden rule': to treat others as one desires to be treated. This text includes more religions but also provides a section for a non-religious tradition as well: Secular-Humanism (SIFC 2011: 48). The religions represented in this document include the seven founding religions alongside Paganism, Jainism and the Church of LDS. The composition of this document made use of focus groups from each community which were carefully balanced to ensure more equitable representation of women and younger people under thirty. Care was taken to avoid the use of potentially offensive quotations (SIFC 2011: 6), but it is evident that each community was given a fair amount of leeway to represent their tradition as they deemed appropriate. For example, the Hindu and Jain sections include representations of swastikas which are a longstanding part of their devotional art (SIFC 2011: 43, 59).

This text does provide contact details for specific religious organizations and congregations based in Scotland. However, the main thrust of its approach is to focus on these traditions as intellectual, ethical lineages founded upon authoritative texts. Each section includes an introduction describing the tradition but is largely devoted to the relevant quotations along with photography or art. Fergus Ewing's foreword emphasizes the need for all communities to contribute to society, and while it lauds diversity, it explicitly critiques the concept of 'mosaic multiculturalism': the idea that each community should lead entirely parallel lives isolated from others and wider society (SIFC 2011: 4).

IFS also collaborated with the Scottish NHS to produce documents aimed at hospital patients and staff. *Reflections on Life* (2011) is over 200 pages long and involves thirteen different religious and 'Belief'[23] (non-religious) groups. This includes the seven recognized world religions, LDS, Brahma Kumaris, Paganism, Humanists but also a section for 'Believers not Belongers': a phrase introduced by the sociologist Grace Davie to describe those who believe in some religious concepts, such as God or life after death, but do not belong to a specific religious group (1994). *Reflections* is arranged by theme rather by tradition and includes inspirational quotations from each tradition on themes such as 'peace', 'healing', 'death and bereavement' and so forth. This text emphasizes words of comfort and wisdom more than moral teachings, as in the case of *Values*. It is quite similar to that text because it largely relies on authoritative texts from each tradition, though the Believers not Belongers' contributions consist mostly of poetry and the Brahma Kumaris offer a guided meditation (NHS Scotland 2011).

IFS have produced a handful of other documents with the NHS including: *A Celebration of New Life* (n.d.) for expectant mothers, *Spiritual Care: A Multi-Faith Resource for Healthcare Staff* (n.d.) and *Religion and Belief Matter: An Information Resource for Healthcare Staff* (n.d.). These were complemented by a more expansive guide *Spiritual Care Matters: An Introductory Resource for all NHS Scotland Staff* (2009).

IFS is committed to numerous progressive global causes, including working with refugees and refugee charities. They have also expressed a strong environmentalist position. The Scottish Inter Faith Council Youth Committee produced a booklet *Our Sacred Earth: A Guide for Becoming More Eco-Friendly in Your Faith Community* (n.d.). This draws on scriptural quotations to inspire readers to be more environmentally conscious but also does offer practical tips. Another key document was produced by the Scottish Government *Belief in Dialogue: Religion and Belief Relations Good Practice Guide* (2011). This text provides specific and pragmatic guidance for how different actors and communities can engage in dialogue and collaborate, outlining the structures that are already in place to facilitate this. IFS also produced a similar, shorter document: *Guidelines for Inclusive Civic Events* (n.d.).

They collaborated with other organizations from several European countries in the Erasmus-funded 'Outside in' project which produced *Transforming Hate in Youth Settings: An Educational Tool and Practice Manual for those Working with Young People* (2018). Along with Interfaith Glasgow, they conducted research on university chaplaincies across the country, the fruits of which was a report: *Interfaith University Chaplaincy Research Project March 2018-May 2019* (2019). They also composed *Untold Stories: Women of Faith: Suffrage, Peace and Human Rights* (n.d.) to celebrate the stories of pioneering women from different religious traditions.[24]

Approach of the book

As alluded to above, the approach of this book is firmly within the non-confessional academic study of religion. It is also indebted to many related fields within the social sciences and humanities, especially the study of nationalism (e.g. see Hutchinson and Smith 1994, Hearn 2006, Özkirimli 2005, 2010, Smith 2010) and the interdisciplinary discussions on secularism (e.g. see Asad 2003, Calhoun, Juergensmeyer and Van Antwerpen 2011, Mandair and Dressler 2011, Mendietta and Van Antwerpen 2011). It will apply models and tools largely drawn from the critical study of religion, especially the critique of the WRP (Smith 1993, King 1999, Masuzawa 2005, Cox 2007, Owen 2011, Cotter and Robertson 2016) and critique of essentialist uses of the categories of religion and religions (see Asad 1993, Smith 1982, 1998, Fitzgerald 1997, 2000, McCutcheon 2001, 2003, Martin 2014). It is methodologically agnostic (Smart 1973 cited in McCutcheon 1999: 216–17), unconcerned with the truth or falsehood of religious claims or which forms of religion (or nationality, or ethnicity, or culture) are valid or authentic.

It is not written from a theological perspective, which means that it is neither committed to nor claims to be speaking on behalf of a religious tradition. It is also not written from an interfaith or anti-interfaith perspective which seeks to promote, defend, reform or oppose interfaith relations. Rather, it seeks to contribute to the understanding of the IFM as a distinct social phenomenon. None of this is a claim to be free from bias or to be necessarily less prone to it than if I were writing from a more committed position. I admitted previously that I am, if anything, inclined to view more pluralist expressions of religion (or non-religion) sympathetically, but this is not a reflection of deep commitment on my part. It is a bias inherited from my upbringing, something to be critiqued and kept in check.

There is nothing remarkable about this, I was born in Scotland's capital (Edinburgh) in 1987 and grew up in the 1990s and 2000s during a time when pluralism had become hegemonic. I am also white, straight, male, cis-gendered, anglophone (albeit familiar with the local Scots dialect) and Scottish from a working class (but far from deprived) background. I imbibed this natal pluralism along with other influences from that context and position, including a broad cultural Protestant influence. It should be borne in mind that this bias also entails a potentially disruptive bias *against* religious identifications that do not conform to this normative pluralism. I have not confessed all of this to take up intellectual arms on behalf of pluralism, or act as its policeman. I contend that focusing on understudied aspects of interfaith relations and the application of a novel methodological toolkit has much potential.

I will not here offer an analytical definition of religion as I have frequently done in previous publications (Sutherland 2012: 53, 2018a: 111, 2017c: 96, 2019: 54–5) and will likely do so again. This is because I will concentrate on the emic (the categories and concepts in general use) rhetorical and ideological constructions of religion(s) employed by IFS, which are quite ripe for examination on their own terms. This is not a disavowal of etic,[25] analytical definitions. Indeed, I will subsequently offer definitions of nationalism and secularism because these concepts are more obscure within their discourse and necessitate clarification to draw them out. Interfaith and normative pluralism were given a clear working definition because their comparative, analytical potential was also deemed to require clarification.

The monograph is written from an avowedly social constructionist position. This means that all identities, institutions, categories and relations usually treated as natural and fixed, are understood to be determined by social actors. These actors are in turn shaped by received but malleable conceptions within a given social context in which specific power relations are prevalent (Martin 2014: 21). The fact that all elements of society are socially constructed (or constructed upon, to give biology, cognitive and environmental sciences their due) should lead to the realization that it does not render any of them all necessarily false or unimportant. Social constructions are as much part of human environments as physical objects (Martin 2014: 27–31), they are constructs like buildings which have to be dealt with, not things which can simply be wished away.

Social constructions are also co-constructed, maintained and reconstructed by many agents, the work of many hands and brains. When successful, they are often reified – treated as independent objects and naturalized, treated as natural, inevitable and timeless when they are human products (Berger 1969: 86, Martin 2014: 28, Koenig and Knöbl 2015a: 7), for example, that humans naturally have religions or form nations, that gender roles are biologically hardwired and so forth. These things could have been constructed differently, they are changeable and dependent on acts of maintenance, much like our built environment. Nonetheless, taking apart or reshaping entrenched social constructions can be a laborious and drawn-out endeavour, one usually carried out with the help of others but whether that doing so is desirable or not is another question.

The social constructionism that I rely on is derived from the sociologist Peter Berger, who identified a three-fold process by which human beings manufacture their social world: (1) externalization, (2) objectivation and (3) internalization. Externalization refers to the way that agents apply themselves and their subjective concepts to their environment, which may include writing books, founding organizations or even simply speaking. These are then 'objectivated' by being introduced into the social environment in which they are now encountered as objects, or features of that environment which have to be negotiated. These are then internalized, becoming a part of the distinctive inner lives of agents, often in different ways which can in turn lead to changes (Berger 1969: 4).

It is also important to state unequivocally that simply because this is a reasonably fresh approach to this material does not mean that it is the correct one. It is also not intended to judge how interfaith relations should be governed, who has a right to inclusion or what is or is not a legitimate religion or part of a contested tradition. In fact, a critical study of the complex power relations, multiple audiences and interests involved in the seemingly innocuous world of interfaith dialogue may show how difficult it can be for IFGs to balance their different principles: inclusion, diversity, equality and accountability to their membership or the public. Indeed, it is an important implication of the social constructionist approach that any alternatives to these would also be shaped by similar constraining conditions and compromises. The social focus of this book means that it does not stipulate the degree to which individuals are enthusiastically committed to the discourses such as the WRP, or nationalism. These are often implicit in their content but tangential to their focus, aims and experiences.

My interpretation will assume that actors mean what they say, unless there is considerable evidence to the contrary (and I never found any) but also that nothing should be accepted uncritically, at face value. I assume that agents are sincere but also that they have multiple motivations, pressures and influences on their actions related to their environment. I will apply the 'hermeneutics of suspicion', reading their texts and statements with an eye for the ways that they reflect and uphold ideological positions and socialization (Gadamer 1984: 317).

Chapter synopsis

Chapter 2 will offer a more robust overview of the history of the interfaith movement (IFM). It will also introduce Scotland as a historical and cultural context, tracing the development of religion from hegemonic Christianity to contemporary diversification and setting the scene of its twenty-first-century devolved political system. This chapter will also outline some key approaches from the study of nationalism that can explain how such a global and cosmopolitan movement can be related to nationalism.

Chapter 3 will analyse the relationship between IFS and the majority Christian tradition in Scotland. It will outline the changes in the relationship between Scottish national identity and Christianity which made space for greater engagement: the shift from Presbyterian hegemony to normative pluralism. The acceptance of an ecumenical Christian identity over denominational ones made it easier to reinforce the conception of Christianity as just one world religion among its peers, along with the secularization of politics and nationhood. However, despite this recognition of formal equality among world religions, I will analyse how the major churches exercised their considerable influence in policing the boundaries of interfaith inclusion through the examples of the Pagan community and heterodox Christian groups.

Chapter 4 will focus on IFS' relationship with religious minorities, beginning with the historic demographic changes which have rendered Scotland into a more religiously diverse nation. It will trace the local roots of the IFM in Scotland in efforts to support newly established immigrant communities, condemn racism and more recently respond to anti-religious (especially Islamophobic) sentiment in the wake of 9/11. This chapter will also analyse the underlying assumptions and categories which can be deduced from IFS' representations of religion, especially the WRP. The tensions between the universalistic conceptions of religions and ethnic-cultural heritage will also be examined.

Chapter 5 will discuss their changing representations of the non-religious population of Scotland and explore the burgeoning field of non-religious studies. The morphology of IFS' representation of the non-religious will be traced from an invisible other, a potential threat, to a dialogue partner represented through the Humanism tradition. *Common Ground*, a conference held between Humanists, interfaith activists and Roman Catholics at the Conforti institute in Coatbridge in 2013, will serve as a clear illustrative example of this changing relationship, especially the development of shared norms and practices between Humanists and interfaith activists.

Chapter 6 offers an overview of the ways that the organization appeals to and reflects a civic-cultural Scottish nationalism to secure religious representation within a changeable devolved public sphere. It will outline the concept of civic-cultural nationalism along with Michael Billig's concept of banal nationalism before analysing a wealth of examples from the case study. This chapter will explore how these forms of public representation of religions have facilitated a close, corporatist relationship with the Scottish Government and civil society. This nevertheless necessitated adapting to and even reinforcing secularization. These themes were most richly illustrated in IFS' engagement with the referendum on Scottish independence in 2014, reinforcing the conception of the 'ultimate sovereignty' of the nation.

Chapter 7 will attempt to show how the analysis of the case study of IFS has something to contribute to the global study of religious pluralism, nationalism and the IFM. It will compare the national context of Scotland with interfaith scene in three other national contexts: India, the United States and the United Kingdom as a broader 'national' context, one which in fact encompasses Scotland. It will reflect on the ways in which even the most global, universalistic and religion-focused movement are dependent on a form of 'glocalisation': adapting these border crossing sentiments to conditions imposed by political and cultural boundaries of one sort or another.

The concluding Chapter 8 will reiterate the core argument of the book that this interfaith organization and, by extension, analogous groups, reinforce a limited form of pluralism rooted in the WRP compatible with a civic-cultural nationalism. It will stress that social scientific studies of interfaith are necessary to show how IFGs, spaces or events are socially constructed in specific environments and framed by the power relations of actors. The book will close with a call for further scholarship and consideration of IFGs within the study of religion.

2

The interfaith movement, religious diversity and nationalism in Scotland and the world

The interfaith movement and its development

The interfaith movement (IFM) is somewhat unusual among diffuse social movements because it is dated so decisively to a single year and location: the Parliament of World Religions at the Chicago World's Fair in 1883 (Brodeur 2005: 43–4, Halafoff 2013: 2, Hedges 2021: 327, Howard 2021: 4). Things are never quite that simple, of course, and the movement owes its genesis to early globalization, European colonial and Christian missionary-led contact between religions as well as the development of comparative religion (or the science of religion) (McCarthy 2007: 15, Womack 2018: 18–19, Howard 2021: 83–6). Scholars in this field such as Max Müller and C. P Tiele (see Sharpe 1986, Capps 2000), along with interest in religion among early social scientists such as August Comte, Herbert Spencer, E. B. Tylor and J. G. Frazer (Morris 1987, Pals 2006), reflected an increasingly global consciousness of religion, albeit dependent on data gathered from empires and often serving those interests (see Chidester 2014). Nonetheless, information about religions across the globe could be accessed that was not always primarily reflected through a confessional or theological lens.

The contact between religious representatives at the Chicago Parliament was in comparison much more egalitarian on the surface than formal contact between religions generally had been. However, like the movement that it produced, the Parliament nevertheless continued to carry strong Christian influences. Unlike the IFM as it exists today though, there is evidence that the aims of the Parliament were much more confessional than they would seem to be at first glance. It was assumed by some of its founding figures that an open, direct comparison of religions would render the superiority of Christianity obvious. Nonetheless, this does not change the fact that different world religions were represented on (roughly) equal footing by their own practitioners with a prohibition on proselytization (McCarthy 2007: 17, Halafoff 2013: 38, Hedges 2021: 327, Howard 2021: 94, 98), and the effects of this among western audiences were very distant from any Christian supremacist intentions.

The fact that the Parliament was defined as a religiously plural space where an attendee could hear from a range of different speakers present their religions in their own words was important in itself. In particular, the Hindu speaker Swami Vivekananda and Sri Lankan Buddhist Angarika Dharmapala left a distinct and lasting positive impression on western audiences (Howard 2021: 97, 117). The very novelty of this event meant that it acted as a model which helped to direct growing awareness and acceptance of diversity into the direct representation of multiple religions (McCarthy 2007: 18). Furthermore, numerous international and national interfaith groups (IFGs) were established in its wake (Halafoff 2013: 38, Pederson 2004: 80–5). The oldest international IFG to survive from before the Second World War was the World Congress of Faiths (WCF) founded in 1936 by Francis Younghusband (1863–1942) following another early interfaith gathering: The Conference on some Living Religions of the Empire held in 1924 London (Howard 2021: 4–5). One of the oldest national IFGs is the Inter-Religious Organization of Singapore, founded in 1949 (Hedges 2019: 8-9, 2021: 327).

The contemporary influence and prominence of the IFM also owe much to the Christian ecumenical movement as well (Halafoff 2013: 38, see Chapter 3). Ecumenicism can be defined as the effort to engender cooperation, maintain a common identity among or even reunify the sects or denominations of a specific religion. It could be viewed as akin to interfaith dialogue but within a single religion. The term is derived from the Greek 'oikumene' referring to the world, or universality. While it can be applied to interreligious relations, references to ecumenicism usually entail the Christian ecumenical movement (Bowker 1997: 303–4, Kesting 2014). This began as an effort to re-forge a unity of purpose among Protestant denominations to consolidate their respective missionary efforts rather than risk losing that influence through rivalry. This led to a famous missionary conference in Edinburgh in 1910 (see Stanley 2012) and eventually to the establishment of the World Council of Churches (WCC) in the 1960s (Howard 2021: 133).

While the Christian ecumenical movement began as a Protestant endeavour, it gradually began to include Roman Catholic and Orthodox participants. For the Roman Catholic Church, this was a result of the liberalization brought about by the Second Vatican Council in 1966, which recognized the legitimacy of other forms of Christianity and to a lesser extent other religions (Womack 2018: 21, Hedges 2021: 328–30, Howard 2021: 5). The Catholic Church may not have joined the WCC (Bowker 1997: 304) but it has developed informal relations with it.[1] At local and national levels though Catholic representatives have mostly joined up with their fellow Christians in ecumenical groups. The significance of this ecumenicism for the IFM was that it allowed Christianity to be represented as a common religion alongside others, promoted the conception of unity in difference and established models of cooperation. It should also be noted that the entrenchment of ecumenicism coincided with changing attitudes among Christians towards other religions and also with religious diversification in many societies in the twentieth century. The WCC met officially with representatives of other religions (Muslim, Hindu and Buddhist) as early as 1970 (Womack 2018: 21, Howard 2021: 214, 236).

The shift from ecumenicism to interfaith was not merely conceptual for many local groups but actually literal. Many local IFGs began as ecumenical church councils which extended their membership, usually first to Jewish, later Muslim and other religious communities (McCarthy 2007: 87, Pederson 2004: 80). Though as we have established the earliest roots of the IFM were global, this higher-level influence had to be combined with more grassroots forces to be effective. The IFM as it exists today could perhaps be described as the fusion of these more high-level, top-down norms and more routine, bottom-up practices rooted in ecumenicism and community activism.

An important thread of continuity throughout the historical development of the IFM is what I have termed the interfaith ethos: that religions should engage in close, harmonious relations and dialogue as an end in itself rather than compete. However, the concerns, priorities and composition of the global interfaith scene have shifted and adapted to changing conditions. The early IFM was characterized by a philosophical focus and was primarily the preserve of theologians and clerical elites (Fahy and Bock 2018: 2, Halafoff 2013: 39). In the years following the Second World War, their key concern was establishing interreligious harmony and peacebuilding, following the experiences of war and the trauma of the Holocaust. 'Judeo-Christian' dialogue was particularly pronounced during this time (Halafoff 2013: 40). These are still important themes in interfaith discourse, and as noted in the previous chapter, organizing Holocaust Memorial Day (HMD) was one of IFS' regular roles until very recently.

This post-war change of attitudes arguably played a significant role in promoting the wider prevalence of normative pluralism and multiculturalism generally, in contrast to exclusionary or assimilationist models of national societies. The post-war context also saw the actual diversification of many societies through transnational migration and religious experimentation, especially among younger generations from the 1960s, for example, western youth converting to Buddhism or forms of Hinduism (Halafoff 2013: 44, 46). Alternative forms of religion and spirituality in western societies do have much older roots but have attained a much greater influence from this time, including the growth of (Neo-)Paganism (see Clifton and Harvey 2004). As the global order at this time was defined by the climate of the Cold War, unsurprisingly nuclear disarmament and peace became areas of greater concern (Halafoff 2013: 41).

However, more grassroots groups concerned with the provision of welfare in different communities began to emerge at the local level. In Scotland the first IFG was Glasgow Sharing of Faiths (GSF), which was born from the work of a former nurse and Church of Scotland missionary to Pakistan, Stella Reekie. She used her competence in the Urdu language to work with recently established Pakistani immigrants in Glasgow but also began to relate to them through shared importance of religion in their lives. GSF was primarily concerned with the pragmatic needs of different communities in the city but at the same time organized an interfaith festival educating the public about elements of these religions known as the 'Presentation of Faiths' (Adamson, Ramsay and Craig 1984).

The late 1980s and 1990s was the period in which IFGs began to proliferate. For example, the Inter Faith Network of the United Kingdom (IFNUK) was established in 1987 (Fahy and Bock 2018: 50, IFNUK 2007: 6) and Edinburgh Inter Faith Association (EIFA) founded in 1989 (Goldblatt 2022). The Scottish Inter Faith Council (SIFC), which would later be renamed Interfaith Scotland (IFS), was created at the end of this period in 1999. The centennial of the World Parliament of Religions was held in Chicago in 1993, which reflected the changing concerns and make-up of the IFM and has been held regularly in different cities across the globe ever since (Halafoff 2013: 3, Hedges 2021: 327–29).

In the 1980s and 1990s the environment, poverty and inequality became key concerns of the global IFM (Halafoff 2013: 42–3). In previous decades, the focus of interfaith dialogue was conceived along an 'east-west' axis, as between the 'Abrahamic' religions of the west and the religions of South and East Asia in order to establish a common philosophical ground (Halafoff 2013: 50). The environmentalism that characterized the movement in the 1980s and 1990s began to include dialogue with the religious or spiritual practices and concerns of indigenous peoples and developing nations, moving to a 'north-south' axis.

Increasingly, practitioners of Indigenous Religions, Pagans and other forms of alternative religion, especially those with environmentalist leanings, became more prominent in the movement (Halafoff 2013: 43, Hedges 2021: 329). Though concerns of peace and interreligious harmony remained significant, especially in response to the entanglement of religion with ethno-national conflicts in the 1990s, for example, in the former Yugoslavia.

The conception that interfaith dialogue was primarily a tool for promoting harmony between religious communities in conflict came back to the fore, especially following the 11 September (9/11) terrorist attacks in New York in 2001 (Halafoff 2013: 71–2, Hedges 2021: 330). Similar terrorist attacks by Islamist terrorists in Bali on 12 October 2002 on the London underground on 7 July 2005 (7/7) cemented a period of heightened public and governmental concern about Islamic-inspired terrorism across the world (Halafoff 2013: 79–80). This led to a period of growing Islamophobia for Muslim minorities living in non-Muslim majority, especially western societies, and further tensions exacerbated by the American and British invasions of Afghanistan (2001) and Iraq (2003), though arguably beginning with the Rushdie Affair in 1989 (see Asad 1990).

In some ways this provided the IFM with a public role, prominence and recognition that they had not previously had, but was often dictated by the concerns of security conscious governments. They also faced an especially uphill struggle particularly to combat Islamophobic prejudices and fears around Islamic terror (Halafoff 2013: 76–8, Dawson 2016b) alongside greater scrutiny on Islamic societies and communities, for example, around the place of women. In the 2000s, this climate of concern about 'fundamentalist' forms of religion meant that this could be projected on to the category of 'religion' as a whole, as exemplified by the 'New Atheist' movement associated most famously with the evolutionary biologist Richard Dawkins.

This period was an intense one for the IFM in western societies. It was a time of growth and growing prominence but marked by prejudices against Muslims in particular and growing antipathy towards religion in general, while religious affiliation and influence continued to decline. Notably, Scotland's Religious Leaders Forum (RLF) was established in 2002 by the heads of the three biggest churches to ensure that religious leaders could maintain contact and collaborate in addressing the public and media on issues such as these (ACTS n.d.: 17–19). In general, the IFM devoted most of its energy at this time to dealing with these issues, and dialogue between the three main Abrahamic religions – Judaism, Christianity and Islam – was the order of the day (Halafoff 2013: 67, Howard 2021: 239).

From the vantage point of the 2020s, these concerns are still present but other issues have returned to the fore, especially environmentalism (Halafoff 2013: 87). All of these different periods of development have influenced the characteristics of the movement as a multilayered phenomenon. The search for common ground, concern with social harmony and other social issues are still significant, as the empirical study of IFS will show. The IFM as it exists today can be fairly characterized as a broadly progressive movement because of its in-built valourization of pluralism and concern with fairness. Nonetheless, it has become a means through which governments of different alignments increasingly relate to religious groups and govern them in a 'hands off' manner. IFGs are also channels through which religions are accessed by civil organizations or the media but have also become a normalized part of everyday social life.

Modelling interfaith within the critical study of religion

So far, I have identified the subject matter and its status as a lacuna within the field, assessing the existing scholarship. It was asserted that this movement, like all others, is socially constructed: dependent on the actions of agents in a given social environment which determines how it operates and presents itself. As the previous section outlined, the IFM is now 130 years old. It has become part of the social environment of many societies. Furthermore, it is a tradition conveying its own authority, resources, practices, norms and identity. It is also a medium through which agents relate to other elements of the social environment, for example, religion, politics, nationhood or global relations, and so forth. In the more general sense of media, there is the tantalizing fact that its outputs include a range of textual and other content.

I did also touch on some of the key themes within the critical study of religion, which could be pursued through further research on IFGs. This would include the construction and ideological usages of the category of 'religion', its naturalization as *sui generis* and pre-eminently authoritative but also as insulated from the vicissitudes of the secular political sphere. The reification of 'world religions', the promotion of elite, institutional and doctrinal forms of religion are still more evident. I have also stressed the importance of placing IFGs in their contexts; enmeshed in their relations with religious, cultural and political conditions, which are local or localized experiences of transnational currents.

There are some important points about IFGs that need to be spelled out, which are not always obvious from the self-presentation of interfaith activists or with a first glance at their content. It is important to state unequivocally that the IFM is not simply what naturally emerges from 'encounters'[2] between religions, when these are conducted in a friendly rather than hostile spirit. Rather, the IFM must be understood as a distinct social movement which has cultivated the practices and norms that influence these 'encounters' which do not merely dissipate afterwords. Especially given that institutional interfaith groups (IFGs), spaces, newsletters, journals, books, blogs not to mention interfaith activists with long careers, continue to exist. It is important, of course, not to reify 'interfaith' in turn and lose sight of the different persons,[3] groups and texts who identify with or are classified under this rubric.

Certainly, for most agents it is likely to be just one among commitments and identities which they juggle, and which come to the fore under different circumstances. For many participants at public events, for example, their participation may not be especially significant at all, but it is an occasion for potential influence. The most dedicated activists at the core of the movement are important to study as well though, for their own sake and because they cast a wider net. Furthermore, the IFM is just one response to the globalization of religion, secularization and religious diversification of societies.

Like other social movements, the IFM has been determined by uneven power relations and changing historical conditions which have made it desirable and advantageous for some more powerful groups to engage with it. That relating closely to the political class has become a common activity for IFGs, more than many religious communities on their own, highlights that they are intent on pursuing political goals. Such engagement increases the likelihood that they will become more influential, as indeed they have become in many societies. This should encourage scholars to reflect on the ideological roles played by IFGs for their participants and external partners, such as politicians.

For majority religions under increasing pressure from secularization and diversification, interfaith engagement potentially offers a new means of defending their influence within the public sphere in a form more palatable to the emerging normative framework. For religious minorities, interfaith participation could be a conduit to greater recognition, legitimacy, formal equality among a group of peers, and the potential to make use of the resources of the powerful. This would attract religions newly established in an unfamiliar society through migration or conversion. To gain acceptance though, religious minorities may be encouraged to adopt what Indian social theorist Gayatri Spivak called 'strategic essentialism': stressing common, distinct characteristics (but compatible with the agenda of those in power) but downplaying internal differences or elements of their religions that are unpalatable to the majority (Eide 2010: 76).

For secular authorities, IFGs are one means of ensuring harmonious relations among citizens and therefore a prosperous, contented society which legitimates their governance. Among civil institutions charged with delivering services to an increasingly diverse population IFGs can aid them in the fulfilment of these roles. Historically, religions have acted as rival power blocks to secular (if not 'secularist') governments; relating to multiple religions ensures that no one can predominate, which mitigates against the potential formation of such a rival power block. My argument is that the representation of religions as global, universal, unbounded bodies of wisdom not only encourages a positive view of religion but also differentiates them from the bounded, locally authoritative sphere of the secular nation. 'Religion' and 'nation' are distinguished so that they can intersect but not wholly merge. They are rendered overlapping but non-competitive.

The IFM is the most concrete form of normative religious pluralism but is just one among many approaches which make ideological uses of the categories of 'religion' and 'religions'. Religious groups can and do pursue other avenues through which to exert influences within national spaces or appeal to cultural identities, many of which are more exclusionary. Nonetheless, appealing to pluralism is especially useful where it has become part of the predominant norms of a given society. In a thoroughly secularized society such as Scotland, it is much more compatible with certain forms of secularism as I will discuss more fully in subsequent chapters (see Hedges 2019: 1-4, 10-13).

It should be noted that these discussions of ideology and strategic operations are not understood to refer to some kind of purely cynical manipulation or necessarily indicate a lack of sincerity among agents. It is simply a recognition that actors operate in a given set of power relations and pursue goals for themselves: individually, and on behalf of groups.[4] This therefore depends on persuading potential allies, partners and publics which depend on recognition and legitimation. Ultimately, this simply means that actors are products of their environment but also produce their environment, demonstrating the contingency of all naturalized boundaries, categories and practices.

Setting the scene: The historical context of Scotland

Before returning to the core case study of Interfaith Scotland (IFS), it will be useful to provide a historical account of the religious, cultural and political development of their 'national' environment. According to some commentators, a distinct characteristic of contemporary Scots' collective memory and myth-making about 'their' past is that it has been left fairly open. It has not been subject to the kind of singular, overriding narratives associated with many nation-states (e.g. the United States) or divided by strong clashing narratives (e.g. France). This has allowed for different periods, symbols and aspects of Scotland's past to be used by different groups for their own reasons. The historian Marinell Ash compared the mythic figures of Scottish history to the peaks of the country's mountains with the connections between them obscured by mist (Ash n.d.: 1 cited in McCrone 1992: 18). The journalist Neil Ascherson compared it to a rubbish heap from which scavengers pick out what they will, in contrast to the well-organized and tended garden of English history (Ascherson 2002: vii–viii). This has allowed different groups to claim and re-forge the myths of the nation to suit themselves, including IFS, without much resistance.

Little is known about the peoples who inhabited prehistoric 'Scotland' or the 'religions' that they may have practiced. Even at this stage though, one of Scotland's contemporary communities – Pagans are associated with it through putative religious sites from this time such as the Callanish standing stones on the island of Lewis (e.g. IFS n.d.: 21). By the Early Medieval period (400–1000 C.E.), the territory that would become Scotland was inhabited by several peoples: the Scots or Gaels in the northwest, the Britons in the southwest speaking a Brythonic language (related to Welsh), the Angles in the southeast speaking a form of Old English and the Picts in much of central, eastern and northeastern Scotland. From the ninth-century Norse from Scandinavia raided, conquered and settled throughout the north and northwest, including the Gaelic heartlands of the Western Isles but more decisively in the Northern Isles (the Orkney and Shetland archipelagos) (Broun 1998: 4–5).

Scots Gaelic is now only spoken by a small minority, with only 2.5 per cent of Scots reporting some skills in the language (National Records of Scotland 2024). It was traditionally spoken in the Highlands and Western Isles and was initially the dominant language of the Kingdom of Scotland. This language is now recognized as an important part of Scottish culture, increasingly institutionalized, for example, in the Scottish Parliament, but unfortunately this has not reversed its decline. The languages of the 'Scottish' (Strathclyde) Britons and the unknown language of the Picts died out, but the Northumbrian English spoken by the Angles developed into the language now known as Scots. This became the dominant language of Scotland from the late Middle Ages until the modern day. This was traditionally spoken in the Lowlands and the northeast of the country and 46.2 per cent of the population has some skills in the language (ibid.). However, its linguistic proximity to English means that it has been to a large extent mixed with, absorbed and pushed out by English, which has been the predominant spoken and written language since the introduction of modern schooling.

The fact that this foundational period of Scottish history could be described as multi-ethnic, and that the majority of Scots are descended from a mixture of these distinct peoples can be used to show that pluralism is not new or alien to Scotland. Sister Smyth has explicitly drawn parallels between this early history and contemporary Scotland in a text produced for the Christian ecumenical group ACTS (ACTS n.d.: 3). This period also witnessed the thorough Christianization of the country associated with numerous local saints, most famously St Columba (Colm Cille) linked with the abbey on the island of Iona. This early period of Christianity has been interpreted as forming a distinct 'Celtic Christianity' the inheritance of which was claimed by later, competing Christian sects. As I will discuss in more detail in subsequent chapters, sites such as Iona have also become pilgrimage sites for interfaith participants as testament to the general religious heritage of the country, which all 'people of faith' can relate to.

Nevertheless, when Scotland became a kingdom, it was firmly aligned with the Roman Catholic Church which legitimated it, recognized its independence and allowed it to claim the apostle St Andrew as its patron saint (Broun 2002: 22–4, 28–9, McCrone 1992: 19). Scottish identity developed through relations with continental Europe but also through frequent invasions, first from Norway and then more frequently from England. The period of invasion by England produced totemic national heroes such as the Scottish rebel leader William Wallace and King Robert I (Robert the Bruce) (see Cowan 1998, Watson 1998).

Scotland was transformed by the tides of Reformation sweeping through northern Europe in the sixteenth century. The Scottish Reformation was led by the emblematic figure John Knox, who founded the Church of Scotland in 1560, commonly known as 'the Kirk' (Scots 'church') (Lynch 1998: 84–5). Knox was a disciple of the radical French reformer John Calvin, who taught that salvation could not be guaranteed either by faith, good works or sacramental rituals because God already determined who is saved or damned from the beginning of time (predestination) (Bruce 2014: 13).

The dominant faction within the Kirk coupled Calvinist theology with a Presbyterian Church structure. This meant that congregations were governed by elders (Gk. 'presbyteroi') who had a say in the appointment of their minister. From the congregational level, representatives are appointed from the bottom-up through presbyteries (equivalent to dioceses in other denominations) to the General Assembly (equivalent to a synod) and headed by a moderator who serves for a year (Brown 1997: 18). Importantly, the Presbyterians rejected the rule of bishops and all traditional sacramental rituals derived from Catholicism.

However, despite the emergence of a Presbyterian-Calvinist hegemony in Scotland, Roman Catholic populations continued to exist, especially in the Highlands and Islands. Alongside them, Episcopalians who maintained a more 'Anglican' form of Protestantism involving Bishops (Gk. 'Episkopoi'), ordained priests and more Catholic-style rituals (but outside the Roman Catholic church) predominated in parts of the Highlands but especially in the northeast (Bruce 1985: 8). The Episcopalians formally seceded from the Kirk in 1711, and while they later joined the Anglican Communion, are a separate church from the Church of England with their distinct history (Bruce 2014: 9, 13, 112, 120). For a long time, Presbyterianism and Calvinism were considered defining parts of Scottish culture and emblematic of the Scottish character, despite the entrenched presence of denominational minorities and the fact that this tradition was really predominant only in the south (Bruce 1985: 8).

This shows how associations between a society and a dominant religion or ideology may depend less straightforwardly on the brute force of numbers, let alone on essential characteristics, than they do on the monopolization of the governance, civic life, communications and representations of that society. Southern Scotland, especially the central belt with the major cities of Edinburgh and Glasgow, has been a centre of commerce and media for centuries, as well as home to the bulk of the population. This has meant that gaining influence within that area entails greater influence over the image of the nation. In the contemporary period, this part of Scotland is also the most religiously, ethnically and culturally diverse area of the country which has facilitated the rebranding of the nation as pluralist. However, while there are still predominantly Catholic and Episcopalian areas of northern Scotland, from the late eighteenth and nineteenth centuries, many areas of the Highlands and Western Isles became staunchly Presbyterian (Bruce 2014: 12, Paton 2002: 97). Ironically, the vigorous, conservative Calvinism of some communities, such as on the Isle of Lewis, contrasts markedly with the secular image of modern Scotland disseminated from the south.

The relationship between the Church of Scotland, national identity and political power would become especially complex in the following century. In 1603 King James VI of Scotland was crowned James I of England and Ireland and henceforth the country's monarchs have resided in England until the present day. Though the three kingdoms had remained independent, they were ruled by the same monarchs. Despite the Scottish roots of the Stuart dynasty, their residence in the largest and most powerful kingdom exerted a cultural and religious influence on the Stuart monarchs, not the other way round. James I and VI was famous for sponsoring the scriptural translation known as the King James Bible, which was prescribed throughout his realms but crucially this was in English, not Scots or Gaelic.

On matters of religion, James and his descendant favoured Anglicanism and sought to impose Episcopalianism in Scotland (Stephen 2002: 69), which was opposed by the powerful 'Covenanter' movement swearing a 'National Covenant' in 1638 to uphold Presbyterianism (Young 1998: 107–10). Following the Wars of the Three Kingdoms, the execution of King Charles I by the English Parliamentarian leader Oliver Cromwell and the restoration of Charles II in 1660, Episcopalianism was once again imposed on the Church of Scotland and the Covenanting movement suppressed (Young 1998: 113–18). However, when James II and VII converted to Catholicism, he was deposed in 1688 by his daughter Mary Stuart and her husband, the Dutch Prince William of Orange, who reigned as co-monarchs: Mary II and William II and III. To gain support in Scotland, they recognized Presbyterianism as the official position of the Kirk (Young 1998: 122).

Following this however, Scotland was unified with England through the Treaty of Union in 1707, which abolished the nation's parliament (until the establishment of the present Scottish Parliament in 1999), forming the United Kingdom of Great Britain. Union with England did obviously lead to greater English influences, but it did not, for the most part, entail absorption into a new, singular British nation (Young 1998: 122–30, Finlay 1998: 145–6). Scots have in different ways continuously asserted a distinct national identity ever since, albeit based around different agendas, symbols and tropes. Furthermore, the Treaty of Union itself guaranteed the independence and pre-eminence of the Kirk in Scotland (Stephen 2002: 68) as well as its separate legal system which insulated Scottish civil society.

The Scots subsequently played a significant role in the emerging British Empire; militarily, administratively, commercially and through emigration, mostly to North America and Australasia. This also entailed participation in the Atlantic slave trade, the subjugation of indigenous peoples and the economic exploitation of colonized territories. The Union opened Scotland up to unprecedented global influences and initially undermined the Kirk's hegemony, providing alternative resources for identity and myth-making for later generations. Scottish intellectuals, some of whom were openly sceptical of traditional religion, played a significant role in the 'Enlightenment', for example: David Hume, Adam Smith and Adam Ferguson (Devine 2012: 65–6, Finlay 1998). Many figures of the Scottish Enlightenment were staunchly Unionist and invested in cultivating a new British identity to varying degrees.

When the last Stuart monarch, Queen Anne, died without heirs in 1714 she was succeeded by the German Prince George I, Elector of Hanover. This sparked another series of rebellions in Scotland to restore the heirs of the deposed James II and VII, whose supporters are known as Jacobites (from Latin 'Jacobus' James) in 1715 and 1745. These risings were most commonly supported by Catholics as well as by Episcopalians. In the 1745 rising, Charles Edward Stuart, popularly known as 'Bonnie Prince Charlie', raised a Jacobite army joined by many Highland clans. The Jacobites were defeated at the Battle of Culloden and Charles Stuart fled, leading to the forceful pacification of the Highlands by the victorious Hanoverians. They enacted further punitive and assimilationist measures by banning the Gaelic language and Highland dress: the kilt and tartan. The opening up of the Highlands and changing economic conditions incentivized many clan chieftains as landowners to evict their traditional tenants to make space for lucrative sheep farms. These 'Highland Clearances' as they came to be known involved the mass deportation of Highlanders from their ancestral lands, moving to coastal fishing villages, the Lowlands, England, North America or Australasia. (Devine 2012: 174–5).

However, this same period witnessed the flowering of the Scottish Romantic movement and myth-making about these events. Jacobites were increasingly viewed sympathetically as a noble but spent force, becoming part of the fabric of Scottish identity; its mythic past, rather than ideological support for a specific dynasty. This was accompanied by a romanticization of the Highlands ('Highlandism'), Gaelic culture and the clans. Cultural paraphernalia such as kilts, tartan and bagpipes became iconic elements of Scottish culture in general. James MacPherson's widely popular poem *Ossian* that claimed to be the translation of a Gaelic epic but was likely mostly fabricated, was an important part of this romantic turn (Nairn 1977: 96, Trevor-Roper 1983: 21–2, Cameron 1998: 177, Devine 2012: 234). Though an often overlooked reason why the trappings of Highland dress and the great highland bagpipes went from being on the fringe to the centre of Scottish identity is likely to be the popularity of the British army's Highland regiments (Devine 2012: 244).

This romantic transformation of Scotland was cemented by the novelist Sir Walter Scott, who wrote sympathetically about Highland clans, the Jacobite rebellions and Scotland's medieval past while reconciling these with Unionism.

Scott was instrumental in organizing the pageantry of King George IV's visit to Scotland in 1822 (known as 'the king's jaunt') which stressed continuity with Scotland's ancient monarchy but also encouraged participants to don Highland dress. This is credited with popularizing the invented tradition of the philibeg or 'short kilt' which is now the national dress of Scotland (Nairn 1977: 96, 115–6, Cameron 1998: 177, Trevor-Roper 1983: 21–2, Devine 2012: 234).

It should be noted though that this romanticism drew on aspects of Lowlands culture as well, especially the Scots language. The romantic poet Robert Burns, who wrote largely in Scots, continues to be regarded as the national poet of Scotland; his poems and songs are hugely significant as cultural touchstones. Furthermore, Burns' Day on 25 January is one of the country's pre-eminent national celebrations. The focal point of this celebration is a meal known as a 'Burns' Supper' consisting of the traditional Scottish dish of haggis, neeps (turnips) and tatties (potatoes) following the recitation of Burn's poem *Address to a Haggis*. Some Burn's Suppers are formal and ritualistic, with multiple stages and the piping in of the haggis, but it will usually include at least the meal and a reading of the poem. This poem and much of Burns' oeuvre express a romanticization of rural Scottish life by valorizing the folkways of its peasantry but also the desire to maintain a distinctive Scottish identity (see Cohen 2000: 161–3).

Burns also expressed rising scepticism about traditional Calvinism, for example, in his poem *Holy Willie's Prayer* which lampoons the doctrine of predestination. While there may have been tension between the Enlightenment and the Romantic movement, both helped to undermine Presbyterian hegemony and the fusion of national and denominational identities. Both of these movements provided alternative bases for myth-making and cultural symbolism among the Scots population, which did not depend on religious affiliation. Crucially, most Scots influenced by these movements would have been Presbyterians. This does not explain how a nation with such a strong Protestant Christian identity becomes religiously plural. While I have stressed that demographic change in real terms is not the only significant factor, it is still important to the process of rendering pluralism a part of lived experience and a tool of social integration.

The religious diversification of Scotland

As has been repeatedly stressed, even at the high points of Presbyterian hegemony, there were always minority populations, especially Catholics and

Episcopalians. Nonetheless, the first stirrings of further religious diversification were among Presbyterians. The effects of the Enlightenment and Romanticism can be viewed as undermining traditional Presbyterianism and paving the way for a more secular society which led to traditionalist reactions. As early as the eighteenth century and into the nineteenth and twentieth centuries, groups of Presbyterians seceded from the established Kirk for a variety of reasons (Bruce 2014: 9–11, Devine 2012: 374–7).

The most dramatic example of secession from the Kirk was the 'Great Disruption' of 1843 led by Revd. Thomas Chalmers at the General Assembly of that year, when Chalmers and over half the ministers in attendance walked out to form the Free Church (Devine 2012: 374–7). The reason for this was that the Kirk had allowed landowners to have a say in the appointment of parish ministers, which was held to be the prerogative of the elders. This accompanied a general religious revival which combined Presbyterianism with the emerging phenomenon of Evangelicalism, which placed greater emphasis on enthusiastic religiosity and missionary efforts in the empire.

By the mid-nineteenth century, Scotland was home to a variety of competing Presbyterian denominations. While this changed the relationship between religion and national identity, arguably this reinforced the associations between Presbyterianism and Scottishness in other ways. This was a period in which public enthusiasm for the Medieval period as a base of Scots collective memory and symbolism associated with Walter Scott waned. Meanwhile, public commemoration and interest in the Scottish Reformation and recognition of figures like Knox and the Covenanters as national heroes became more prominent. Chalmers and famous Scottish missionaries, such as David Livingstone, also became icons for many. By the late twentieth century though conditions had observably changed again, as there was a notable lack of enthusiasm for Reformation history (Lynch 1998: 82–3, Devine 2012: 364).

The biggest change in the religious demographics of Scotland was increasing immigration from Ireland, especially following the Potato Famine (1845–1852), which greatly bolstered the Catholic population (Devine 2012: 518–22). The Catholic community shifted from a small minority, primarily in the Highlands and Western Isles, to a sizeable segment of the populated mostly concentrated in the cities and towns of the Lowlands. Unfortunately, this led to persistent sectarianism and anti-Irish racism in some communities which was considered endemic to Scottish society, though it has become less pervasive in recent decades and is now more often associated with football rivalries than religious observance (Bruce 2014: 54–5), though still a live issue (see Devine 2000,

Bruce, Glendinning, Paterson and Rosie 2004, Rosie 2004, Geoghegan 2013). The reunification of most Presbyterian churches, including most Free Church congregations, with the Church of Scotland in 1929 was arguably an attempt to maintain Protestant hegemony and rooted in fear of Irish Catholics (Brown 1997: 39). An infamous report was presented to the General Assembly of that year: *The Menace of the Irish Race to our Scottish Nationality* (Bruce 1985: 46, Brown 1997: 39, Edwards 2012: 140).

Other nationalities, such as Italian, Polish and Lithuanian immigrants, further added to the Catholic population from the late nineteenth century onwards (Devine 2012: 518–522). This was paralleled when many Poles came to Scotland after the Second World War and more recently in 2004 through the European Union's Freedom of Movement policy, most of whom were Catholic (Piętka-Nykaza 2018: 126). Also in the late nineteenth century, Ashkenazi Jews began to make their home in the country (Devine 2012: 18–22), adding to the tiny Jewish population which existed beforehand and making a non-Christian religion increasingly visible in a homogenously Christian society.

The Enlightenment and Romantic movements have played their part in providing alternative norms, myths and symbols which were less specifically Protestant or even Christian, which could be widely shared without denominational commitments. Subsequently, during the Enlightenment period, leading philosophers and especially Scottish scientists and their discoveries or inventions became a point of pride for many Scots (Fernandez 2000: 123–5). As we have noted, the Jacobite period and the history of the societies of Highland clans could also be drawn on as a mythic and symbolic resource. This provided Scots with a rich and adaptable body of cultural symbolism and tropes which could be taken on and adapted by newly established communities, for example, the creation of tartans representing minority communities.[5]

The twentieth century, especially following the Second World War, saw the further secularization of Scottish society and greater diversification. From 1948 onwards, people from Britain's former colonies in Asia, Africa and the Caribbean began to settle in larger numbers in the UK, some making their way to Scotland (see Devine and McCarthy 2018). The nationalities who settled in Scotland at this time included Pakistanis, Indians (see Bonino 2018), Bangladeshis,[6] Chinese (see Bell 2018) and Sri Lankans, along with further Jewish migration (see Evans and McCarthy 2018). As noted earlier, Polish and East European immigration to Scotland increased in the 2000s, and there was an increase in African immigration in the same decade (see Piacentini 2018: 178).

This has obviously greatly diversified the religious landscape of the nation because these new immigrant communities brought their religious identities and practices with them. Different Muslim, Hindu, Sikh and Buddhist congregations were established (Bruce 2014: 14–15, Devine 2012: 563–4). The more visible they became, the more they were included in the civic life of local areas, the more the conception of public religion in Scotland shifted from being purely Christian. As noted earlier, the first IFG in Scotland, Glasgow Sharing of Faiths, was founded by Stella Reekie in 1969, an organization which engaged with the public of Glasgow and organized an annual interfaith festival. This was the same period in which Scotland was becoming much more culturally secular, church attendance was declining and increasing numbers of Scots were claiming to be non-religious (Brown 1997: 174).

This combination of diversification and secularization was arguably a fertile environment for the development of new forms of religion. Younger Scots who had been raised Christian were increasingly able to explore new and alternative forms of religion[7] or none (see Bruce 2014: 3–4, 15, 109). As in many western societies, there was growing interest in Buddhism, sometimes leading to conversions, especially after the Tibetan Kagyu Samyé Dzong established the large purpose-built monastery of Samyé Ling in Eskdalemuir in Dumfries and Galloway in 1967 (MacKenzie 2011). It also led to the development of more home-grown forms of alternative religion, such as Paganism and New Age or holistic spirituality, such as the Findhorn foundation established near Tomintoul in Aberdeenshire in 1972 (see Sutcliffe 2000, 2002).

As of the 2022 census,[8] the largest single religious identification (identification in relation to the category of 'religion') is for the first time in recorded history no religion at 51.1 per cent, rising from 36.7 per cent in 2011. Christians overall 38.8 per cent, the Church of Scotland specifically 20.1 per cent and Roman Catholics 13.3 per cent are the largest religious groups according to the census (National Records of Scotland 2024), which means that Christians have lost the slight majority 54 per cent they had in 2011 (National Records of Scotland 2013: 4). The population of non-Christian religious minorities is just under 4 per cent which can be broken down as follows: Muslim 2.2 per cent, Hindus 0.55 per cent, Pagans 0.35 per cent, Buddhists 0.28 per cent, Sikhs 0.20 per cent, Jews 0.11 per cent and others 0.23 per cent (National Records of Scotland 2024).

Nonetheless, the proportion of non-Christian minorities is substantially higher in the major urban areas of Glasgow, Edinburgh, Dundee, Aberdeen and surrounding settlements. All of these communities have become more visible in recent decades and have punched above their weight in gaining recognition, though IFGs such as IFS have played a role in securing this. So far, I have discussed the changing religious and cultural developments of Scottish national identity but will now bring this account up to date with the contemporary political context and the politicization of nationality.

The contemporary politics of Scotland: Autonomy, independence and nationalism

One of the defining characteristics of Scotland after 1707 has been that it is a non-independent nation, one of the paradigmatic examples of a stateless nation (see Guibernau 1999, Anderson and Keil 2016). It has been part of a fairly centralized unitary state since then, officially known as the United Kingdom of Great Britain and Northern Ireland since 1922, or more informally as the United Kingdom. At the same time, a distinct and highly potent Scottish national identity has been maintained, which is informed by the sense of a long, continuing history. It has also been buffered by its distinct legal system and since the nineteenth century a distinct education system and civil service (Devine 2012: 307, Keating 2005: 3–4).

This was in spite of the fact that Scotland not only lacked independence but any kind of autonomous or devolved legislature until 1999, the decline of its traditional languages (Scots Gaelic and Scots) and the absence of other characteristics which might serve as hard cultural bulwarks against assimilation into a common British nationality (McCrone 1992: 174). The most surprising absence of all though is that for much of Scotland's modern history and unlike many parallel cases, it lacked any kind of strong form of political nationalism, which only became politically ascendant in the twenty-first century.

However, it would be easy to underestimate the importance of a more diffuse cultural nationalism buffered by Scotland's autonomous civil institutions and encoded in cultural symbolism. An important part of this cultural nationalism is a vivid sense of nationhood which is ineffable but also pervasive:

> As an inclination found widely across the political and social spectrums, however nationalism has appeared more as a lament for the continuing denial of the integrity and authenticity of Scottish nationhood, in the long wake of the loss of the Scottish nation-state … It is essentially a *cultural* nationalism that has some similarity to nationalistic and other reactions that follow from a popular perception of the denigration of a culture by a powerful neighbour … In

this sense, Scottish nationalism is a statement of *identity*, the potency of which is separable from – independent of – its more partisan political programme. (Cohen 1996: 803, emphasis in original)

The power of this sentiment is also backed up by recent census data, 73.7 per cent of census respondents reported Scottish as their nationality. The data is more refined than this would indicate because respondents were able to identify with multiple national identities and report the degree to which they identified with each. This shows that a clear majority not only identify their nationality as 65.4 per cent as 'Scottish only' and 'Scottish and British' 8.2 per cent, with 13.9 per cent as 'British only'. While exclusive Scottish identification has grown slightly from 62.4 per cent in 2011 so has exclusive British identification from 8.4 per cent in 2011, this was at the expense of dual identification, which was at 18.3 per cent in 2011 (National Records of Scotland 2024). This reflects greater polarization among the Scots population over identity related to but not identical with the divide over the question of independence. Overall though, greater identification with 'Scottishness' has been steadily growing while the significance of 'Britishness' has been in decline, a clear trend from the 1990s at least (see McCrone, Morris and Kiely 1995: 172).

Identification with a common Britishness, though not necessarily implying a lack of national identification with Scotland, was much more powerful earlier in the twentieth century. A strong British Unionism was at a particular high point associated with both world wars and the development of the comprehensive welfare state in post-war Britain (Devine 2012: 4). This means that historically this was not a linear shift from the primacy of British to Scottish identity because both have fallen and risen in salience in different periods, but they have also been reconciled and syncretized in different ways as well. The pronounced rise in identification as Scottish over British has been correlated with the recent ascendancy of Scottish nationalism, but this nationalism has older roots and also taken on different agendas and profiles.

Graeme Morton has argued that the concept that nineteenth-century Scotland lacked a nationalist movement misses the point that Scottish nationalism was historically largely Unionist; its energies were directed into maintaining a distinct Scottish nationhood conceived as an equal partner in the Union (and empire). Scottish national heroes such as Wallace and Bruce were viewed as ensuring that Scotland was not conquered and incorporated into England but rather had to be negotiated with through the Treaty of Union (Morton 1998: 164–70). Atsuko Ichijo has also shown that in contemporary

Scottish politics, Unionist political parties emphasize a distinct form of Scottish nationalism in recognizing Scotland as a nation within the Union and claim to work for its distinctive interests (2012: 24).

Nonetheless, the question of Scottish home rule, whether Scotland should be granted an assembly or parliament along with the other 'home nations', periodically arose. The issue of home rule continued to bubble away under the lid of the unitary state of the United Kingdom. The post-war UK however was a strongly centralized state defined by strong social democracy, an industrial economy and trade unionism (Devine 2012: 630). This was also the beginning of decolonization: the break-up of the British empire with the independence of India and Pakistan in 1947, though Ireland had become independent in 1922 and a republic in 1936. This means that questions of autonomy and independence were never far below the surface during this period.

However, the decline of British industry in the 1960s greatly affected Scotland, especially because Glasgow was the centre of shipbuilding in the United Kingdom. Frustrations at the lack of autonomy and the fact that Scotland's distinct laws were made in London not Edinburgh, led to growing clamour for a devolved legislature and steady growth in support for independence. Labour continued to dominate Scottish politics in the twentieth century, as the Liberals had done in the nineteenth century and the Scottish National Party (SNP) has so far in the twenty-first. The SNP were founded in 1934 and have been the major pro-independence party ever since but were politically insignificant until the latter decades of the twentieth century. In 1967 the SNP candidate Winnie Ewing won the Hamilton by-election, their first serious breakthrough which saw support begin to rise and make them an electoral threat (Keating 2005: 55, Devine 2012: 325, 574).

A referendum was held on the establishment of a devolved Scottish Assembly in 1979 under a Labour government. A majority voted in favour of devolution, but the government had stipulated that those who did not participate in the referendum were classed as voting 'no', which meant that the proposal was defeated (Ascherson 2002: 105–7, Devine 2012: 621). The SNP were incensed by this, and their MPs triggered a successful vote of no confidence in Prime Minister Jim Callaghan in the House of Commons. In the same year, a general election was held in which the radically right-wing Conservative Margaret Thatcher became the prime minister. Her government ushered in the Neoliberal age and buried the post-war Social Democratic one; privatizing government-owned industries, cutting the welfare state, successfully breaking the power of trade unions during the miner's strike and shifting the United Kingdom from an industrial to a financial and service-based economy. These policies especially affected many communities in Scotland along with Wales and northern England, who had largely opposed them (Devine 2012: 591–4).

The Conservative Party dominated UK politics for the next eighteen years, despite receiving little electoral support in Scotland. This bolstered Scottish nationalism (within and without the SNP itself) because it provided a figure to rally against, the 'Thatcherite other' (Mitchell 2005: 23), and accentuated political divisions between England (at least as a whole) and Scotland. Scottish MPs could be characterized as impotent, consistently outvoted in the House of Commons by Conservative MPs representing an English majority who could nonetheless impose policies opposed by most Scots (Ascherson 2002: 107). A crucial factor that is easy to take for granted is the persistence of a distinct Scottish national identity, as characterized by Cohen. This has plausibly rendered Scotland's majority opposition to the policies of the government as a case of one nation dominating another, rather than one area having different electoral tendencies to the majority.

After decades of campaigning by a coalition of groups drawn from across Scottish society, including churches, to keep the issue of devolution alive (Ascherson 2002: 116–21, Keating 2005: 13, on its relationship to religion, see: Sutcliffe 2004), this finally became a possibility with the election of a Labour government under Tony Blair in 1997. A referendum was held again in the same year, and the proposal was the establishment of a full parliament with tax raising powers and without any stipulations regarding voter turnout. A clear majority of 63.48 per cent voted for devolution, and the new parliament was opened in 1999 with Labour's Donald Dewar as the inaugural first minister (Ascherson 2002: 171, Keating 2005: 18, Devine 2012: 631). As noted previously, IFS was founded in the same year which demonstrated the organization's rootedness in the context of devolution.

In 2007 the SNP became the largest single party in the Scottish Parliament, forming a minority government under Alex Salmond. This marked a shift in political relations within the devolved United Kingdom because for the first time the ruling parties in Holyrood and Westminster (the names given to the Scottish and UK parliaments, respectively) differed. It was also the first time that a pro-independence party had become the largest party. The SNP subsequently won a landslide in 2011,[9] a year after the Conservative came to power again in Westminster.

This gave them the legislative power they needed to push for a referendum on independence, striking the Edinburgh Agreement with Conservative PM David Cameron to hold a referendum in 2014. The lead up to the referendum was defined by campaigning by two cross-party groups: 'Yes Scotland' (pro-independence) made up of the SNP and the Scottish Greens, and 'Better Together' (Unionist), made up of the Scottish Conservatives, Scottish Labour and the Scottish Liberal Democrats. It was also marked by public debates and saturated media as well as everyday life for the Scottish population (on the referendum and religion, see Rosie 2014).

The proposal for independence was defeated, the 'no' position won by a clear margin at 55.30 per cent but 44.70 per cent voted 'yes', a quarter of Scottish voters.[10] However, this did not mean that the question of independence or Union ever went away. The SNP continued to enjoy high electoral support in the Scottish Parliament. More surprisingly, the SNP also won a landslide in the Scottish seats in the UK Parliament in 2015, becoming the largest group of Scottish MPs at Westminster.[11] Despite this electoral success, they have had little control over wider developments and have faced increasingly hostile Conservative UK governments.

Two years after the independence referendum in 2014, a UK-wide referendum was held on the UK's membership of the European Union (EU) in 2016. A majority of Scottish voters (62 per cent) supported the 'Remain' position, to continue to be part of the EU and notably before the 2014 referendum they had been warned that an independent Scotland could be shut out of the EU. However, a slim majority of the UK electorate voted in favour of the 'Leave' (withdrawal) position at 51.89 per cent, which came to be known as 'Brexit' (a portmanteau of 'British' and 'exit'.[12] The United Kingdom finally withdrew from the EU in 2020, and so far, the SNP's efforts to capitalize on this to drive up support for a second referendum on independence have not been successful. They have also been unable to persuade increasingly more right-wing Conservative governments whose support base is increasingly Leave voters in England, nor the UK's Supreme Court, to allow them to hold one. It is not clear that the pro-independence position would be endorsed by a majority of the Scottish electorate if one was held.

IFS have commented very sparingly on the issue of Brexit in comparison to their extensive coverage of the 2014 independence referendum (see Chapter 6), but they did present information about the spike in hate crimes against ethnic minorities which followed it. It was noted that this had largely not affected Scotland but they cautioned against complacency on the issue. Notably, Dr Sier during the now annual summit between the FM and IFS, took the opportunity to thank the then First Minister Nicola Sturgeon for her leadership during the Brexit process (IFS 2017: 4, 6).

Since then, people across the world were affected by the Coronavirus epidemic which forced societies across the globe to go into lockdown and then return to a degree of tentative normality. This was also the subject of repeated clashes between the Scottish and UK governments, but also forced groups like IFS to change their practices (see IFS Summer 2020), though they have returned to face-to-face meetings and more routine practices.

Nicola Sturgeon resigned over a scandal about SNP party finances, for which she was briefly arrested (though not subsequently charged) (Nicolson 2023). Humza Yousaf became the first Muslim First Minister but has faced diminishing support for the SNP, which has been in power for sixteen years in Holyrood and has depended on a coalition agreement with the Scottish Green Party. When Yousaf chose to end the power-sharing agreement with the Greens this triggered a vote of no confidence in the Scottish Parliament, which led him to resign in turn. Following this, the former SNP leader John Swinney ascended unopposed to the role of First Minister and these are the uncertain and unsteady conditions of Scottish politics at the time of writing (Cook and McCool 2024). Conditions may be about to shift again as Labour won in a landslide in the UK general election on July 4th of this year, winning a majority of Scottish MPs and are likely to make considerable gains from the SNP in the Scottish Parliament. Having discussed both the histories of the IFM and the development of Scottish nationalism, a question remains: how on earth does it relate to nationalism, as I claim?

On nationalism: How on earth does it relate to interfaith dialogue?

For many readers, interfaith dialogue and nationalism may intuitively seem to have nothing to do with one another. It is understandable that casual observers might perceive this to be the case, but it reflects unreflective assumptions and surface-level appearances. Part of the problem is that 'nationalism' in the popular understanding is often equated with supremacist, exclusionary or xenophobic sentiment (Calhoun 2007: 7), which would stand in stark contrast to the IFM. At the very least, it is usually associated with overt political movements which most IFGs would not risk endorsing. It is undeniable that the IFM has a broadly progressive character for the most part which has explicitly critiqued supremacism, racism, prejudice, exclusivism and isolationism. It has been equally clear in its broad support for diversity of all kinds, multiculturalism and especially religious pluralism. The IFM is not only a global movement of interlinked IFGs but can be characterized by global consciousness and concerns; IFS is no exception to this.

Nonetheless, nationalism is commonly understood to be much broader than this within the academic study of nationalism or nationalism studies, one which I have argued that religion scholars should adopt when approaching nationalism (Sutherland 2017a). 'Nationalism' is often understood to be the ideology that undergirds the system of 'nation-states' but also which allows representatives of 'stateless nations' to make national claims (Halliday 2005: 528–9, van den Berghe 1981: 62, see also Guibernau 1999, Anderson and Kiel 2016). It can also refer to the historical process as well as the specific political movements which brought about this situation.

Elie Kedourie defined nationalist ideology as composed of two core claims or assumptions: firstly, that the world is naturally divided into 'national' communities and that nationhood is the legitimate basis for statehood (Kedourie 1960: 9). Despite the notable processes of globalization since the late twentieth century, we continue to live in a world where the authority of sovereign states; independent territorial units, which Max Weber famously defined as having a 'monopoly of the legitimate use of violence in a given territory' (Dunne and Schmidt 2005: 172), is paramount. This legitimacy is based on their claims to represent their population (Halliday 2005: 529). This differs substantially from the claims of most pre-modern states to have received a divine mandate to rule their territory or even simply by virtue of conquest (Gellner 1983: 13–16, Anderson 1983: 19–20). Agents of modern states do not claim to represent their rulers but their citizenry.

This form of legitimation does not automatically equate to nationalism specifically, but this makes nationalism an attractive ideological support for the state. It is easier to base these claims to speak on behalf of a populace if that population is conceived as bound together and differentiated by certain characteristics, that they are a 'people', a 'nation'. This is why many states claim to be 'nation-states'.

However, to be successful, this depends on a degree of acceptance by that population. The agitation of national movements through a range of cultural and political projects, education systems teaching national history (Gellner 1983

27, 31, 33–4) and mass media help forge and maintain these national identities (Anderson 1983, Billig 1995 109–22). The content that these institutions impart is a common 'national' history, symbolism, myths and culture; represented most obviously by the flag. Nation-building projects can be undertaken not only by states for their benefit but also by non-state actors who may not always respect established borders and often agitate for independence from or unification of existing states. In turn, ruling elites of any new nation-states will be subject to these same pressures. All successful nationalist projects, regardless of their origins, are dependent on a back and forth between elites and the masses.

It is not the case, however, that all modern states claim to be nation-states and some recognize multiple nations within their borders (see Seymour and Gagnon 2012, Anderson and Keil 2016). Occasionally, where there are entrenched national identities within some parts of the state, it may be easier to present the state as a 'family' or 'union' of nations in order to manage that diversity. Even the most homogenous nation-states (and substate national movements) have to manage the inevitable centripetal tendencies which arise among a large group of people: recognizing regional, local or other differences within that common 'national' community. When states adopt a 'plurinational' identity this can convince some citizens who identify with sub-state nationalities that they are nonetheless better together as part of a common polity. This is one particular theme which speaks to the study of religious diversity; normative pluralism, interfaith dialogue and different forms of secularism are also means of managing diversity.

Though still wider than many popular understandings of nationalism, one of the more restrictive definitions of nationalism within the literature was offered by the pioneering scholar Ernest Gellner. He defined nationalism as a principle and movement aiming to make the political and cultural community congruent (Gellner 1983: 1). This means that more specific characteristics of nationalist movements have been omitted, for example, whether they are 'left' or 'right', 'religious' or 'secular'. Nationalism for Gellner refers to programmes for national unification or secession, for example, Sinn Féin in Ireland and the SNP in Scotland.

Anthony Smith has offered a slightly broader definition as movements for national unity, independence or autonomy (Smith 2010: 9), which in Scotland could include the campaign for devolution. Nonetheless, I regard Kedourie's approach to be most useful for my purposes. Nationalism involves the categorization of bodies of people as 'nations', the understanding that they have a right to self-determination and that these are the legitimate forms of an overarching political community. This is the mentality which underlies the different relationships that have developed between contemporary religious diversity and national claims. As Liah Greenfeld argued, the 'nation' has replaced 'religion' as the overarching category into which different communities must fit (Greenfeld 1996).

Nationalism is also commonly divided into 'civic' and 'ethnic' forms, though an analytical typology, it is a more refined version of Hans Kohn's normative distinction between 'eastern' and 'western' nationalism, which argued for the moral superiority of the latter (Kohn 1994). 'Civic' forms of nationalism are those which define the characteristics of the nation through citizenship, common laws, inhabitation of a given territory and often core values, for example, liberty, fraternity and equality. 'Ethnic' nationalisms are those which define the nation through membership in an ethnicity, genealogical descent, common culture or indeed religion (Smith 1986: 134, Özkirimli 2005: 22–8, 2010: 35–6, Sutherland 2017a: 11, 2017b: 75-7). The problem with this typology, especially the latter type, is that it lumps together very different concepts (race, ethnicity, religion and culture) in an uneven fashion, which is also implicitly normative. It is in certain respects a more sophisticated version of the popular but spurious distinction between nationalism and patriotism.

Indeed, civic nationalism is most readily identifiable with the most established western nation-states, especially as the allusions to the national values most clearly apply to the United States and France. The cultural components of some national movements were often responses to cultural assimilationism, repression or subaltern status within larger states. Culture may have been the main unifying factor in the absence of the kind of institutional power that established nations could take for granted (Chatterjee 1986: 2, 1993: 6–8, see also Kaviraj 2007). It has been pointed out by several scholars that this typology obscures the strong cultural and historic components of even the most prototypical examples of civic nationalism: the role of the French language, for example, the sense of continuity in a historic territory and so forth (Smith 1986: 134, Özkirimli 2005: 22–8, 2010: 35–6, Sutherland 2017a: 11, 2017b: 75–7).

Nonetheless, this can potentially be a useful dichotomy if it is not used uncritically or rigidly and is understood to form a spectrum. It can draw attention to the factors or features which are emphasized by a nationalist movement, party or actor. I will show that the elements emphasized in IFS' literature can be classed as both civic and cultural which is why I claim that they express and relate to a civic-cultural nationalism. This does not mean that they espouse any kind of exclusionary or monocultural nationalism, but their representations of Scottish nationhood are not merely cultural in the implicit sense of civic nationalism but saturated with cultural references. These cultural references are used to associate different communities with Scotland, combining the traditional culture of the nation with expressions of cultural diversity to bind them together.

Having discussed the contested contours of nationalism, that still leaves the question of what differentiates nations as groups of people from other types of communities operating in the modern world. For a definition of nations, I will draw on the work of the path-breaking scholar of nationalism Benedict Anderson: nations are imagined communities conceived as at once limited and sovereign (Anderson 1983: 5–6). This does not mean that nations are imaginary but rather that they depend on the sentiments of the people who make them up; it is the self-conception or identity of a group. All communal identities applied to a great number of people who could never personally interact are imagined in this sense, for example, religions. What distinguishes nations is that they are conceived of as sovereign, having the right to self-determination, but also having their restricted claims to a bounded territory. Nationalist claims are by definition not global or universal in this sense because beyond the borders of the nation are other nations (ibid.). The most belligerent nationalists may claim lands beyond their current or recognized territories, but they legitimate this by arguing that it is historically or culturally part of their homeland, for example, the Russian legitimation for their invasion of Ukraine.

The most difficult category to disentangle from 'nation' is doubtlessly 'ethnicity'. Anthony Smith, for example, has defined ethnicities (*ethnie*) as a named human population with a set of myths, memories, symbols and values bound to a specific homeland (Smith 1986: 32). Though it is perhaps not always the case that ethnic groups have the same clearly demarcated territorial claims as those made on behalf of nations, territorial associations are rarely absent. Even in the case of ethnic minority communities formed through immigration, they continue to relate to homelands, sometimes modern nation-states (e.g. Pakistan, Lebanon) and may continue to support national projects in the homeland, which Smith calls 'vicarious nationalism' (Smith 1986: 151).

The concept of ethnicity is frequently used interchangeably with race or genealogical descent, but this clashes with the more cultural approaches championed by leading scholars of ethnicity. This assumption about ethnicity can repeat the same arbitrary normative civic-ethnic distinction, by casting nations as open, fluid and inclusive, while ethnicities are cast as fixed, exclusive, and based on descent. While myths of historic origins, collective memories and fictive kinship have been claimed about both ethnicities and nations, this does not automatically mean that they are closed. The Norwegian anthropologist Frederik Barth emphasized the importance of permeable boundaries as key to the maintenance of different ethnic groups. He observed that 'personnel' would often successfully move between ethnic categories by negotiating and taking on the boundary markers which distinguished ethnic belonging in different contexts (Barth 1969: 9–15).

It is also important to recognize that in the contemporary world, people often hold multiple ethnic affiliations, and new ethno-cultural categories periodically arise, especially as a result of globalization. Craig Calhoun gives the example of an emerging Asian (or Asian-American) identity in the United States, which would be less salient in the context of Asian societies themselves (Calhoun 2007: 160–1). All collective identities reflect the creativity and contextual adaptability of human beings but also highlight that when new identities arise, if they become salient and internalized by the agents, they are not necessarily any less powerful than long established ones.

The key difference between ethnic and national identities as I would define them, is not how exclusive or open they are. Rather, I would distinguish them according to the importance placed on sovereignty over a bounded territory by a sizeable portion of their population. The question remains how to classify cases like Scotland, Catalonia or Québec when the population is divided over independence but at the same time commonly regard themselves to be a nation. I would argue that they can be defined as nations regardless of whether their members agree on how their collective identity should be institutionally reflected if they largely hold an underlying conception that their community carries an 'ultimate sovereignty', a right to self-determination over their 'homeland'.

Whether nations have attained statehood, whether a majority desires it, or whether they appeal to 'civic' or 'cultural' features; national identities can and have been combined with multiculturalism and normative pluralism as well as more exclusionary projects. The relationship between pluralism and nationalism has been underexplored, but a synthesis of pluralism and nationalism is likely to be common, perhaps the norm. For example, the anthropologist Thomas Hylland Eriksen has written about how a common national identity is reinforced in Mauritius through public displays and performances of the different ethnicities of the island and their cultures (Eriksen 2002).

Nationalism as a common, but a very broad discourse upholds the vision of a world made up of nations and their ultimate sovereignty over their 'homelands'. This acts as the basis for different, competing political projects but also the complementary endeavours of different interest groups in a society. It is this broader nationalism with which IFGs have to negotiate with most of all because it is pervasive and informs the self-understanding of different actors in that society. Even if they try to avoid specific national political projects, this kind of nationalism cannot be avoided so easily when it defines the identity of the land and people as well as the authority of its government.

Michael Billig argued that most nationalism is in fact 'banal' rather than belligerent. It is experienced as part of the background of everyday life in which national belonging is continuously reinforced through the reproduction of symbols of the nation (flags lying unnoticed and unattended, sport strips, maps of the national territory, currency etc.) and everyday references to it as well as a world populated by nations (Billig 1995: 5–8). Common language, the 'small words' or deixes in media and indeed everyday conversations, for example, 'we', 'they', 'our nation' or indeed 'the government', also continuously reference the boundaries of the national community (Billig 1995: 94).

IFS and other IFGs operate in that environment and deal with governments whose authority is based on claims to represent the nation. Their members are also residents of the nation and may also express these sentiments themselves. Interfaith texts are one type among many types of sources which reinforce and encapsulate the ways in which pluralism is actively constructed and adapted. Nonetheless, these discourses reaffirm the ultimate sovereignty of the national community over its limited territory, even if it pales in comparison to the universal and timeless features attributed to the world's religions.

3

Heritage and partnership:
Interfaith Scotland's representation of
Scottish Christians

Introduction

In Chapter 2, we discussed how the interfaith movement (IFM) as a phenomenon can be related to the broader development of religious pluralism and more counter-intuitively to nationalism. In the four subsequent chapters of this book, we will empirically ground this broader analysis through the case study of Interfaith Scotland (IFS). This chapter is concerned with the organization's representation of Christians and Christianity. How was IFS able to integrate the most powerful and historic majority religion into its paradigm of one nation of many faiths?

There were three intrinsic challenges to including Christians in an interfaith framework in Scotland. Firstly, Christians until very recently formed a majority of the Scottish population and an overwhelming majority of 'people of faith', meaning that representing them proportionately would have entailed Christian domination. Secondly, the major churches at least, are still powerful and entrenched within Scottish society: possessing shared identity, language, practices and norms recognizable to most Scots. This means that Christians may not have perceived any benefits to joining an interfaith organization because even smaller and less established churches can potentially draw on this common heritage. Thirdly, the sheer number of distinct churches means that if each were represented separately, Christians would also dominate numerically in a different sense.

> For the Churches the question of Christian membership was much discussed: should membership be … ecumenical … or from different Christian denominations[?] … [T]here was now concern that the council would be

unbalanced … And yet if the Churches were represented by ACTS, individual
denominations might not take the council seriously.[1] (ACTS n.d: 16)

The desire and difficulties in striking a balance between representations of a
common identity and representing diversity will be a significant theme for this
chapter and the book as a whole. The incorporation of Christians, especially
the major churches, carries the risk of domination but also potential access to
their resources, knowledge, contacts and influence within the country. Christian
churches can help to legitimate interfaith relations and the public presence
of religious minorities. Furthermore, the realization of the Scottish interfaith
movement's vision of constructing and normalizing the view of Scotland as a
multi-faith nation depends on the incorporation of the largest religious category.

The three challenges outlined earlier, the numeracy, power and diversity of
Christians in Scotland, would seem to be fairly difficult hurdles to overcome. It
begs the question, why were Christians interested in getting involved with the
interfaith movement at all? Christians would have to be motivated to accept a
fairly diminished status in relation to both their broader religious tradition and
denomination. It is important to acknowledge that Christian involvement in the
Scottish interfaith movement can be explained largely by the fact that Christian
individuals and institutions were instrumental in establishing it in the first place.
However, that leaves the question of why they would invest energy and resources
in doing so.

Before discussing the specifics of Christian relations with the interfaith
movement, it will be useful to briefly reintroduce the characteristics of
Christianity in Scotland. According to the last census in 2022, self-identified
Christians were the largest single religious group at 38.8 per cent but lost their
slim majority of 54 per cent from the previous census in 2011. The largest
single denomination is the national church – the Church of Scotland which
represents 20.4 per cent of Scots falling from 32.4 per cent in 2011. The second
major denomination is the Scottish Roman Catholic Church which represents
13 per cent of the population and other Christian groups make up 5.1 per cent
(National Records of Scotland 2024).

The Scottish Episcopal Church is quite a bit numerically smaller but is usually
included as the third major church because of its historic position within the
country, especially in certain regions. The Episcopal Church is part of the
Anglican Communion and related to the Church of England with which it is
sometimes confused. It does include English migrant populations but stresses its
institutional and historical distinctiveness from its English counterpart (Bruce

1985: 8, Bruce 2014: 9, 13, 112, 120). Other forms of Christianity in Scotland include Presbyterian churches which split from the Kirk, known as the 'Free Churches' (Bruce 2014: 9–11, Devine 2012: 374–77). There are also a range of denominations commonly found throughout Britain including Methodist, United Reformed, Baptist, Pentecostal, Orthodox, Congregationalist, Plymouth Brethren, Quaker (The Religious Society of Friends) and other Christian congregations. Despite the considerable differences between all of these groups, however, their description as 'Christian' would now be considered fairly uncontroversial.

The approach taken in this book though largely follows the self-designation of the actors, institutions and communities themselves. It only diverges from that for explicit, analytical purposes or to make historic connections clear. This prerogative is never intended to 'correct' the designation of the community, and it is not the remit of this book to police whatever is deemed authentically Christian. Therefore, Christian will here also include groups considered marginal within Christianity or not considered Christian at all by some. This would include the Church of Jesus Christ of Latter-day Saints (LDS, colloquially known as 'Mormons'), Jehovah's Witnesses, the Family Federation for World Peace and Unification (FFWPU, colloquially known as 'Moonies') who identify as Christians. For historical and analytical reasons, I will discuss Unitarians (the SUA) as well whose membership diverges in their identification with the label.

This chapter will argue that Interfaith Scotland's construct is specifically 'Interfaith Christianity' and is not representative of all Christians in the country. It will analyse this through three key concepts: *ecumenicism*, *pluralism* and *secularism* to explain how and why it emerged as it did. The data relevant to this discussion will include the official institutional representation of Christians in the organization and depictions of Christianity in the literature. Important themes will include how commonalities and differences are stressed or downplayed, and especially how Christianity is rendered into a single world religion equivalent to others. I will discuss how interfaith relations have formed part of the strategies that Christians have used to negotiate the religious diversification and secularization of Scottish public life, as well as the entrenchment of normative secular-pluralism. The dominant forms of Scottish Christianity have undoubtedly been reshaped, but they have been able to adapt from a position of comparative advantage by embracing these ideologies on their own terms. Nonetheless, it should be stressed that this has genuinely involved acceptance of a less pre-eminent status.

Christianity in Scotland from foundations, to sectarianism, to ecumenicism

As stated in previous chapters, Scotland has been overwhelmingly Christian from the origins of Scotland as a recognizable cultural or political entity until the late twentieth century (Bruce 2014: 1). A great store of the literary, artistic, cultural, symbolic and built heritage of the nation is Christian or strongly tinged by Christianity (Broun 2002: 22–4, 28–9). Scotland's patron saint, St Andrew and his symbolism are important national symbols: St Andrew's x-shaped cross is reflected in the nation's flag (a white x-cross on a blue background), and St Andrew's Day on 30 November is considered a national day. The obvious Christian origins of this flag though have not impeded its reinterpretation and application by different communities because it is now chiefly of 'national' rather than 'religious' significance.

The long Christian history of the country does unquestionably and unavoidably impact contemporary Scottish communities in various ways. Nonetheless, the significance of that history depends on the perceptions and interests of actors in the present. That history can be employed for different ideological and theological projects. It can and has been utilized to exclude or marginalize non-Christians, but for IFS, acknowledging that history allows them to repurpose it as a foundation for a religiously plural society (e.g. IFS Summer 2014: 6–7). Complicated histories do not have simple or clear-cut import in heterogeneous societies because these histories are far less static or homogenous than they are often presented to be.

Nonetheless, as acknowledged previously, it would also be fair to suggest that Scottish society was homogenously Christian until the late twentieth century, and the dominant Presbyterian tradition exercised a hegemonic influence until then as well. Until recently, Scottish culture and identity were strongly, if not completely, associated with the Calvinist, Presbyterian tradition. As outlined in the historical section of Chapter 2 the Roman Catholic community began to grow due primarily to immigration from Ireland in the nineteenth century (Devine 2012: 518–22). The existence of Catholics as a larger ethno-religious minority provided an *other* against which such a Scottish Protestant identity could be asserted. This led to persistent anti-Catholic and anti-Irish discrimination in the country and sectarian tensions, as well as segregation between different Christian traditions in Scotland (see Devine 2000, Bruce et al. 2004, Rosie 2004). Had this scenario continued, it would likely have made it difficult for Christian groups to have been able to work together, let alone to accept a *common* position alongside other religions.

However, Catholics in Scotland became increasingly integrated in the mid- to late-twentieth centuries through shared experiences of the world wars, the redevelopment of cities and dispersal of previously fixed urban communities and through the rise of an educated Catholic middle class (Bruce 2014 49–50). Along with this, the changing attitude of the Catholic Church towards other denominations following Vatican II is significant (Womack 2018: 21, Hedges 2021: 328–30, Howard 2021: 5). Since that time, the issue of sectarianism has persisted but has been roundly condemned by all elite institutions which explicitly or tacitly encouraged it, such as the government, media and above all, the churches. It has shifted from a relatively pervasive, tacitly normative attitude in Scottish society to one widely reviled, pushed to the margins of acceptable discourse. It is now much more related to football rivalries than to active religious convictions (Bruce 2014 54–5). Nonetheless, it has not vanished (Geoghegan 2013) and especially for the purposes of this book, it is a crucial part of the historical background of discussions of religious and inter-religious relations in the country.

From the 1960s onwards as with much of the western world; the culture, politics and society of Scotland became increasingly secular (Brown 1997: 174). In a more general sense though, it also meant that the shared norms and default position of the average Scot were no longer Presbyterian, Protestant or even Christian. Beginning in the late 1940s and especially after the 1960s, the religious landscape of Scotland was affected by immigration from former colonies of the British empire, especially South and East Asians, who brought their religions with them. Along with the small Scottish Jewish community, these peoples established active Muslim, Sikh, Hindu and Buddhist communities (Bruce 2014: 14–15, Devine 2012: 563–4, Devine and McCarthy 2018). This decline in Christian influence, increasing diversification coupled with secularization in Scotland and the wider world can help explain the increasingly ecumenical relations among Christians, including across the Protestant and Catholic divide (see Edwards 2012 138–40). The increased integration of the Catholic Church and lay communities, who were, by this point, very long established, was crucial to this process.

Christian membership in interfaith Scotland

While the interfaith movement (IFM) or something analogous to it could have potentially developed in various ways, the fact is that Christians have been particularly foundational and influential in shaping it as a global movement. This was true from its very beginnings in the Chicago Parliament of World Religions in 1893 to the flowering of local interfaith groups across the western world (Brodeur 2005: 42–53, IFS n.d.: 4). Many of these groups began when representatives of non-Christian religions were invited to meetings with members of different churches (Pederson 2004: 80). The pervasiveness of this pattern demonstrates the point that this section will particularly stress, that the IFM globally, nationally and locally has been dependent on the success of the Christian ecumenical movement.

Ecumenism, alongside pluralism and secularism, is one of the three core concepts this chapter will use to analyse the development of Interfaith Christianity in Scotland. The term is derived from the Greek *oikumene*, meaning 'of the world' and refers to efforts to represent and encourage collaboration between Christian churches, denominations and sects. It encourages identification with 'the (world) Church' in the broader, universal sense over and above specific churches. Ecumenism can also be used by scholars to refer to parallel processes within other traditions and as a kind of intra-faith analogue to interfaith (Bowker 1997: 303–04, Kesting 2014).

Much of Christian history has been marked by periods of hegemony and by intense competition between rival denominations. Christian ecumenicism is a relatively modern phenomenon which reflects both of those tendencies in surprising ways and which has significant ties to Scotland. The 1910 Edinburgh Missionary Conference played a landmark role in encouraging this ethos and fostering stronger relations between denominations, though it was not the first such event and was exclusively Protestant (Stanley 2012: 113). Its lasting impact was perhaps encouraging identification with broader Christian aims and identity over and above institutional or denominational ones (Bowker 1997: 303–04, 646–7). On a global scale, it anticipated the formation of the World Council of Churches (WCC) in 1948. It has developed a closer, working relationship with the Catholic Church since Vatican II even though it is not formally a member[2] (Bowker 1997: 304). Furthermore, ecumenical bodies in many nations, such as Scotland, as we shall see, do include Catholic representatives.

As discussed earlier, Christians, both Catholic and Protestant, laity and clergy, played a foundational role in the local as well as global IFM. The first interfaith group in Scotland, Glasgow Sharing of Faiths (GSF) was founded in 1969 by a former Church of Scotland missionary to Pakistan (Adamson, Ramsay and Craig 1984: 1–2, 26). Christians also founded the Interfaith Network for the

United Kingdom (IFNUK) through the work of Brian Pierce in 1987 (IFNUK 2007: 6, Pearce 2012) and local groups such as Edinburgh Interfaith Association (EIFA) by the late Professor Frank Whaling, in 1989 (Goldblatt 2022). Most crucially for us, the Scottish Inter Faith Council (SIFC), later Interfaith Scotland (IFS) was established by a Roman Catholic nun, Sister Isabel Smyth OBE SND (IFS n.d.: 5). As Sister Smyth pointed out in her interview with me, the contribution of Christians, including herself and Stella Reekie, to the foundation of IFM in Scotland was vital. She explained this by the simple demographic fact that there were many more Christians in Scotland at the time than members of other religions, but also that this was a time when Christians were becoming more open to interreligious relations. This openness to dialogue was itself a reflection of a post-Vatican II and WCC context, which further highlights the connection between interfaith and ecumenical relations (Sister Smyth personal communication, 20 June 2016).

The Scottish Religious Leaders Forum (RLF) was also established in 2002 by the heads of the three major churches: the Right Revd. Finlay MacDonald – Moderator of the Church of Scotland, Cardinal Keith O'Brien – Archbishop of Edinburgh and the Most Revd. Bruce Cameron – Primus of the Scottish Episcopal Church. The RLF was established to maintain contact between Scotland's religious leadership following the terror attacks of 11 September 2001 (ACTS n.d.: 17–19, SIFC August 2009: 11). Before the RLF and the establishment of the Scottish Parliament, the UK Government's Secretary of State for Scotland met bi-annually with the heads of the three major churches (Sister Smyth personal communication, 20 June 2016). It is testament to the changing environment of modern Scotland that now the first minister of a directly elected Scottish Parliament meets with representatives of many religions (e.g. IFS September 2012: 4). Nonetheless, in line with the developments discussed in this chapter, it was those same church leaders who proved instrumental in making this a reality.

In Scotland, most churches are members of an ecumenical body founded in 1990 called Action of Churches Together Scotland (ACTS n.d.: 10). Notably, the membership of ACTS and Christian membership of IFS overlap almost completely. The following churches are members of both organizations: the Church of Scotland, Scottish Roman Catholic Church, Scottish Episcopal Church, Religious Society of Friends, the Methodist Church in Scotland, Salvation Army – Scotland and the United Reformed Church: Synod of Scotland[3] (see also Sutherland 2017b, 2017c, 2018a).

ACTS includes two members who have not joined IFS: the Congregational Federation and the United Free Church. There are three identifiably Christian members of IFS who are not members of ACTS: the Scottish Unitarian Association (SUA), the Church of Jesus Christ of Latter-day Saints (LDS) and the Family Federation for World Peace and Unification (FFWPU). Lastly, there are churches which are not members of either, including the Free Church of Scotland or any Baptist, Orthodox, Pentecostal, Plymouth Brethren, Jehovah's Witness or Seventh Day Adventist churches (see Table 3.1).

The Kirk and the Catholic Church had interfaith departments well before the creation of the Scottish Inter Faith Council (SIFC now IFS), but an organization called the Churches Agency for Interfaith Relations (CAIR) played a major role in bridging ecumenicism and interfaith involvement, especially for smaller churches. CAIR was founded in 1995 and grew out of the Kirk's Community and Race Relations group, which was extended to include representatives from other denominations (ACTS n.d.: 10). This development also reflects the notable shift in public discourse in many countries from an emphasis on racial, ethnic or cultural inclusivity to a greater emphasis on religious pluralism. CAIR was disbanded in 2014 because of its overlap with Christian representation in IFS (ACTS n.d.: 12, 16). Historically speaking, we can view this as a specific institutional example of the shift from Christian dominance to normative pluralism through ecumenicism.

If there was still a deep antipathy or few formal or informal ties between Christian denominations, then cultivating a wider sense of commonality and shared interests with more diverse groups would have been difficult. It must be stressed though that the success of ecumenicism in Scotland has not depended on all Christians. Ecumenical relations necessitate a willingness to tolerate some divergence and stress on a common identity as a shared framework.

The reluctance of some churches to engage with ecumenicism and interfaith relations could be explained by the fact that many small churches were the products of secession due to theological and political disagreements (Bruce 2014: 9–11, Devine 2012: 374–7). While the difference between them and the major churches may once have been fairly specific, the gulfs between splinter churches and the Christian 'mainstream' have widened because the 'mainstream' is always a shifting phenomenon which can rapidly leave certain groups behind. The protean and socially constructed character of contemporary mainstream of Scottish Christianity does not mean that it lacks distinctive, relatively cohesive characteristics within this particular historical context.

Table 3.1 Christian membership of interfaith Scotland and action of Churches Together Scotland

'Founding (Christian)' members of IFS	Members of IFS and ACTS	Former 'Associate' (Christian) Members of IFS	Members of ACTS not IFS	Members of Neither
Church of Scotland	Church of Scotland	Church of Jesus Christ of Latter-day Saints (LDS/'Mormon')	Congregational Federation	Free Church of Scotland
Scottish Roman Catholic Church	Scottish Roman Catholic Church	Family Federation for World Peace and Unification (FFWPU/'Moonie')	United Free Church	Other Presbyterian churches
Scottish Episcopal Church	Scottish Episcopal Church	Scottish Unitarian Association (SUA)		Baptist churches
United Reformed Church: Synod of Scotland	United Reformed Church: Synod of Scotland			Orthodox churches
Salvation Army – Scotland	Salvation Army – Scotland			Jehovah's Witnesses
Religious Society of Friends ('Quaker')	Religious Society of Friends ('Quaker')			Evangelical churches
Methodist Church in Scotland	Methodist Church in Scotland			Pentecostal churches etc.

Informally, these interfaith-ecumenical denominations are all part of the established landscape of British Christianity, though there are variations in that landscape among the nations and regions of the UK. This is defined by long residence and similar theologies, values, practices, aesthetics and cultural outlook; even if on the surface these may appear to be quite different 'liberal' and 'conservative', 'high' and 'low' church forms of Christianity. The landscape itself and the mainstream within it differ from what we would expect to find in other Christian majority societies, for example, the United States, Romania, Zambia or the Philippines but are somewhat similar to many Anglophone former British colonies such as Canada, Australia or New Zealand.

Roman Catholicism was long presented as 'foreign' or quite specifically as 'Irish', despite the presence of long-standing Catholic minorities, against which 'British' and 'Scottish' Protestantism was defined. Within this 'ecumenical establishment' (Parsons 1993: 28) there are groups which are quite distinct from the mainstream, such as the Quakers or Religious Society of Friends who are highly divergent from other Scottish Christian groups in terms of ecclesiastical structure, ritual, aesthetics and theology. Nonetheless, they have been easy to incorporate because of their pacifism and openness to dialogue, as well as their long habitation (see Dandelion 2008). This is likely the reason that they have been accepted by more dominant churches. There are also numerically very small groups, such as the Methodists in Scotland, who are nonetheless theologically and culturally similar to other denominations. To this we can also add some newer denominations, such as the United Reformed Church founded in 1971 (Bowker 1997: 1005). On the other hand, as we shall see, certain Christian groups are neither well-established in Scotland nor mainstream within Christianity.

The Scottish Unitarian Association (SUA), the Church of Jesus Christ of Latter-day Saints (LDS) and the Family Federation for World Peace and Unification (FFWPU) are three members of IFS which could be classified as Christian by certain definitions. Until the constitutional change in 2022, they were not classified as 'Christian' members of IFS and were designated as 'associate members'. All three of these groups can be characterized as non-traditional or non-mainstream within Scottish and global Christianity. The Unitarians were first established in England but have had a presence in Scotland since the nineteenth century. Though the LDS and FFWPU could be characterized as 'non-indigenous' and as New Religious Movements (NRMs) (see Barker 1989), especially in this context. All three could be classified as unconventional or heterodox in their doctrines and practices. This also places them outside of the particular world religions model used by IFS and alongside other marginalized religions such as the Brahma Kumaris and the Scottish Pagan Federation (SPF). The existence of NRMs was explicitly acknowledged within the literature to explain this former distinction between 'founding' and 'associate' members.

> The Churches … remained clear that there should be a recognition of the distinction between major historical world religions and newer religious movements. (ACTS n.d: 16)

Nonetheless, this reveals the ingrained influence of the world religions approach, any church recognized as partaking in the common characteristics of Christianity as a tradition can seemingly claim that heritage as part of a 2000-year-old tradition. It does not matter that these churches deviate from each other and were produced by localized historical developments within the long timespan of world Christianity. Nonetheless, new churches who deviate from what is accepted as integral to that tradition, even if they also inherit much from this common tradition, are treated as wholly new. This is in spite of self-identification with Christianity as a global, historical tradition. The fact that the LDS, founded in the 1820s is classed as an NRM while the Iona Community (IC) founded in 1938 and the United Reformed Church (URC) founded in 1971 are not considered 'new' is significant. If the date of foundation is not the marker between 'historic' Christian groups and 'new religions', then what is? We will examine the characteristics of the three Christian Associate Members to ascertain how this boundary is policed.

The Family Federation for World Peace and Unification (FFWPU) is probably the most controversial and was for most of its history has been known as the Unification Church. It was founded as the Holy Spirit Association for the Unification of World Christianity by South Korean Revd. Sun Myung Moon (1920–2012), who claimed to be the Messiah. Followers of Unificationism have been popularly known as 'Moonies' after their founder. This religion came to prominence during the 'cult' scares of the 1980s, and the Church was often accused of brainwashing, though this claim has been unsupported by scholarly research and refuted by the high turnover in membership even in its heyday. One of its defining practices was the staging of mass weddings, often officiated by the Revd. Moon and his wife (Barker 1989: 213–14, Chryssides 2012). The identification as Christian and with Christianity as an explicitly global, multi-denominational tradition is evident through their nomenclature. After years of membership in the organization, there are indications that they have become more accepted, Dr Sier officially opened their new 'Peace Embassy' in Glasgow on 18 November 2022 (IFS Spring 2023: 13).

The Church of Jesus Christ of Latter-day Saints (LDS) commonly known as the Mormon Church was founded in the US state of New York by Joseph Smith (1805–1844) in the 1820s (Shipps 1987: 151–61), notably predating the establishment of the Baháʼí Faith by several decades (see IFS n.d.: 18). Smith claimed to be a prophet and to have received a revelation from an angel called Moroni and a new set of scriptures – *The Book of Mormon*. These texts purport to recount the history of several lost tribes of Israel in North America (Shipps 1987: 3). After a period of persecution, Smith led his community to what is now the US state of Utah, which continues to be the seat of the LDS and the area with the highest concentration of its followers (Shipps 1987: 60). The Church infamously encouraged polygamy early in its history but has actually forbade the practice subsequently (Shipps 1987: 167). They are also famous for their active missionary endeavours, all LDS youth are expected to engage in a period of missionary travel, which has made them more visible than many NRMs. The LDS is quite active in the interfaith movement and more recently received attention in the newsletter because they staged a 'West End' style musical called 'Our Story Goes on' in Edinburgh and Fife for SIFW (IFS 2018: 19). They also contributed their own chapter to *Values in Harmony* but as a separate entry from Christianity, both entries will be examined in more detail below.

The Scottish Unitarian Association (SUA) was founded in 1813 (Chryssides 1998: 86) and is part of a tradition generally known as Unitarianism and as Unitarian-Universalism in the United States (Long 2000: 46–51). The SUA is in many ways a very different case from the FFWPU and LDS. Unlike these organizations, they do not possess strong hierarchical structures or conservative social teachings. They were initially an amalgam of liberal and theologically heterodox groups within Protestant Christianity who espoused Unitarianism and often Universalism (in the United States they were explicitly a conjoining of organizations defined by these doctrines, Chryssides 1998: 23, 34). Unitarianism (*sensu stricto*) is the doctrine that God is one undifferentiated being, as opposed to mainstream Christian Trinitarianism, the doctrine that God is a being made up of three distinct persons: the Father, the Son (Jesus Christ) and the Holy Spirit (Long 2000: 46). Universalism is the doctrine that Christ's resurrection ensured the salvation of all human beings regardless of faith, deeds or observance (Long 2000: 49). Within Christian theology, one might say that it is as far as one could possibly get from traditional Calvinism.

Historically speaking, one can view Unitarianism (*sensu lato*) as a kind of counter-cultural fringe within liberal Protestantism. Both of these doctrines have been expressed by heretical Christian groups and thinkers for centuries, but the first Unitarian chapel was opened in London in 1774 (Chryssides 1998: 9, 19). Nonetheless, this doctrinal openness has meant that the extent to which they are defined by doctrinal positions within a Christian theological spectrum is no longer clear-cut (Chryssides 1998: 33–4). Members of Unitarian congregations are now free to hold whatever religious positions they wish alongside the three core principles of freedom, reason and tolerance, and may also be members of other communities (Chryssides 1998: 5–7, 50–1). They also have very few common rituals besides the lighting of the chalice, which is their core symbol (Chryssides 1998: 54–6, 94–5). Unitarianism in modern times can be considered to be a 'post-Christian' religious community whose membership does not all identify as 'Christian' regardless of its historical origins (Chryssides 1998: 78–9). However, unlike many diffuse forms of alternative spirituality, they have maintained a communal, congregational structure (Long 2000: 49–50).

These three cases are quite distinct, but there are certain commonalities which can be observed. Firstly, none of these groups are part of the WCC or ACTS and are evidently outside of the Scottish Christian mainstream (either rejecting or adding to the doctrines and theologies shared by most Christian groups). Secondly, the controversial characteristics of both the FFWPU and LDS mean that the possibility that they could have the same level of influence as the mainstream churches could lead to a loss of public credibility either for IFS or the churches. As we shall see later in the chapter, IFS may have given them associate membership because of actual or anticipated pressure from the major churches, who did in fact exert similar pressure in relation to the SPF. However, it is also likely that as IFS have become more established, less dependent on the churches and non-mainstream religious groups have become more accepted that these concerns dissipated over time, which facilitated the reform of membership in 2022.

The SUA are not controversial to anywhere near the same extent (though this was not always the case and may still be controversial in more conservative circles) or in the same ways. Their Unitarianism and post-Christianity put them at odds with Christian denominations, but their universalism and multi-faith ethos are likely shared by liberals within those denominations. It should be noted though that Quakers also hold unstructured services (Dandelion 2008: 48–52), are open to highly individualized interpretation (Dandelion 2008: 65–7), and some Quakers have also identified as post-Christian (Dandelion 2008: 67–8). Arguably, Quakers have a greater public profile and entrenched institutional involvement in the ecumenical movement which has ensured that they continue to be recognized as Christian. Notably, Unitarians had associate member status in the British Council of Churches, and when this was reorganized into the Council of Churches for Britain and Ireland (now Churches Together Britain and Ireland), their application for full membership was denied (Chryssides 1998: 79). However, in many local interfaith groups such as EIFA, the Unitarians have full board representation but one distinct from Christianity.[4] In this case perhaps, the classification of Unitarianism as something distinct from Christianity appears to be mutual rather than imposed by the majority. It is notable that when IFS abolished the two-tier system and introduced the three classifications ('Abrahamic', 'Dharmic' and 'Other Faiths and spiritual traditions') that LDS were classed as 'Abrahamic' and the FFWPU and SUA as 'other faiths and spiritual traditions'.[5]

As with other identifiable traditions, Christianity has been rendered into a world religion with distinct characteristics, norms and values shared by all groups classifiable as Christians, which are considered more significant than differences between them. This is evident within and reinforced by IFS' literature, through documents such as *The Guide to the Faith Communities of Scotland* and *Values in Harmony*. The Christianity section of the *Guide* introduces the origins of the religion, the role of Jesus Christ and affirms a Trinitarian position:

> Christians believe Jesus to be the Son of God … following in the way of Jesus who revealed the forgiving love of God for all people and God's concern for human beings. (IFS n.d: 8)

It affirms the divinity of Christ with a tacit acknowledgement that this is not completely universal: 'for many he is understood as an incarnation'. The section also rather ingeniously glosses over some of the biggest doctrinal and ritual controversies within the tradition, between adult and infant baptism and a 'symbolic' or 'sacramental' understanding of the communion (or eucharist) ritual (IFS n.d.: 8–9).

In *Values*, the success of ecumenicism is demonstrated by the fact that ACTS is the sole contact provided for all Christians in Scotland. The stress on continuity and Christian heritage within Scotland is represented by the photo of Iona Abbey and Celtic crosses (SIFC 2011: 28), '[a] centre for pilgrimage for Christians of many diverse background (SIFC 2011: 29)'. The abbey reflects ancient Christian monasticism but is owned and used by the ecumenical Iona Community, founded by a Church of Scotland minister, the Revd. George MacLeod in 1938. The Christianity section conveys support for a multi-ethnic and multicultural Christianity, summed up by the famous quote from Galatians

3:28: 'there is neither Jew nor Greek (cited in SIFC 2011: 31). There are also quotes supportive of ecumenicism and against sectarianism:

> Today there are many different traditions and churches within Christianity. Regrettably, Christian history has suffered the scandal of division. Thankfully, today many Christians are actively seeking to work more and more closely together ... The aim is to re-establish unity among all of Christ's followers – a unity which encompasses the rich diversity found among our many and valued Christian traditions. (SIFC 2011: 29)

Nonetheless, this broad church still has walls. The LDS section of *Values* is notably fronted by a photograph of an LDS Cathedral in Preston, in the northwest of England, which conforms to traditional church architecture. They use their section to affirm the golden rule, using the exact same quote, Luke 6:31, as the Christianity section (SIFC 2011: 33–4).

> The Church of Jesus Christ of Latter-day Saints is a Christian faith with Jesus Christ at its head. We believe that the gospel, preached by Jesus Christ in ancient times, is restored to earth and continues to be directed by Him through a living prophet and twelve apostles. (SIFC 2011: 34)

It goes on to affirm Trinitarianism and the significance of the Old and New Testaments alongside the *Book of Mormon*. The example of Jesus is invoked in a way that expresses their Christian and interfaith credentials while also acknowledging their distinctiveness (SIFC 2011: 33–4).

Christians and pluralism

Ecumenicism was a vital step in integrating Christianity into the Scottish IFM. It encouraged cooperation as well as regular, harmonious relations between Christian churches and acceptance that they are Christians first and foremost before they are members of denominations. This was crucial groundwork for the acceptance of an equal status with other religions deemed equivalent to that common Christian tradition. In practice, this has actually entailed the acceptance of a formally diminished status in certain respects.

The historical background of ecumenicism in Scotland has been a period of declining church attendance, declining Christian identification and eroding denominational identities as a result (Bruce 2014: 3–4). This makes the acceptance of the ecumenical establishment much easier to understand. Nonetheless, this does not necessarily make the leap from this ecumenicism to interfaith an obvious one; especially given how much Christian churches and individuals have actively facilitated the inclusion of religious minorities rather than simply participated alongside them. It would have been quite possible for this Christian unity to have been constructed *against* the other and in defence of an exclusionary vision of the national public sphere. A desire for ecumenical relations and an antipathy towards interfaith dialogue has been expressed by, for example, the former Moderator of the Free Church of Scotland, Revd. David Robertson:

> Church leaders are continually pleading for unity. We in the Free Church long for Christian unity – but it must be Christian … It is impossible to be united with those who would deny the very basics of the Christian faith. (Robertson 2016)

The enthusiastic acceptance of religious pluralism can also be viewed as reinforcing the distinct characteristics of this ecumenical Christianity in relation to those left outside of the mainstream or who have refused to adapt to the new consensus. Certainly, IFS depends on an influential segment of Christians accepting the value of dialogue on an equal basis with members of other traditions. IFS benefits from and encourages this interfaith Christianity to secure their position against exclusionary forms of Christianity. These mainstream churches use interfaith engagement to demarcate themselves against these exclusionary forms of Christianity and to further push them out of the public representation of modern Scottish Christianity.

This section of the chapter will be concerned with the ways in which this Christian pluralism is reflected, represented and reinforced in IFS' literature. As with many other groups, visible Christian representation in the literature, through photography, can be difficult to gauge. Certain religious groups are associated with particular ethnic heritages which are represented through dress, music, dance, food and visual arts, which are used to visually express both multiculturalism and interfaith relations. Christianity is complex in this regard because it includes much of the white Scottish majority but is also made up of people from a range of ethnic backgrounds. Furthermore, while Scottish Christianity as noted is tied to the heritage of Scotland in various ways, Scottish cultural identity is no longer bound to it in any exclusive or propriety sense. The presence of tartans, kilts or for that matter saltires cannot be taken to represent Christians or Christianity specifically at all.

One manner in which the presence of Christians and Christianity is visually expressed in photography though is through the vestments of Christian clergy, especially in photos of the Religious Leaders Forum (RLF). This is in many ways highly representative of interfaith because it includes Christian clergy in dialogue or standing together with representatives of other religions who also bear identifiable religious garb – Sikh turbans, Jewish skullcaps (*kippah*), Buddhist monastic robes and so forth. Nonetheless, it is also not completely representative because this includes members of the clergy or institutional authorities within these traditions, not ordinary lay membership. In cases where lay membership is more predominant, it can be impossible to tell what religion participants are affiliated with. IFS often actively circumvents this by explicitly stating what tradition participants represent, whether they have a formal role in doing so or not. Despite these efforts, this information cannot always be ascertained. In many ways Christian affiliation, at least in interfaith circles, is still the implied norm or default position of many participants (though in certain cases this can be taken to be the non-religious, secular and religiously apathetic publics).

Another way in which the presence of Christianity is visually represented in the literature is unsurprisingly through churches. Places of worship, explicitly multifaith and civic spaces are all common venues, and there is a preference for a variety of different, purpose-built places of worship. However, the number of purpose-built non-Christian places of worship such as gurdwaras, temples or synagogues in Scotland is still comparatively low, especially outside of the main cities. Even many non-Christian places of worship were converted from former churches and bear those architectural features. In general though, interfaith events and meetings often take place in churches or include visits to Christian sites because there are far more of them and they are found throughout the country.

Nonetheless, this has not been much of a stumbling block for IFS in their construction of Scotland as one nation of many faiths. In interfaith events, multiple churches or Christian sites may be involved, but other places of worship can be utilized along with them to create a sense of distinct, diverse and active communities worshipping alongside each other. Neighbourhood places of worship can also be perceived as the most immediate, accessible layer of a kind of sacred national landscape along with major sites of pilgrimage and even described in terms of a 'pilgrimage to sacred sites in Scotland' (SIFC August 2009: 9). This sacred landscape embeds Christian and non-Christian sites together from visits between a local church and mosque to pilgrimages to Iona and Samyé Ling (e.g. SIFC September 2010: 8, IFS Spring 2013: 15, IFS Summer

2014: 5). This makes the Christian character of many historic Christian sites part of a common heritage for 'people of faith' in Scotland.

The theme of pluralism is particularly evident in Christian self-representations in documents such as the *Guide* and *Values*. In the *Guide*, under the heading 'concerns of the community', no issues specific to Christians have been mentioned (IFS n.d.: 9). This suggests a community far less threatened by prejudice (especially in comparison to the Jewish and Muslim communities) and without any kind of resentment about diversification. Some Christians would no doubt have used this section to attack perceived prejudices against Christians (and of course prejudice against certain sub-groups such as anti-Catholicism does continue to exist) or perhaps used it as a platform to lambast secularism, but this is not how interfaith Christianity presents itself.

> They believe in the presence and support of God's spirit among all … many Christians find common cause working together with others for the good of communities at local, national and international levels. (IFS n.d: 9)

Values' Christian section introduces the characteristics of the tradition, including that they share the Hebrew Bible with their 'Jewish brothers and sisters' (SIFC 2011: 29–30). The scriptural and other quotes are used both to express their perspective and affirm commonalities with other traditions, 'we trust that these [quotes] will resonate with the insights and values of other traditions' (SIFC 2011: 30).

> These values are shared by many people in our world. The majority of Christians seek to live in harmony with adherents of other faith traditions and philosophies. For the Christian, the reason and purpose of those values is centred in Jesus Christ, God who is love. (SIFC 2011: 29)

Many of these scriptural passages can be interpreted as legitimating interfaith Christianity, including the acceptance of a diminished status. Some illustrative examples include: "encourage the faint hearted, help the weak, be patient with them (1 Thessalonians 5:14)," and "[do] not seek your own advantage but that of the other (1 Corinthians 10:24)." "[I]n humility regard others as better than yourselves. Let each of you look not to your own interests, but to the interest of others (Philippians 2:3–5)," and "[l]ive in harmony with one another; do not claim to be wiser than you are (Romans 12:16)" (SIFC 2011: 30).

The LDS section affirms support for all, 'regardless of race, religion or culture'. It presents the Church's interfaith credentials along with its right to independence of belief and worship. The founding prophet Joseph Smith and the contemporary prophet are invoked as authorities to demonstrate this (SIFC 2011: 35–8).

> We claim the privilege of worshipping Almighty God according to the dictates of our conscience, and allow all men the same privilege, let them worship how or what they may. (Articles of Faith 1:11 cited in SIFC 2011: 38)

> The world in which we live is filled with diversity. We can and should demonstrate respect towards those whose beliefs differ from our own (President Thomas S. Monson, October 2008, Prophet of the Church of Jesus Christ of Latter-day Saints, cited in SIFC 2011: 38).

The question remains why have Christians used their position to promote pluralism and other religions, even to the point of using their allotted space to legitimate interfaith sentiment rather than express unique concerns or address stereotypes about themselves? Part of the reason for this will likely be simply that they have accepted and internalized pluralist values along with other segments of the population. To the extent that this is true, it will influence their self-perception: that modern religions are expected to espouse pluralism and engage with interfaith dialogue, just as contemporary nations are expected to be multi-faith (Greenfeld 1996: 177).

However, embracing and espousing this increasingly powerful and pervasive ideology will also carry certain advantages in the public spaces in which it has become predominant. This allows them to operate within and help shape this pluralism, to secure influence and achieve other political goals. The possibility that ulterior motives may inform Christians' interfaith engagement does not change the fact that they are actively and regularly participating in these relations. Participation will inevitably have an influence on their outlook and ways of working. Furthermore, motivations may change over time as discourses and practices are internalized. It should also be noted that not all Christians have in fact accepted these values or been irresistibly drawn or pushed into interfaith relations, as we have seen.

Regardless of why interfaith relations were pursued, it would have been counterproductive for them to have dominated these relations too much. This can help explain why many of the quotations invoked in the Christian section of *Values* stress humility. Given the power imbalance between Christians and religious minorities; it has been necessary for the former to help the latter secure their position, attain visibility and amplify their voices. This has encouraged active efforts to facilitate IFGs which can help to explain the foundations laid by individual Christians such as Reekie or Smyth and the institutional support given by the major churches. It has involved the sharing of their considerable resources and using them to help religious minorities achieve more recognition. None of this could have been achieved had each church insisted to be represented individually on all such occasions, or Christians insisted on representation according to their proportion of the population.

Another broad explanation for this has been the emergence of a common 'faith' agenda. Consciousness of the shared religiousness of these different traditions in a secular public sphere, that they may share some of the same interests and be subject to the same stereotypes or negative press, has developed. This ethos conforms closely with the WRP which views religions as sharing analogous features such as codified doctrines, authoritative scriptures and ethical teachings and has helped Christians to accept other religions on an equal basis. Rather like the processes which produced ecumenical Christianity in Scotland, this form of pluralism into which the former has been integrated has been used to exclude as much as to include.

The former two-tier system

The dominance of the world religions paradigm (WRP) within the organization became particularly entrenched in 2012 through the introduction of the two-tier' system of membership, which was abolished in 2022. The two-tier system distinguished 'founding' members who were recognized as part of one of the major world religions and 'associate' members who were not. Along with this, a representative system was introduced where communities classified under one of the seven founding traditions nominated a representative on the board. This system is still in place and means that there is one Christian representative among all of the different denominations, but the two-tier system is no longer in place because there is no division between (full) membership and associate membership. Nonetheless, membership is still sorted into three categories: 'Abrahamic', 'Dharmic' and 'Other Faiths and Spiritual traditions.[6]

The roots of the former two-tier system can be traced to the early days of the SIFC, when the Scottish Pagan Federation (SPF) applied to join the organization. They held 'observer' status until 2012, for a decade until they became an associate members along with the Christian groups discussed earlier and the Brahma Kumaris. The best documentary account of this comes from a text produced by ACTS and written by Sister Smyth, which itself reveals the interrelationship between Christian ecumenicism and Christian interfaith participation. The relationships between these religions are discussed in fairly essentialist terms, which nonetheless leads to contrary responses. The document expresses a strong desire to ensure that dialogue between the 'major world faiths' is achieved, which it is implied could be scuppered if too many groups are included. Conversely, a genuine fear is expressed that 'bona fide' religious groups may be excluded (ACTS n.d.: 16). In my interview with her, Sister Smyth explained that there was considerable shock when SIFC received a membership application from the SPF. She admitted that they had not anticipated that groups calling themselves 'religions' outside the six or seven major world religions would be interested in joining the council. The former two-tier system was adopted as a compromise (Sister Isabel Smyth personal communication, 20 June 2016).

Christian interfaith activists were split on the issue of Pagan membership, Jewish and Muslim representatives refused to take a side while the Buddhist and Hindu communities staunchly supported the SPF. The latter were intrigued by the presence of what appeared to them to be a native western form of polytheism (John MacIntyre personal communication, 30 October 2016, SIFC 2003). Crucially though, the Church of Scotland and the Scottish Roman Catholic Church were officially opposed, and the Kirk even threatened to withdraw (SIFC 2003). This demonstrates the unofficial power and influence exerted by the most powerful churches over interfaith relations and smaller religious communities. During my interview with John MacIntyre, he related that some Christians appeared to fear that they would be demographically challenged by the still fairly numerically small Pagan community, especially among Scotland's youth. He opined that this may have reflected a subconscious discomfort with the fact that Paganism did not originate outside of the western world but within it, which challenged the status of Christians as 'hosts' to other communities (John MacIntyre personal communication, 30 October 2016).

Conversely, neither they nor the Pagans themselves lack awareness of the modernity of Paganism as a movement, but all parties appear to recognize Paganism as a contemporary incarnation of pre-Christian religion (SIFC 2003). Also, even those attempts at exclusion undergird a commitment to a kind of pluralism. It is notable that these same values were successfully taken up and mobilized by the SPF and their allies, which proved difficult even for such powerful actors to resist. It is evident, though, that Christians are concerned about changing demographics and that there is some trepidation about the likely loss of majority status and loss of influence.

Christians and secular Scotland

The third factor shaping Scottish interfaith Christianity is secularism. The secularization of the Scottish public sphere has been an environmental factor in the integration of Christians with other religious groups. The acceptance and promotion of interfaith relations have also entailed the acceptance of a certain form of secularism. The right of religious groups to access and influence the national public sphere is frequently asserted in the interfaith literature but never as an exclusive or preeminent right (e.g. IFS Summer 2014: 7). The process of secularization and promotion of religiously compatible forms of secularism are interrelated, the latter is a means of adapting to the former by presenting an alternative model of secularism to 'militant' (religion-excluding) secularism.

Secularization includes increasing non-religious identification, declining Christian affiliation and church attendance. The churches, especially the Kirk have been unable to maintain a normative hegemony over Scotland (Bruce 1985: 216, Brown 1997: 174, Lynch 1998: 82) and have thus made common cause with other religious groups to build alliances and resist further disempowerment. This has led them to espouse the importance of 'faith' or 'religion' in general rather than Christianity in particular. The fact that their position in Scottish public life is increasingly shared makes it more defensible because they deflect accusations that they dominate or enjoy special privileges which may appear especially unwarranted in an increasingly secular society. Public statements coming from the RLF or IFS (e.g. IFS Summer 2014: 7) will be received differently by the Scottish public, including the non-religious and religiously lukewarm than a similar statement coming from the Kirk or even ACTS alone. Smyth expressed her view that Christians had to learn that they shared a home with multiple religious communities and had to share their voice with others (Sister Isabel Smyth personal communication, 10 June 2016).

For the churches, sharing their resources and supporting religious minorities has entailed accepting a form of secularism because it involves accepting that national public spaces do not belong to any one group in society. Increasingly, the ways that religions are represented are primarily through IFGs: IFS, the RLF and local groups. This is quite different from the certain forms of secularism, such as Laicism in France, which strictly police religious expression in the public sphere (Casanova 2011: 57–60, Fernando 2014). This form of secularism is one that I have labelled the Northwest European model which can coexist even with established churches but where the shared culture, norms and bases of public life are not determined by any one religious identification. Politics and public life are still separate, differentiated from religion, but religions are entitled to make use of and influence public spaces (see Taylor 2011a, Taylor 2011b, Hedges 2019: 5). Though, there are also largely unwritten rules about what degrees or forms of religious expression are considered acceptable.

The secularization of day-to-day politics and public culture means that Christians are less able and inclined to dominate public life. The progressive growth of an explicitly non-religious population which has become the majority and eclipsed membership of the national church for a decade, is an important factor. This could also bring with it the threat of a more exclusionary form of secularism, as unlikely as that seems at this time (see IFS Summer 2013: 12). We also need to understand all of this within the context of devolution and an emerging Scottish public sphere which has potential effects on the place of religious groups in the country (see Sutcliffe 2004).

It is also notable that devolved Scottish politics have become somewhat more institutionally secular than UK politics (though they are substantially similar in other ways). This is also informed by the possibility that Scotland may become an independent country, especially with the political ascendency of the SNP and the 2014 referendum on independence. This brings with it uncertainty about the future constitutional make-up of Scotland and what position religion will have within it.[7] It is also true that devolution did genuinely change these relationships in certain limited respects. While the UK parliament in Westminster continues to be officially opened with Christian prayers, the Scottish parliament is officially opened with a ritual called 'Time for Reflection'. This involves a representative of religious or non-religious group providing a pre-approved talk for the MSPs (Bonney 2013: 425–42, 431–8).

Changing times inevitably invite scrutiny on established ways of doing things, especially perceived privileges. One area of controversy has been the influence of the Kirk on non-denominational schools, including the provision of Religious Education (RE) and the inclusion of non-elected voting Kirk representatives on local education boards. The Kirk has explicitly defended this by pointing to the fact that they have invited members of religious minorities to join these boards in their place in some areas (Munro 2013). Even these fairly limited privileges have been shared and are certainly no longer taken for granted.

Scottish politics is thoroughly secular because politicians acquire their authority by claiming to represent the entire Scottish population, and being Scottish is no longer synonymous with being Christian, Protestant or Presbyterian. 'Religious' and 'national' identities have been further differentiated. However, as we have seen, the power of public representation is not completely equal.

Christians have continued to have a larger influence on religious representation and this has also meant that the non-religious are not represented in quite the same way. Though, we have seen similar attempts to relate to and even promote non-religious involvement through the inclusion of Humanists. The Kirk worked with the Humanist Society Scotland (HSS) to propose that the religious services held in schools, entirely within the Kirk's prerogative, be changed to 'Time for Reflection', which also links schools to the Scottish parliament (Fraser 2013). Christian contributions to the IFS literature can also be viewed as legitimating secularism in certain respects. Romans 13:7 is invoked, which urges that respect, honour and taxes be paid to the authorities and 1 Peter 2:17's injunction to '[h]onour the Emperor (SIFC 2011: 30)', can both be viewed as encouraging and acceptance of and cooperation with secular authorities.

Christianity has had a huge influence on the foundations and heritage of Scotland as a nation, as well as on IFS, the wider IFM and the WRP, which it espouses. Nonetheless, they genuinely have lost their hegemonic influence over Scottish society. Other groups have continued to build on their foundations, and Christians pitched in to help with them, but they have had to cede ground to allow this to happen.

Conclusion

This chapter traced the ways in which Christianity has been woven into Interfaith Scotland's vision of Scotland as one nation of many faiths. Christianity is imbricated with the history, symbolism and culture of Scotland to a degree no other religion can match. It is made up of multiple denominations with a common overarching religious identity which presented a particular challenge to represent them without them dominating. The fact that Christians played such a role in the foundation of the interfaith movement (IFM) has meant that they had the motivation to overcome this challenge.

This depended on the prior development of ecumenicism, to ensure that denominations were actually capable of cooperating within the IFS and accepting common representation. It also necessitated the acceptance of a model of pluralism based on the WRP which placed Christianity on an equal footing with other world religions, stressing their shared membership in this category rather than insisting on demographic or separate representation. In practice, this has been a means of preserving Christian influence and access in a secularizing nation with an emerging, dynamic political system. It has been advantageous to cultivate a desirable form of secularism (as with pluralism) which has been easier for them to adapt to, even if they genuinely did have to adapt in the process.

As we have seen though, this has reflected their greater power and security, which has sometimes been used to exclude. The relationship between ecumenicism and interfaith has alienated many conservative Christians, but it has also been used to marginalize Christians actively involved in interfaith who are not part of the ecumenical establishment. Pluralism has been based on the WRP which has in a certain sense shaped other religions into analogues of Christianity, moulded into a cruciform shape, and this same paradigm has been used to further marginalize groups which do not fit into it. It is to those other religions which we will discuss in Chapter 4 of this book.

4

Unity in diversity: Interfaith Scotland's representation of Scottish religious minorities

Introduction

In Chapter 3, we discussed the influence of the country's traditional religion – Christianity, in shaping the public representation of religious pluralism in a secularizing society. Christians, or the dominant factions within modern Scottish Christianity, constructed interfaith relations on their own terms but still had to adapt to these new conditions themselves. This included emphasizing the broader tradition over specific denominations and representing it as equivalent to a handful of 'world religions'. We also discussed how aspects of the nation's Christian heritage have been given new significance as the common heritage for Scots 'people of faith'.

This chapter will focus on Interfaith Scotland's (IFS) representations of non-Christian religious minorities (see Sutherland 2018b). While Christians were vital in its establishment, the inclusion of identifiably distinct religions is IFS' *raison d'etre*. This chapter will trace some of the themes of the last chapter: how these traditions were reconstructed as equal dialogue partners which are identifiable, accessible, relatable and quotable. It will show how these processes operated with ingrained assumptions about religion and how some voices were amplified or muted.

Religious minorities have been cast as distinctive contributors to national life by cultivating a positive image of religion in general. IFS promote a conception of the relationship between religious pluralism and national identity as one of unity in diversity or one nation of many faiths (and cultures). This is an integrationist rather than assimilationist model of pluralism, encouraging minorities to preserve a distinct identity while partaking in a common 'national' and an overarching 'religious' identity.

The ways in which religious minorities have been represented in these ways will be broken down according to three broad concepts: *'religion'*, *'ethnicity'* and *'nationality'*. These three categories are each intertwined and often overlap, but nonetheless are not interchangeable in their emic or etic use. The fact that these categories are so complex and intertwined makes their treatment as non-overlapping in the IFS literature particularly telling.

For the most part, these categories differentiate the types of groups one can belong to rather than function as identities in themselves (though 'religion' is occasionally an exception). For example, 'Hindu' and 'Buddhist' may refer to huge global populations which include many sub-groups (e.g. Vaishnavi and Triratna, respectively), but nonetheless do refer to a group of people and their traditions. Categories such as 'religion', 'ethnicity' and 'nationality' though, despite general emic use, refer to types of groups. While these are not obscure terms, they are still somewhat abstract. They are classifications of classifications (see Smith 2000).

The typical emic use of these categories might entail that, for example, one could be a Scot by birth or residence (nationality), an Iranian by ancestry and shared culture (ethnicity) and a Bahá'í in terms of beliefs and practices (religion). Things are considerably more complex than that neat picture would suggest though, as this person might hold an Iranian passport, and even if they had dual citizenship, there is currently no Scottish passport to hold. They may have dual Iranian and British nationalities but identify as Scottish because of their exposure to Scottish culture. The Scots can be classed as an ethnic group as well whether this is understood in terms of ancestry or culture. Members of all these three groupings can also be thought of as having shared norms, practices and worldviews, not just religions. There is considerable overlap between certain ethnicities and religions to the point that some religions are classed as 'ethnic-religions', which creates a tension with the dominant world religions model.

Nonetheless, these three categories do serve a particular purpose in contemporary society, allowing actors to account for multiple forms of belonging even if they cannot be neatly separated in practice. As these are emic concepts in Scottish society, they may allow actors to make sense of the multiple types of connections and differences that they have with others. Using our previous example; the shared the experience of growing up or living in Scotland as a 'nation', a shared Iranian 'ethnic/cultural' background and connections with Bahá'í 'co-religionists'.

The key point for the purposes of this chapter is that these three categories are treated very differently. Religion and nationality in particular are treated as non-overlapping and non-competitive, while ethnicity is often a more implicit, residual category which can be loosely related to religion but is often not treated as a significant part of it (even if lived reality often undermines this). These three categories can be treated as distinct forms of belonging which do not threaten each other because they do not compete on the same ground. Understood in this way, one would not be expected to choose between being, for example, Scottish and being Sikh but there are circumstances where groups have been pressured to make similar decisions.

Nonetheless, the statements, practices and self-representations of interfaith participants cannot always be so neatly classified. Tensions between multiple affiliations are not necessarily always reconciled in the same way. As such, the 'religion' constructed in the literature tends to fit certain religions more closely than others, namely the most universalistic ones, for example, the Bahá'í Faith, Islam and Buddhism. Other communities have stronger ties to ethnicities, especially Judaism, Sikhism and Hinduism. However, all have been cast in a universalistic mould, all have some ethnic ties and all have been related to Scottish national identity in different ways.

Religious minorities in Scotland

Despite the ambiguity around these categories, it is relatively easy to specify what is meant by religious minority here. In the context of Scotland, it refers to a non-Christian religion, a group which is deemed by themselves and others to be religious but not Christian. As always, the boundaries between religious traditions are complex but unlike some communities discussed in Chapter 3, these groups placement outside of Christianity is largely uncontroversial.

Despite decades of diversification and secularization, religious minorities still make up a small proportion of the population. Muslims are the largest religious minority community at 2.2 per cent, Hindus 0.55 per cent, Pagans 0.35 per cent, Buddhists 0.28 per cent, Sikhs 0.20 per cent each, Jews 0.11 per cent and 'other' at 0.23 per cent (which would include Bahá'ís etc.). Religious minorities together made up just under 4 per cent of the Scottish population in 2022 (National Records of Scotland 2024) compared to 9 per cent in England and Wales.[1] Nonetheless, it is noteworthy that they make up a much larger proportion of the urban Scottish population than in many rural areas. In Na hEileanan Siar (Gaelic 'The Western Isles') the total number of recorded affiliation with non-Christian religious groups was 276 out of a population of 26, 140 while the Muslim population of Glasgow alone is 48, 766 (National Records of Scotland 2024).

Membership of interfaith Scotland

IFS currently divides its membership into three categories 'Abrahamic', 'Dharmic' and 'Other Faiths and spiritual traditions', and there is now no tiered system of membership. These three categories (Abrahamic, Dharmic and Other) are broader and more inclusive than world religions categories which the organization formerly stressed. They do to some extent reflect historic origins and relations between different religions but they are still limited in some ways as well. The category Abrahamic stresses the fact that Abraham is recognized as a prophet within Jewish, Christian, Islamic and Bahá'í traditions (Bowker 1997: 10–11) and that these religions have a common 'western' origin. Dharmic is applied to religions of South Asian origin based on the Sanskrit term *Dharma* which is used in traditions such as Hinduism, Buddhism, Jainism and Sikhism, which is commonly (if controversially) used to translate the Latinate term religion (ibid.: 275–6). The introduction of an additional category has allowed them to include groups which are less easy to categorize within the WRP and recognize them on an (at least formally) equal basis.

Nonetheless, these kinds of neat classifications can still obscure the relations that have existed among religions and encourage the kind of broad, universalistic approach to religious representation of the WRP. For example, many Scottish Muslims are of South Asian Pakistani and Bangladeshi heritage and traditional South Asian Islam (and Christian and Jewish) practices have been influenced by the 'Dharmic' religions of the region. In fact, Sikhism emerged from the hybridity between Hindu devotionalism (*bhakti*) and Islamic mysticism (Sufism) in the fifteenth century Punjab (ibid.: 899–900). The emphasis on the category Abrahamic reinforces Muslim communities' connections with other western religions first and foremost, through scriptural sources. Different groups in modern Scotland are similarly subject to mutual influences between themselves and wider society, including secular-pluralism, nationalism and the WRP.

Nonetheless, the representation of the world religions is still ingrained through both the system of board representatives and the ways that categories once alien to the WRP have been reconstructed through it. The seven founding traditions (along with representatives of women and of young people, a co-optee and an interfaith expert) continue to have a specific representative on IFS' board. Aside from Christianity, the six remaining founding traditions are: the Bahá'í Faith, Buddhism, Hinduism, Islam, Judaism and Sikhism.[2] Each of these traditions is represented by one member of the board each and in IFS' literature they are largely discussed as singular, overarching traditions which can obscure the diversity and dissent within each.

Until the abolition of the two-tier system of membership in 2022, the minority associate members included the Scottish Pagan Federation (SPF) and the Brahma Kumaris of Edinburgh and Glasgow. The former is indubitably distinct from the seven traditions mentioned, while the latter are closely connected to Hinduism but claim to be open to all forms of religion (Barker 1989: 213–14). Given their small proportion of the population, the position of the six founding non-Christian religions reflects their global establishment much more than their position within Scotland.

The World Religions Paradigm

The pluralism emphasized by IFS is limited and structured by its institutionalization of the WRP as well as its reproduction of world religion categories within its literature. This entails emphasizing a handful of religions perceived to have global standing and rendered equivalent to each other and to Christianity: the Bahá'í Faith, Buddhism, Hinduism, Islam, Judaism and Sikhism (Masuzawa 2005: 2–3, Cotter and Robertson 2016: 2). It also entails that the identity formed from the broader religious tradition overrides whatever distinctions or divisions exist within them e.g. sects, denominations, factions, movements, tendencies and so forth (Mauzawa 2005: 9–10).

'World religions' are portrayed as having a common essence expounded within codified teachings and canonical scriptures (Cox 2007: 88, Cotter and Robertson 2016: 9–10). This reinforces their equivalence and legitimates their representation by a single board member and description according to analogous features, often fitting an Abrahamic, even Protestant mould. In this conception, religions are made up of a globally dispersed population bound by personal conviction, philosophically elaborated doctrines and ethical commandments traceable to founders, great personages and canonical texts (Masuzawa

2005: 17–18, Cotter and Robertson 2016: 6). Some of these features were not entirely lacking but were given inflated importance by European scholars and missionaries, as well as indigenous elites responding to them (who were usually the ones who possessed these resources already). These conceptions were then exported throughout these religions' diasporas and became further entrenched, especially in Christian majority societies (King 1999: 107, Martin 2016: 70–1).

The category of world religions usually includes the so-called 'big 5:' Buddhism, Christianity, Hinduism, Islam and Judaism. As Cotter and Robertson point out, the Abrahamic religions are often listed first. Other religions which are variously added to the list include Daoism, Confucianism, Shinto (or sometimes 'Chinese' and 'Japanese religions'), Sikhism, Zoroastrianism and sometimes catch-all terms for the rest such as 'indigenous' or 'new religious movements' (NRMs) (Cox 2007: 1–2 Cotter and Robertson 2016: 2). The Baháʼí Faith, along with Rastafarianism, are examples of newer religions which are frequently included. In the Scottish IFM and IFS specifically the Faith has attained that recognition quite securely. Stella Reekie specifically invited the local Baháʼís into Glasgow Sharing of Faiths (GSF) (Adamson, Ramsay and Craig 1984: 27); they are one of the 'founding' traditions and the Director Maureen Sier is also Baháʼí.

As Jonathan Z. Smith argued, the world religions category is a recognition that a religion is perceived to be powerful in a particular part of the world and that it cannot be ignored or sidelined in the eyes of the Christian West (Smith 1993: 294–6). These traditions were those considered worthy of study, dialogue and recognition even if this was for purposes of conversion or colonial governance. These are the religions acknowledged as active agents in history, as world, region or nation shaping, unlike the largely local groups which cannot command the same influence or numbers. Religions which have not attained this status or often rendered invisible or are else treated as homogenous, even interchangeable with each other (ibid.).

Though, non-Christian religions have been represented and shaped through Christian categories rather than purely on their own terms, this is not obvious to the casual observer. Furthermore, this does not mean that their distinctiveness was eradicated, merely blended or re-ordered. While this equality was dictated by the powerful, it necessitated the recognition of the other as equivalent and formally equal. This means that Scotland's religious minorities have not primarily attained recognition as specific communities but as representatives of more abstract, global categories. The number of Buddhists in Scotland does not matter, the fact that Scottish Buddhists are the living representatives of a major world religion is what matters. This highlights the role that religion can play in the dynamics between globalization and nationalism; while there may be a tension between these phenomena, in the twenty-first century they are often intertwined. By being graced with the presence of the major world religions, the status of the nation is elevated globally.

The WRP is appealing to IFGs because it embeds the conception of religions as equal and analogous entities. This entails that good faith efforts to engage in dialogue between them will easily become fair and fruitful. This conception of religion is powerfully visualized in the common interfaith symbol, the interfaith tree, in which the symbols of religions are represented as the leaves of a single tree. This implies that while religions are produced by distinct branches, they share common underlying roots and that together offer shade and fruit to humanity. One important example of its use though, was the planting of a tree outside of St Mungo's Museum of Religious Life and Art in Glasgow in 2009 to commemorate IFS' foundation in 1999 as the Scottish Inter Faith Council (SIFC) (SIFC March 2010: 10).

The conception of 'world religions' has been directly referenced on occasion as well. Dumfries and Galloway interfaith group instituted a 'World Religions Day' which drew on prayers and readings from different traditions (SIFC February 2011: 4, IFS Spring 2013: 8). At these events, members of different religions were encouraged to 'acknowledge the similarities between different faiths' and 'the fundamental oneness of faith' (IFS Spring 2015: 25). Iain Stewart of EIFA gave a talk to primary school children on the common threads of the world religions, introducing them to the 'the similarities and foundations that bond all belief systems together (IFS Spring 2013: 9)'.

Interfaith Scotland and religion-making[3]

How then does IFS specifically construct 'religion' and 'religions' according to this model? To analyse this process, I will outline and then substantiate the largely implicit assumptions within their documents and activities. I am certainly not claiming that they are unique or foundational in this regard; rather, they are influenced by, draw on and exemplify wider processes. They are simply one local, limited albeit underappreciated example of how a specific understanding of religion is being (re)constructed, disseminated and reinforced for a given audience.

I have identified eight characteristics which can break down IFS' implicit definition of religion. These include the conception that religions are defined

(1) *substantively*, by identifiable, intrinsic features and (2) have an *essential* nature, they are also depicted as (3) *sacred*, (4) *institutionalized*, (5) *intellectual* or *philosophical*, (6) *ethically-focused* (7) *traditions* which are (8) *universal* in scope. The last four characteristics especially exemplify the WRP discussed earlier.

I describe this definition as implicit because it is compiled from the assumptions inherent in what or who is included in IFS and the claims or convictions which they express about religion in the literature. This definition has also been translated into academic language but this is not intended to leave the reader with the impression that this is any kind of explicit or rigid model, held by all relevant parties in all circumstances. These characteristics simply aid in the break down and analysis of their disparate statements and actions. The fact that they have a definition, and that this definition differs from many academic ones including mine (Sutherland 2012: 53, 2017c: 96), is not meant to imply that they are mistaken. To do so would assume that they are not contributors to the social meaning of 'religion' and that there is an external, fixed and observable entity for them to be mistaken about.

By stating that IFS implicitly defines religion (1) *substantively*, I mean that religions are characterized by belief in, claims about or relations with their commonly assumed foci – the 'supernatural': gods, souls, afterlives and so forth (Platvoet 1999: 252–3). This is reflected in their summaries and descriptions of religions as related to belief in God or gods. A partial exception is Buddhism with acknowledgement of its non-theistic status, but belief in reincarnation, the search for enlightenment and the superhuman qualities of the Buddha are confirmed (IFS n.d.: 6–7). Buddhism is certainly distinguished from representations of the non-religious and the Humanist tradition, for instance, (see Chapter 5). It is notable that many beliefs and practices based around similar claims are left out though: alternative and holistic spirituality ('New Age'), Reiki, astrology and so forth because these lack many of the features discussed later in the text.

For IFS though, religion is understood in (2) *essentialist* terms, not merely as a classificatory tool but as involving ingrained, distinct essence or fixed characteristics. Religion and religions are things in themselves in this understanding, not merely categories applied somewhat arbitrarily (usefully or not) to myriad social relations and cultural products. Religion is qualitatively distinct from other elements of society and culture; it is *sui generis* and distinct even from parallel secular systems (Martin 2014: 37–8). Sister Smyth argued during her interview with me that religious communities should be allowed to have their own specific conversations and questions alongside those they shared with other groups (Sister Isabel Smyth personal communication, 20 June 2016).

Religions are also treated as (3) *sacred* or organized around sacralized beliefs and norms. Religious identities, beliefs and practices are of deep personal and communal importance (see Durkheim 2001). Religion is explicitly equated in much of the literature as concerned with a 'weighty matter' in some documents (Scottish Government 2011: 45) and has also been explicitly differentiated from personalized spirituality (Xaverian Missionaries of the United Kingdom and United States 2013: 6). One possible reason for this is the fact that many common alternative spiritual beliefs and practices do not form a concrete, distinct communal or personal identity. In the eyes of IFS and the Scottish Government, they do not require representation.

Religions are also (4) *institutional*; they can be represented fairly comprehensively through organizations and spoken for by authorized leadership. IFS membership is entirely composed of other organizations which must have charitable status and a constitution (Maureen Sier personal communication, 18 November 2015). One of the flagship institutions which IFS helps to administer is the Religious Leaders Forum (RLF) (ibid.). Religious leaders may all vary in their roles, titles, rationale and means of (and barriers to) assuming office, but they are recognized as functionally equivalent spokespeople.

> Can I tell you the one about the Minister, the Priest and the Rabbi? Actually my story also includes the Sikh Ghani, the Buddhist Monk, the Tibetan Lama, the Hindu priest and the Baha'i – that's me – among others! *Alan Forsyth* [sic]. (SIFC August 2009: 11)

This reference to a common genre of joke about religious officials reflects the common western religious norm among Protestants, Catholics and Jews but simply opens it up to include more diverse traditions. These figures are further legitimated by mutual recognition and recognition by bodies such as IFS (and the Scottish Government, who largely defer to them) as the authoritative spokespeople for 'their' religion. Religious leaders of whatever form are thus differentiated from the laity, the larger mass of adherents and have been enshrined as the voices of that tradition (see point 7).

The last four characteristics are bound up quite closely with the world religions approach discussed earlier. Religions are discussed primarily according to their (5) *intellectual* components, including bodies of doctrines or teachings, philosophical or theological concepts and usually religious texts, especially canonical sources. Historically, these aspects of the tradition were quite often the preserve of a small literate, clerical elite, but they have become more widely read due to rising literacy and modern communications technology (King

1999: 62, Cotter and Robertson 2016: 8–9). Nonetheless, the influence of Christian, especially Protestant, conceptions of a foundational and authoritative canon was considerable.

The WRP encourages the conception of texts and doctrines as key to understanding the motivations of practitioners. The fact is though that not all religions have a central universally agreed-upon canon equivalent to the Bible or Qur'an. The mere fact that there are texts within a tradition can be misleading for social scientific or historical studies of religion but useful for interfaith purposes. For example, at an interfaith service celebrating the late Queen's Diamond Jubilee in Aberdeen, unspecified 'Hindu scriptures' could be slotted into place alongside readings from the Bible and Qur'an into a basically Christian format (IFS September 2012: 13). Though the fact that this model fits Abrahamic religions more closely continues to have an impact. For example, the practice of scriptural reasoning widely used in local interfaith circles in Scotland usually involves drawing out similar themes in the Qur'an and the Bible, including on one occasion with regard to Abraham himself. Nonetheless, practitioners have raised the possibility of extending this to the scriptures of other religions and perhaps non-religious traditions (SIFC February 2011: 12, IFS Summer 2014: 11).

This intellectual focus contrasts with other possible emphases, such as on practices, birth, upbringing or communal participation. Religions are seemingly boiled down to a coherent set of ideas rather than communities primarily made up of natal adherents which have accrued multiple, often incoherent batches of beliefs and customs. The appeal to doctrines, philosophies and texts cultivates a more systematic, coherent and more stable image. Another reason that interfaith activists make use of texts is that, at least in translation, they can easily be replicated and selectively appropriated to fit the needs of different contexts.

Regardless of how doctrinal and scriptural a religion is, there are few hurdles to depicting it in this way. This is because the proliferation of literacy in the modern world means that there are mountains of publications and web resources; insider and outsider, popular, journalistic and academic, about any religion. This approach also means that it is possible to represent religions even if none of its members are actually present in the country let alone at the local interfaith meeting. For example, Skye Faiths Together (SFT) held a 'Vigil for the Planet' in Portree which made use of quotations labelled as Bahá'í, Buddhist, Christian, Daoist, Hindu, Islamic, Jewish, Native American, Quaker and Sikh sources, while it is unlikely that most of those practitioners were in attendance (SIFC March 2010: 3).

Religions are presented not only as coherent, finely-honed intellectual traditions but also as systems of information first and foremost, which can be appealed to (if not as they would likely admit, fully grasped or fairly represented) by anyone regardless of their background or status. Practitioners, especially religious leaders, are depicted as possessing much greater understanding and moral rights to speak for their religions but this could be interpreted as reflecting their deep immersion in a tradition and its concepts, as much as their localized social relationships. This characterization applies to both 'missionary' and 'non-missionary' or 'ethnic' religions. Ernest Gellner identified this 'context-free' communication as characteristic of industrialized (and we can add globalizing) societies, where information is standardized, technical and replicable rather than steeped in local nuances unintelligible to outsiders (Gellner 1983: 52–61).

Religions are also cast as overwhelmingly (6) *ethical*, not just in the sense that religions are essentially benign but also that these traditions are specifically concerned with teaching ethical behaviour. Furthermore, they each individually preach an ethical system which is universal and mutually compatible with each other and secular public life. In particular, the so-called 'golden-rule', – to treat others as you would wish to be treated. This was given particular attention by interfaith commentators, contributors from specific religions and Scottish Government ministers in *Values in Harmony* (SIFC 2011). This document also demonstrates the ethical characteristics of religions and their commitment to pluralism through quotations and appeals to various authoritative sources in parallel with each tradition.

As with other attributes of the WRP, this universalizes the features of specific religions. All cultures have had ethical systems, but these have not always been the preserve of religions, which have often been governed by pragmatic needs. As always, these processes are of course much bigger than Scotland let alone IFS but there are reasons why IFS has exemplified and reinforced them. Stressing the complementary benign influences of religions; as expressing fundamental, universal values, places them outside or above political or ideological disputes. This makes IFS not simply a partisan interest group but a moral voice in public life speaking for all Scots and all humankind.

Religions are also identified primarily as (7) *traditional*, contemporary religious communities that are expressions of well-established, often ancient lineages which legitimize their modern representatives. A 'bona fide' religion is one which can demonstrate such a connection and is informed by references to it, which means that more *ad hoc* or newer beliefs and practices are less legitimate. For newer religions then, establishing connections to older lineages, cultivating a distinctive authoritative lineage or both are the means of gaining such recognition.

Nonetheless, there is some recognition that these global traditions need to be localized and indigenized. This makes them more accessible and influential, as well as underscores the need to include them in Scottish public dialogue as equals. It is important that religious minorities are also represented as Scots, even if the Scottish circumstances of these communities are often given less emphasis than their global linkages.

In the *Guide*, the reader is given information about the Bahá'í Faith, the Brahma Kumaris, Buddhism, Christianity, Hinduism, Islam, Jainism, Judaism, Paganism and Sikhism. Notably, the founding religions are ordered alphabetically followed non-alphabetically by the then associate members and with the one religion mentioned without any representation in IFS – Jainism, placed last. Each religion is described through equivalent categories: basic beliefs, customs and practices, places of worship, main festivals, food and diet and concerns of the community. It is striking that a document entitled *Guide to the Faith Communities of Scotland* does not offer details about specific communities located in Scotland (IFS n.d.). Instead, it describes each in the highly general terms analysed earlier. *Values* does include some contact details and additional content discussing the place of religion in modern Scottish society but otherwise presents religions in a similar fashion (SIFC 2011).

It is not my task to specify where each religion begins and ends, but rather to (re)describe and analyse actors' assertions about, interpretations of and mobilizations of these categories. There are disagreements about which groups but also what elements – practices, sacred figures or other elements properly belong to a given tradition. The Brahma Kumaris could be classed as 'Hindu' because they were founded in India by a practicing Hindu – Dada Lekh Raj, who claimed to be an incarnation of Shiva. Nonetheless, they also declare that participation in their communities, centred around the practice of Raja Yoga is open to all religions and that they are not a religion (in parallel with another Hindu-originated movement with a following in the west – Transcendental Meditation founded by Guru Maharishi Mahesh Yogi) (Barker 1989: 213–14). This is the likely reason that they were formally classified as associate members rather than as Hindus.

The boundaries around each tradition are constructed and contested, even if they are presented as natural and self-evident (Sutcliffe 2016: 26). These boundaries can therefore be strengthened or weakened, moved, renegotiated but in all cases are difficult to police. Religions also frequently draw on influences from other traditions and even make claims about them, which may contradict members of that community. This can be especially fraught when claims about a given tradition by representatives of an alien one become integral to the latter.

For example, Hindus have claimed the Buddha and the prophets of other religions as divine avatars equivalent to Krishna, Rama and so forth (IFS n.d.: 10–11). The Bahá'í prophet Bahá'u'lláh is held to be the latest in a long line of prophets who founded the world's major religions (ibid.: 18, SIFC 2011: 15). This is an expansion of the Islamic claim that Muhammad was the final prophet in a lineage which includes major figures from the Hebrew Bible and the New Testament (IFS n.d.: 4, 12). This also usefully highlights the fact that Christianity added its own sacred figures – Jesus and his apostles and scriptures to those they inherited from Jewish tradition. The commitment of interfaith organizations to the conception of complementarity and to empower members of religions to speak on their behalf (albeit in limited and structured ways) can thus lead to quite discordant texts. Nonetheless, these tensions are rarely if ever addressed, or even recognized beyond the basic acknowledgement that the religions are different from each other.

In the *Guide* for example, the Buddhist section explicitly denies the divinity of the Buddha, whom it is state that Buddhists do not really worship at all. The non-theistic characterization of Buddhism is affirmed by the stated rejection of creator gods (IFS n.d.: 6–7). This contrasts with the Hindu sections' claim that the Buddha is one among many incarnations and images through which God can be worshipped. The Hindu section is especially fascinating because it exhibits a strong desire to depict Hinduism as a religion relatable to its counterparts but also as exemplary of a religious universalism which would potentially absorb them. Despite the massive diversity of Hindu beliefs and practices, and the degree to which its classification as a single religion is debated, it is consistently presented in interfaith circles as one which possesses a clear set of tenets. It is reflected in events such as a public lecture given by the priest of the Glasgow Hindu Mandir on 'the essence of Hinduism'. The Hindu section of the *Guide* also describes it in monotheistic and pantheistic (or monistic) terms, as worshipping a single God in multiple forms and that God is present in all beings. Key concepts such as karma, reincarnation and avatars are also introduced but its lack of dogma is also touted (IFS n.d.: 10–11). The Hindu section of *Values* embodies many of the aforementioned tendencies but also acknowledges different deities, meaning that it can be read as polytheist, monotheist and pantheist/monist at once (SIFC 2011: 39–44).

Despite its marginalized status, Paganism has been described in both terms analogous to other religions as well as in ways which reflect their claims and self-image:

> Paganism has its roots in the indigenous, pre-Christian religions of Europe, evolved and adapted to the circumstances of modern life. Its re-emergence in Scotland parallels that observed in other Western countries. (IFS n.d. 20)

It is always described as an ancient pre-Christian religion, but it is also reconstructed according to the mould of the WRP. In *Values*, disparate sources are utilized to construct a common, intellectual tradition. These sources range from ancient Babylonian writings, classical philosophers and famous contemporary Pagan authors such as Starhawk (SIFC 2011: 69). As with representations of Hinduism, the tension between the heterogeneity and sense of a historic, global tradition is reworked to stipulate that these are in fact integral parts of that overarching tradition. Similarly, the lack of doctrines is highlighted, but shared norms are outlined: environmentalism, religious pluralism and a rejection of proselytization (IFS n.d.: 21).

The position of the SPF within IFS is perhaps unsurprising; they are a religious group which has become more visible and normalized in recent decades. They may be small in number, but they are increasingly recognized as part of the mix of contemporary western religious pluralism. Their use of common labels, nomenclature, symbols and practices such as specific festivals means that they have not been all that difficult to fit into IFS' conceptions of religion. They are somewhat alien to the WRP but not so alien that they cannot invent a tradition in parallel with other religions without much difficulty. This is in marked contrast to the looser melange of practitioners which make up much of the alternative religion and spirituality.

Features 4–7 are also ones that draw a boundary between 'religion' and much of the alternative 'spiritual' milieu. One partial exception to this is the inclusion of a section in the NHS document *Reflections on Life Matters* for 'Believers not Belongers',[4] those that do have 'religious' belief but do not 'belong' to any particular community or congregation. This section does not outline any particular beliefs and is composed of an assortment of poems and reflections (NHS Scotland 2011: 11). Nonetheless, even this bears the hallmarks of the ways in which traditions have been reified – emphasis on texts which can be cast as of deep personal significance for this category of people, to be treated as authoritative and representative of them.

There is also a marked tendency for alternative spiritual practitioners to appeal to different religious traditions, which means that in a sense they converge with IFS in their understanding of the differences between religion and spirituality (just as interfaith activists do not view themselves as forming a 'faith'). Aberdeen Interfaith Group once held a workshop with a member of the 'New Age' Findhorn community (see Sutcliffe 2000, 2002) who led them in a ritual called a 'Harmonic Temple' which combined practices from four different religions (SIFC March 2012: 6). The very eclecticism of such practices is grounded in a perception that there are bounded and codified repertoires which can be tapped into.

Lastly, religions are taken to be (8) *universal* or universalistic, they are of global importance, transcending all localized boundaries, and rendered into equivalent characteristics (doctrines, ethics, scriptures etc.). This means that they can be reproduced anywhere, potentially by anyone, which also means that they are potentially open to anyone who subscribes to these doctrines and can complement more limited, localized identities. Those religions which are universalistic, transcultural, textual, belief-centred and monotheist fit this model most closely; and there are two minority traditions which closely correspond to this model: Islam and the Bahá'í Faith.

The Bahá'í Faith is a tradition which is avowedly universalistic in different ways: it is very internationally spread in accordance with its staunch internationalism, advocating the establishment of a world government and accepting most world religions as previous divine revelations. It is also comparatively modern, founded in Iran in the nineteenth century by the prophet Bahá'u'lláh (1817–92) (see Bowker 1997: 120–1), which means that it can perhaps fit more easily into contemporary religious pluralist, interfaith ethics:

> May Fanaticism and religious bigotry be unknown ... and the religions of the world enter the divine temple of oneness. (Compilations of *Baha'i World Faith*, p. 256 cited in SIFC 2011: 15).

> A religion which does not conform with the postulates of science is merely superstition. (Abdul Bahá, *Divine Philosophy*, p. 82 cited in ibid: 18)

> Religious truth is not absolute but relative. (Shoghi Effendi,[5] Summary Statement – 1947, Special UN Committee on Palestine, cited in ibid).

Judaism and Sikhism on the other hand are monotheistic and possess canonical scriptures (the Torah and Guru Granth Sahib, respectively) but they are overwhelmingly non-missionary religions which are both also classified as ethnicities. In interfaith literature their universalistic tendencies are usually accentuated, as previously noted with Hinduism (alongside the emphasis its monotheistic tendencies at the expense of others).

Richard King has argued that the modern construction of Hinduism as an inclusive, common religion for Hindus appealed selectively to specific sources to present it as the most universalistic religion (King 1999: 93–8, 103–7). This gave it a comparative advantage in competition with the claims of Protestant missionaries who claimed to represent the most universal religion. The Hindu and Baháʼí versions of universalism without assimilation mean that they can recognize and include multiple religions without the necessity of conversion.

Some minorities can present themselves as exemplary of the interfaith value system more easily than the majority. Those groups that have specifically had to adapt and even contort themselves to fit a set of norms dictated by a dominant group have sometimes become versatile in utilizing those norms. Even many firmly ethnic religions can emphasize universalistic strands and present their particularity as reflecting a respect for the validity of other communities.

For example, Judaism, the paradigmatic example of an ethnic religion can draw on certain strands within the tradition to present it in universalistic terms or to actively work within universalistic discourse. For example, the non-proselytising characteristic can be recast as avowedly pluralist rather than exclusivist: 'Judaism does not seek converts, believing that non-Jews should follow their own path (SIFC 2011: 62)'. Conversely, this does not mean that those universalistic elements were inauthentic or that modern ethno-religious groups have not also internalized some thoroughly universalistic norms. This was reflected in a sermon given by Rabbi Mark Solomon at an interfaith Shabbat service in Edinburgh:

> All men and women, of every colour and creed, of every race and nation, are our brothers and sisters … Like brothers and sisters, we should feel a sense of common identity … For God, who created us, cares for all of us; therefore we should care equally for one another. (IFS Spring 2015: 8)

Judaism is also similarly discussed frequently in the language of 'faith' in the broad sense (i.e. beyond simply using the term) rather than as ethno-cultural heritage. For example, the IFS newsletter reported on the local activities of the Reform Jewish organization Limmud and one particular event dubbed, 'my Jewish journey', in which members of the Jewish community discussed their analogous faith journeys with a practitioner of Tibetan Buddhism and a Christian (IFS Spring 2015: 7).

In the case of Buddhism, the practice of meditation and its philosophical aspects are most prominently represented. The fact that it is to some extent non-theistic (or presented as such)[6] in western discourses has allowed it to fill a distinct niche: supplying practices which can be safely shared among a multi-faith audience which are perceived to be beneficial and interesting, without compromising anyone's beliefs. For example, AIFG invited a Buddhist monk to give a talk on Buddhism and participants held a discussion afterword about how to apply Buddhist insights into their lives (IFS Summer 2013: 9). Despite the continuous replication of the equivalence of religious traditions, there are few parallels with the ways that other religions (including Christianity) are engaged with. One would not expect to find a similar discussion, at least in a staunchly interfaith milieu, about how one can apply insights from another religion directly into one's life (as opposed to, finding common resonances between another religion and one's own).

For many minorities, the category of religion can be a means of connecting with other communities but also with the traditional majority. It implies that elements of cultural practice and inheritance are vitally bound to a global ethical system and cosmology of utmost importance, which must be respected locally and nationally. Religion can serve as a useful means of defending controversial practices such as Kosher and Halal methods of animal slaughter. Regardless, this feeds into broader societal discussions of the place of religion in modern public life and the perceived rights or privileges which it imparts. Religious minorities may benefit from the sanctuary usually provided by the category, but their inclusion can also legitimate the position of the former majority in a secularising nation. This is achieved by appealing to a certain form of secular argument about the rights of different groups but also reinforces the secular norm that no one group has propriety rights over civic-political structures or national identity.

Christians may have laid the discursive and institutional groundwork, but minorities' intrinsic importance to interfaith relations provides them with a space and status. They have also demonstrated agency in their use of and adaptation to these structures and a say over the ways in which they have been represented, even if this is limited to certain groups and actors. They may have been subject to the influence of particular discourses, but they have often shown an ability to master them more fully than their more dominant counterparts, for example, presenting themselves as more universalist and pluralist. Even thoroughly ethnic religions have been able to recast their core characteristics as interfaith virtues, using this to delegitimize assimilationism or proselytization.

Responding to religious prejudice in a post-9/11 world

A central remit of IFS has been to develop harmonious relations between religions and to secure influence and access to the Scottish public sphere for them. An important part of this has been addressing prejudice and harmful stereotypes against religion and against specific religions. IFS addresses both of these issues but does not sharply distinguish them either. This can be explained by the context: a secularizing society whose constitutional arrangements, including the place of religion within it, are uncertain.

Religious minorities are especially vulnerable because their position in society is less secure, and their norms and practices are more 'alien' to both the 'religious' and 'non-religious' populations. Muslims have been especially victimized after the 11 September terrorist attacks. Some communities are actually positively stereotyped (which produces its own problems for the affected community), most notably Buddhists. These different images of minorities though reflect their comparative lack of control over their image. Nonetheless, minorities have become more secure through processes of further diversification, the entrenchment of normative religious pluralism in Scotland and indeed through interfaith activism. Nonetheless, these conditions meant that making common cause with the then Christian majority was desirable. Similarly, the hegemonic security of the Christian population has been seriously eroded to the point of becoming the largest minority, which made this desire for connection mutual.

However, increasingly visible interfaith relations and the shared category of religion in general can have deep ramifications for all communities under that rubric. Negative stereotypes about some religions can and have been projected onto others. It has therefore been advantageous for religious groups in a stronger position to help defend those in a weaker position. This can include aiding, facilitating and highlighting the contributions made by minority communities but especially for IFS, cultivating a positive view of religion as essentially ethical. They have directly addressed stereotypes of religions and explained (though never explained away) expressions of religion which engender negative press. This also legitimates IFS as a vital link for the public with different communities who want to better their society and the lineages of moral wisdom which they carry with them.

The Al-Qaeda terrorist attacks on the World Trade Centre on 11 September 2001 greatly altered the image of Islam and religion among western publics, though it drew on long-standing antipathies rooted in Christian Islamophobia and to a lesser extent secularist struggles with Christian churches. Religion was stereotyped by popular critics such as the 'New Atheist' authors in the 2000s as associated with violence, intolerance, authoritarianism and terrorism, but Islam was usually singled out as especially problematic.

Nonetheless, the Scottish Muslim community is regarded by some of its members and by others as well integrated and even a model for Muslims in other parts of the United Kingdom[7] (Azam 2015). However, Islamophobia is still a serious issue in the country (Rodger 2015). Repeated media coverage of cases of terrorism and extremism can act as unrepresentative grist to that mill. For example, the case of a young Scottish Muslim woman, Aqsa Mahmood, who travelled to Syria in 2015 to wed an ISIS soldier, nicknamed 'the Jihadi bride' was extensively covered in the Scottish media (Settle and Braiden 2015). Another example was related to inter-Muslim conflict, when a Glaswegian Ahmedi Muslim shopkeeper was killed by a Sunni Muslim who had driven up from Bradford (Swindon 2016). Both the Scottish Sunni Muslim community and IFS responded to this event through public expressions of sympathy with the Ahmedi community and condemnations of violence.

IFS' efforts to cultivate a diverse and benign image of religion have been highly astute. As I indicated earlier, they have been careful to avoid any kind of denial of religiously motivated violence or intolerance. They have not made any attempt to assert that it is not real religion, instead they emphasized that it is not representative (which most scholars would agree with e.g. Cavanaugh 2011) because the essential foundations of religion are benign, as represented by practices such as aid work or indeed interfaith relations themselves.

The pervasiveness of Islamophobia has meant that IFS has been eager to promote the work of Muslim activists in addressing that prejudice: educating the Scottish public about Islam, engaging in charitable endeavours and building solidarity with other communities. In 2013, Rose Drew of Interfaith Glasgow and several other interfaith activists were invited to discuss the rise in religious prejudice, especially Islamophobia, with the then First Minister Alex Salmond (IFS Summer 2013: 4). Islamic charities such as Islamic Relief have been highlighted (IFS Summer 2013: 6). More specific examples include the endeavour by a group of mosques in Glasgow to collaborate with a Christian charity to distribute leftover meat from *Eid al-Adha* celebrations to the homeless (IFS Summer 2013: 12, IFS Spring 2014: 10). The *Guide* also stresses the importance of *Zakat* or annual almsgiving to the poor as one of the five pillars of Islam (IFS n.d.: 12–13).

One Muslim interfaith activist, Muhammad Omar, a former member of the IFS Youth Committee and Refugee Officer, visited schools in Shetland both to talk to pupils about interfaith work and his own religion. He highlighted Islamic teachings about altruism and generosity. Omar also stressed his openness to questions (IFS Spring 2014: 15), which has been echoed in accounts of interfaith outreach by other Muslim activists. This is likely informed by a popular stereotype of religious people, especially Muslims, as highly sensitive, quick to take offence and closed-minded.

There were several examples of extensive educational outreach by Muslim groups to the public, most of which sought to address the stereotype of Islam as oppressive to women. A Muslim woman's group in Kirkaldy, Jewels of Islam, held monthly open days to allow visitors to freely discuss controversial topics such as the place of the hijab (headscarf worn by some Muslim women) and marriage in Islam (IFS Summer 2013: 6). In 2014, the group met with Malala Yousafzai, a Pakistani campaigner for women's education who survived being shot by the Taliban as a schoolgirl (IFS Spring 2015: 25). This also served the purpose of highlighting a female Muslim role model. Another Muslim women's group Amina Muslim Women's Resource Centre also sent representatives to discuss myths about Muslim women. They also created an exhibit at the Scottish Parliament called 'I speak for myself!' (IFS September 2012: 18).

Addressing the perception of women in Islam was one of the key themes in the quotations chosen for the Muslim section of *Values*:

> Muslims believe that all men and women are created equal. A Muslim woman has the same duties in her religion as a man.
>
> *Women are the other half of men.* (Hadith)
>
> *The most perfect amongst you is the one who has best manners and kindest to his wife* (Hadith) [sic] SIFC 2011: 53).

The sincerity of either these specific activists or the IFS themselves is not in doubt. Nor is their desire to promote the welfare of the Scots population or help the Muslim community at large tackle Islamophobia. However, their statements or ways of framing these events are ripe for analysis and demonstrate the essentialist understanding of religion that has become central to their worldview. The desire to redress prejudices is refracted through their construction of religion and which also lines up with efforts by Scots Christians to adapt to their loss of hegemony.

With the suggestion that there is no place for religion apart from the privacy of home and place of worship ... Would advocates of a secular Scotland want ... Church Action on Poverty or Islamic Relief to stop caring? (IFS Summer 2013: 12)

Some religions do not have such associations, and in the case of Buddhism, for example, it is subject to positive stereotypes in a manner which can be characterized as romanticized to the point of exoticism and indeed orientalism. The fact that Buddhism has been commonly bound up with ethno-national and other forms of conflict, intolerance and terrorism in parts of Southeast and East Asia (Jerryson 2017) has often been ignored (Ramey 2016: 48, Siddiqui 2016). For those engaged in the business of defending and promoting the image of religion, these positive images of some can be put to use, just as negative stereotypes of others need to be combatted for the good of the whole. The *Guide* section on Buddhism certainly reinforces the pacifist and compassionate image of the religion (IFS n.d.: 7).

Religious minorities, ethnicity and nationalism

The diversity of modern Scotland is largely the result of immigration from former British colonies from the mid-twentieth century onwards. There is also considerable overlap between the 'religious' and 'ethnic' minority populations, as exemplified by the largest minority community – South Asians, especially Pakistani Muslims, many of whom are second, third or fourth generation Scots (Devine 2012: 563–4). The former SNP First Minister Humza Yousaf is a second-generation Scots Pakistani and a practicing Muslim. South Asian migration to Scotland became significant from 1948 and increased in the 1960s and 1970s (ibid.). The first interfaith group in Scotland – GSF was founded through the work of Stella Reekie with immigrants in Glasgow, facilitated by her ability to speak Urdu because most migrants to the city were from Pakistan.

IFS strongly supports multiculturalism as well as religious pluralism and often reports on multicultural celebrations alongside specifically interfaith events. The latter also tend to incorporate other aspects of cultural diversity to complement explicitly religious elements, including food, music, dance and art which help to substantiate and visualize diversity. Nonetheless, unlike religious diversity, these representations of cultural diversity are noticeably depicted broadly and are not clearly bound to the representation of groups. This cultural diffusion can cement the discursive transformation of a relatively ethnically and culturally homogenous nation into a plural one.

It is true that cultural practices or objects are usually distinguished to an extent either by national or by large regional labels: African, Arabic, Chinese, Indian and indeed quite commonly Scottish. In fact, a key feature of multicultural and interfaith events in Scotland is the combined and sometimes hybridized use of elements of Scottish traditional culture with the cultural heritage of ethnic minority groups. This has also encouraged all peoples in Scotland to access and take on Scottish cultural identity as their own, just as Scotland has been remade as multicultural.

On the surface, their depiction of ethno-cultural and religious diversity may seem similar, but they are substantially different. Their depictions of religious traditions may be somewhat abstract but they are nonetheless sharply distinguished from each other as well as tied to institutionalized groups and leadership. Their representations of cultural diversity do acknowledge origins but are otherwise unbounded and diffuse; there is no concerted effort to relate them to specific communities or lineages. Attendees at interfaith events are usually explicitly stated to be members of a given community or perhaps bearers of a tradition (or ism).

Nonetheless, most practitioners do not neatly separate 'religious' and 'ethnic' components of their lives, if these categories are acknowledged by them at all. This means that while interfaith literature has its emphases and interests, which may be largely unconscious, representing diverse religious groups cannot help but depict their wider cultural ties as well. This is especially true for religious minorities due to their recent migration histories and overlap with Scotland's ethnic minorities. Though the WRP approach and the increasing presence of converts in some communities have loosened these bonds to some extent.

Islam may be a global, transnational and multi-ethnic religion but while there are white Scottish and other converts to Islam, the majority of Muslims in Scotland are immigrants or the descendants of immigrants from Muslim-majority countries. Most Scots Muslims are of South Asian, primarily Pakistani origin, though there is a substantial Bangladeshi community. This is reflected, for example, in the fact that the Edinburgh and East of Scotland Pakistan Association was at one point a Muslim member of IFS (IFS Draft Report: 30). There are also communities with origins in other parts of the Muslim world, including different Arabic-speaking nationalities, Turks, Iranians, Malaysians, Somalis and Muslims from other parts of Africa.

The Sikhs are overwhelmingly of Punjabi origin and, as discussed earlier, are also classed as an ethnic group (Thomas 1993a: 209–10). Similarly, as elsewhere, most Hindus have roots in different parts of India though this includes different ethno-linguistic groups, but it is also sometimes asserted to be a common overarching ethnos as well. The Indian connections and internal diversity are demonstrated by the two Hindu members of IFS: the Glasgow Hindu Mandir and the Hindu Temple of Scotland, in Rutherglen, the latter is specifically associated with the South Indian community.[8] There are Hindu converts in Scotland, but these have mostly joined specific Hindu NRMs such as the International Society for Krishna Consciousness (ISKCON, popularly known as 'Hare Krishnas'), which unlike more traditional forms of Hinduism seek to proselytize, especially in the west (Thomas 1993b: 193–4).

Depictions of the Hindu and Sikh communities as well as most Muslims are inseparable from the South Asian cultures in which they are enmeshed. Interfaith events frequently include renditions of South Asian music, including popular Bollywood songs (IFS Spring 2013: 10) as well as overtly devotional music such as Hindu bhajans (SIFC March 2012: 2) and other visible, auditory or edible expressions of the cultures of the subcontinent.

Though they have been longer established in Scotland than most other minorities, the Jewish community is also of immigrant heritage and is largely descended from Eastern European (Ashkenazi) Jews who immigrated from the late nineteenth century onwards (Devine 2012: 518–22). This migration history has been a means of building solidarity with other minorities. The Edinburgh Jewish Community Centre attached to the Edinburgh Hebrew Congregation in Salisbury Road held an event in 2014 for immigrants to the city, who were invited to share their personal and familial stories of coming to Edinburgh (IFS Summer 2014: 13).

Buddhists in Scotland are a mixture of people of East Asian and Southeast Asian descent and converts from white Scottish or other backgrounds. The two Buddhist members of IFS are the Tibetan Buddhist Kagyu Samyé Dzong (part of the Karma Kagyu tradition) and the western-origin Triratna Buddhist Community (formerly known as Friends of the Western Buddhist Order). There are other Buddhist communities in Scotland though, including Thai and Sinhalese (the majority ethnic group of Sri Lanka) Theravadins, which are largely composed of immigrants or their descendants. One Buddhist group which is not a member of IFS but has participated in some interfaith events and has been reported in the literature is the majority Sinhalese Scottish Buddhist Vihara (SBV) led by the Venerable Rewatha. IFS reported on its tenth anniversary celebrations in 2012, which included a mix of Scottish and Sri Lankan themes and was attended by representatives of the Sri Lankan consulate (IFS September 2012: 6).

Immigration narratives, cultural heritage and constructions of the original as well-adoptive homeland have been important to the histories and concerns of minority communities which have been reflected in their depictions. Local interfaith groups have frequently hosted public events discussing immigrant experiences (SIFC March 2012: 2, IFS September 2012: 17). The CEO of the Scottish Refugee Council (SRC) John Wilks addressed the IFS AGM, which I attended in 2015. The SRC was also formerly a member of the IFS.

One of the most important annual events held by IFS since 2012 is Holocaust Memorial Day (HMD) on 27 January. For obvious reasons, the Jewish community plays a central role in these commemorations due to the genocide committed against European Jews, as well as Roma, homosexuals and the disabled by the Nazis during WWII. HMD also commemorates victims of other genocides, such as the Armenian genocide in 1915, Cambodia in the 1970s, Rwanda and Bosnia in the 1990s as well as Darfur in the 2000s (IFS Spring 2013: 18, IFS Spring 2015: 20) and most recently ISIS' genocide against Yezidis in Iraq (IFS Spring 2019: 5). The key role played by representatives of the Jewish community in commemorating and interpreting these events reflects the enormous numbers of Jews murdered in the wartime Holocaust and the seismic impact it had on post-war conceptions of and responses to genocide. In interfaith circles it also reflects the fact that this history is bound so closely to a specific religious community.

There are many specific examples of the ways in which interfaith commemorations and reportage of HMD include representatives of the Jewish community who weave aspects of Judaism or Jewish culture into them. For example, when Rabbi David Rose gave a talk on the Holocaust to school pupils in Edinburgh and read out the Jewish prayer for the dead (IFS Spring 2013: 14). During HMD events, both IFS and Jewish leaders often deftly move between acknowledgement of the importance of these commemorations for specific communities and their wider relevance for humanity. In practice, the audience is the Scottish or local public, and these serve to inculcate pluralist values more immediately and ultimately to ensure that these events are not repeated here and now (exemplified by the phrase "never again"). The fact that HMD does not focus exclusively on the Nazi Holocaust but highlights multiple genocides demonstrates that the Holocaust was far from unique, similar events can and have been repeated in different circumstances.

For interfaith groups, this helps to impart the fact that different groups can be vulnerable to state or majority persecution and that different religions share common interests. It is a powerful reminder of the need for tolerance and coexistence, the value of dialogue as well as public rights and representation for different religions. This traumatic history has also been used to highlight the role of 'people of faith' in responding to persecution and can be used to point to connections between communities. One example of this is an article in the newsletter written by the Church of Scotland, Reverend Andrew Sarle, whose German-Jewish father had fled to the United Kingdom and whose distant ancestor was a Rabbi (IFS Spring 2015: 29, ACTS n.d.). Similarly, in the case of the Bahá'í community, Maureen Sier has written about her husband Nick Sier's Jewish relatives who were murdered in the Holocaust (IFS Spring 2015: 21).

Another core role of IFS has been to integrate religious minorities into a shared Scottish public sphere and civic structures supported by these liberal-pluralist values in opposition to supremacism, intolerance and exclusivism. These shared norms encourage a common sense of ownership and participation in the common good defined by Scottish civic nationalism, which can be contrasted with the nationalisms which contributed to war and intolerance. This can be associated with IFS' (and the government's) desire to integrate but not assimilate religious minorities into the nation. This in turn can allow religious minorities to articulate their interests, defend their rights to practice their religion and critique prejudices or stereotypes about them. For example, the Scottish Council of Jewish Communities (SCoJeC) created their government-funded 'being Jewish in Scotland' project the findings of which were publicly presented in Edinburgh in 2013 and Peebles in 2014. Participants in the project conveyed both experiences and concerns around anti-Semitism but also expressions of belonging to Scotland (IFS Spring 2014: 11, IFS Spring 2015: 15).

As mentioned earlier and discussed at length in Chapter 6, this emphasis on civic nationalism is also strongly associated with and supported by the use of Scottish cultural heritage alongside specifically civic forms of belonging. An illustrative example was IFS' coverage and engagement with the 20th Commonwealth Games held in Glasgow in 2014, especially the ceremonies surrounding them in which IFS was a leading participant. IFS held a multi-faith service for the opening of the games which included music from a Sikh children's choir wearing tartan outfits (IFS Summer 2014: 10). One more recent case of the embedding of Scottish and interfaith symbolism within the practices and symbolism of a South Asian religious community was literal. The IFS logo was included within a Shiva *lingam* at a service at the Hindu Temple of Scotland held in English and Sanskrit (IFS 2017: 11).[9] A crucial means by which religious minorities are represented as belonging to a common Scottish national identity in the literature is giving local events a national significance. For example, the opening of the first purpose-built gurdwara in Glasgow:

> [The Gurdwara] is also inherently open to everyone of any religion or no religion … it will serve as a focal point for us to engage with the wider Scottish population. (IFS Spring 2013: 14)

As discussed previously, the emphasis on the shared category of religion can open up and diversify the storehouse of largely Christian historical sites which are also considered part of the nation's heritage and link them to the more immediate level of local places of worship. These themes were conveyed in a newsletter article where a Muslim woman reflected on her visit to Iona, stating that the Christian services she attended 'shone a light on God's path'. She added that she did not think that she had the 'right to dismiss the truths that others hold dear' and that 'being from the UK, my faith is Islam my culture is not' (IFS Spring 2014: 22–3).

While they may still occupy a somewhat marginal position and took years to gain entry, one interesting feature of the increasing acceptance of the Pagan community is the recognition of their claims to pre-Christian sites such as the standing stones of Callanish on Lewis. In fact, Callanish was used to symbolize them in the *Guide* (IFS n.d.: 21). There is considerable evidence that Pagans have become more accepted as interfaith participants across Scotland. It is common for the display or even making of religious objects, symbols, foods and art forms (depending on restrictions of course) to become part of the public activities at interfaith events, especially for children. The painting of 'Pagan stones' has become one of these regular activities (e.g. IFS 2017: 26). IFS organized an interfaith pilgrimage with the Edinburgh Women's Interfaith Group to places of worship in Glasgow for World Interfaith Harmony Week 2022, which included a talk by the interfaith officer of SPF Linda Haggerstone, who shared her poems on the festival of Imbolc (IFS Spring 2022: 23). Most strikingly, when the SPF interfaith officer who had campaigned for SPF to be included in IFS (SIFC) John MacIntyre retired from his post, he was feted in the IFS newsletter, they praised 'his immense contribution to the role', and offered thanks for:

> all his hard work in ensuring Paganism is recognised and included among the other faith traditions within the interfaith umbrella. (IFS 2018: 33)

Conclusion

IFS has helped to facilitate minorities' integration into Scottish national public life. It is a common Scottish identity, sometimes implicitly and explicitly, that these groups have been encouraged to integrate into. This has involved active participation in Scottish civil society and expressions of a national identity informed and symbolized by the country's traditional culture. There is evidence that religious minorities have been able to capitalize on the entrenchment of normative pluralism to secure their interests and gain a degree of influence. At the same time, it is quite probable that minorities, as with much of the majority have internalized and espouse this worldview independently.

The demographics of religious minorities in Scotland overlap considerably with those of ethnic minorities as well as histories of immigration to the point that these simply cannot be neatly separated. While IFS supports multiculturalism it does not lay as much stress on ethnicity preferring general conceptions of cultural diversity which inform and enrich the religions and the nation. Their understanding of religion is an example of the WRP which emphasizes doctrines, ethical wisdom and systematic traditions distinguishable from each other but complementary and comparable to one another. These religions are global and trans-historical bound to, but somewhat separate from the communities which practice them and are constructed as equal collaborators. They are also separate from diffuse forms of spirituality and from secular worldviews. These world religious traditions inform and influence the nation for the better, even while they transcend it. This means that they do not challenge its mere bounded sovereignty (or ultimate right to self-determination).

5

Rivals or collaborators? Interfaith Scotland's representation of the non-religious

Introduction

In previous chapters, we saw how Interfaith Scotland (IFS) constructed a world religions discourse through its texts and institutional representation. A common ecumenical Christianity was constructed; equal and analogous to the Baháʼí, Buddhist, Hindu, Jewish, Muslim and Sikh minority traditions. In all cases, the emphasis was placed on the wider tradition and less on the communities which align with them. Groups which do not conform to or are not part of the mainstream of one of these traditions were either ignored, marginalized or shaped to fit this mould. Fundamentally, IFS have a remit to represent 'people of faith', to defend and articulate their common rights and interests as well as highlight their contributions to society. As such, they can claim to represent the Scottish population: its traditional Christian majority and religious minorities. They can now also claim that they have found a place for newer and less conventional religions. However, this leaves one significant gap in their representation: the number of Scots who do not claim to be religious who grew throughout IFS' development and who now form the majority.

According to the 2022 census, the self-identified 'non-religious' are now not only the largest single group but form an overall majority at 51.1 per cent which is larger than all combined Christian categories 38.8 per cent and all Scots who have identified with a religious label 42.72 per cent (National Records of Scotland 2024). While the recent census is something of a milestone, these trends have been evident for decades, including during IFS/SIFC's twenty-five-year history. By the previous census in 2011, non-religious affiliation 36.7 per cent was lower than Christian affiliation overall 54.4 per cent, but was already higher than identification with the Church of Scotland at the time 32 per cent (National Records of Scotland 2011), which is now only 20.1 per cent (National

Records of Scotland 2024). This has certainly made this population increasingly difficult to ignore since then.

The category of 'non-religion' is complicated. It can include more active and more passive disavowals of religion. Identification with certain labels such as atheist, agnostic and Humanist are generally also classed non-religious without the need for further clarification (Cotter 2020: 21–4). If it was held to include those who identify with religious labels due to their family background but who neither participate in a religious community nor claim to believe in their religion's supposedly core tenets (Cotter 2020: 4), then it could be enlarged even further.[1] On the other hand, many self-identified non-religious people claim to believe in traditionally 'religious' concepts like God or the afterlife or engage in practices such as prayer, divination or magic (Cotter 2020: 31–2). This population is generally known as the 'spiritual but not religious' (SBNR). This highlights the ambiguous and contested nature of social categories, even the supposedly fundamental dichotomy between the religious and non-religious or the seemingly objective distinction between majorities and minorities.

Most of the non-religious are white and of Christian heritage (Bullivant 2017: 10 cited in Cotter 2020: 28) which will continue to have an influence on their understanding of religion and normative views about acceptable or unacceptable expressions of religion. Nonetheless, we also must take seriously their espousal of distinct identities, worldviews and ethical systems. Unlike previous periods of Scottish history, the non-religious are no longer novel nor must they struggle to be understood or accepted. However, they have not developed anything like the institutional frameworks, resources or even cohesive identities and ideologies of Christians or many religious minorities.

Turning back to IFS, their initial attitude to the non-religious appears to have been disinterest to the point that they largely ignored them. Over time, they have increasingly acknowledged and related to that population, or rather their selected representatives. This relationship has developed from a distant and indirect one to an increasingly regular and cordial one. This chapter will analyse the development of IFS' representation of the non-religious through three key stages, though these are not strictly chronological but rather interrelated steps of a process. These steps are: (1) the *acknowledgement* of the non-religious, (2) the quest for *common ground* and (3) the recognition (but also construction) of, as well as ongoing dialogue with a non-religious (belief) tradition: *Humanism*.

Initially references to the non-religious in IFS literature were very thin on the ground, conspicuous by their absence. Many of their educational endeavours towards the Scottish public could be interpreted as addressing an implicitly non-religious (or at least secularized) audience. A certain kind of non-religious position was directly addressed in their critiques of what they call 'militant secularism'. However, IFS participated in a Scottish Government working group: the Scottish Working Group on Religion and Belief Relations (SWGRBR) with the Humanist Society Scotland (HSS) from 2008. There was a gradual process under way in which Scotland's authorities recognized Humanism as equivalent to religious groups and sought to accommodate it on equal terms. This is part of the reason that IFS actively participated in dialogue with Humanist representatives and incorporated Humanism as a tradition into some of their documents.

The analysis of the cultivation of common ground between IFS and the non-religious will focus on a case study: the *Common Ground* conference held in Coatbridge at the Catholic Conforti Institute in 2013. This is because it was recorded in detail through proceedings published by the organizers: the Xaverian Missionaries of the United Kingdom and the United States. It offers a clear account of the efforts to construct a shared normative framework between interfaith and non-religious groups but also the ways in which their representation of the population is limited and based on self-selection. This has culminated in a joint effort to construct a recognized common tradition for the non-religious equivalent to the world religions but distinct from them. It is also shaped by the language of the 2010 UK Equality Act by using the category of 'belief' to denote groups legally protected on an equivalent basis to religions, to further identify Scotland as one nation of many faiths and none.

Non-religion and the non-religious

The category of 'non-religion' is perhaps more nebulous than the category of 'religion' itself. Non-religion can be classified as a negative, relational and oppositional category (Campbell 1971: 21, Bullivant and Lee 2012, Day, Vincett and Cotter 2013: 2, Cotter 2020). It is a negative category not in the sense of being pejorative, but that it is defined by the absence of religion (Lee 2015: 50 cited in Cotter 2020: 55). For scholars interested in the emic use of language, it is relational because its use will vary according to what the positive category (religion) means for a given group or in a given context. It is oppositional because both categories exclude the other (Quack 2014: 441). In some ways, this oppositional category is less disruptive to many normative models of religion than things which are on the category's fringes, for example, new religious movements, alternative spirituality and so forth.

However, non-religion has increasingly become a positive self-designation for some. This was rendered plausible by the fact that for several generations it has been relatively common for many Scots to identify as non-religious without necessarily having left a religion. It will be useful at this point to distinguish between everything not specifically classified as 'religious' and groups or agents understood by themselves or others to have specifically 'non-religious' identities, worldviews, institutions and values (Quack 2014: 441). The latter can be distinguished by the use of a capital 'N' as Lois Lee advocated (Lee 2012: 131 cited in Cheruvallil-Contractor et al 2013: 176) while the former is probably better referred to as 'secular' (Lee 2015: 39 cited in Cotter 2020: 24).

There are also many groups, institutions, identities and value systems which are secular in this sense rather than Non-religious: Dundonians, Liberal-Democrats, Scottish rugby team supporters, Blues music fans and so forth. These kinds of groups replicate the secularity of Scottish society at large because membership is differentiated from the question of religion. Those groups such as the Humanist and ironically some Secularist groups and labels such as atheist, are not simply secular in the above sense because they entail an explicit rejection or disavowal of religion (Campbell 1971: 27, Lee 2015: 31 cited in Cotter 2020: 21). Antagonistically or not, that label is thus related to the question of religious identity in a way that the above secular examples are generally not. Some Non-religious agents imbue that designation with distinctive significance, developing or taking on related practices and norms but for many it continues to be a largely negative designation, an indication of who they are not. In both cases though, there is at least an explicit, conscious disavowal of the category of religious. Whether positive or negative, for IFS the rise of this category raised the question of how to relate to this group.

An invisible other

One of the principal remits of IFS is to promote an active role for religious groups in the public sphere and to provide a forum for dialogue between them. It is unclear what the position of the Non-religious should be within this. Close reading of IFS' literature has revealed a subtle and gradual shift in their attitudes towards the Non-religious over time but initially, they appear to have largely ignored them.

It must be acknowledged though, as outlined in earlier chapters, that the interfaith movement (IFM) may have roots in the late nineteenth century but only became more widespread and influential from the late twentieth century on. The development of ecumenical relations between Christian churches, the establishment of minority communities in western societies and the developing relationships between them, has absorbed their attention. They may have assumed earlier in their work that interfaith relations would be of exclusive interest to religious people.

In the *Guide*, for example, the Non-religious are not mentioned at all in its discussion of the 2011 Census despite their record growth. The discussion also leans towards a highly optimistic interpretation of the figures on religion, equating religious self-identification with 'membership' of religious communities, for example. The *Guide* also argues that religious statistics may actually be undercounted because religious identification is a voluntary question in the census (IFS n.d. 5). This may be true, but it does not consider the reverse position, that many people may tick a box because of their family background but may not be observant, believe in religious doctrines or even consider themselves religious in their day-to-day life (Cotter 2020: 4). Non-religion is here conspicuous by its absence and is depicted as an invisible other, against which religion is implicitly measured but not thought about as a category among the populace. The problem for IFS is that they claim to be a national body who work for the benefit of all Scots and yet were unsure how to relate to a group who even then, represented over a third of the population. The undeniable fact of the growing Non-religious population is something that they did not ignore for long and their own principles likely encouraged them to try to 'making a difference through dialogue' with their Non-religious neighbours.[2]

The militant threat

Another explanation for IFS' growing acknowledgement of, and efforts to relate to the Non-religious was because they viewed them as a potential threat. In the late 2000s, the so-called 'New Atheist' movement gained unprecedented public prominence through the authors Richard Dawkins, Chrisopher Hitchens, Sam Harris, Daniel Dennett and Ayaan Hirsi Ali. They were notable for their scathing attacks on religion but also for encouraging active identification as atheist (see Wolf 2006, Zenk 2013, Cotter 2011, Cotter, Quadrio and Tuckett 2017). When IFS began to respond more regularly to anti-religious sentiment, the New

Atheist movement was probably past its heyday but nonetheless was still part of the discourse around religion. The likely reasons that IFS began to decry militant secularism more commonly from the early 2010s were probably a combination of the long hangover from the emergence of New Atheism (and the post-9/11 climate), coupled with their awareness of the coming independence referendum and possibility of constitutional change.

It should be noted though that despite their alarm at 'militant secularism' they were always careful to avoid indiscriminate broadsides against a whole segment of the population. They never condemned the Non-religious as a group of people, and their critiques were always addressed to perceived attitudes among that population. It is likely however that when IFS address negative stereotypes about religion as a whole rather than prejudice against specific religions, that the Non-religious are the presumed source of these prejudices. A good example of this is the way in which they touted the success of their school visits in tackling anti-religious sentiment, by quoting from pupils: 'I hadn't realised that religious people were NORMAL (sic)!' To which they added:

> Interfaith Scotland's youth have worked as wonderful advocates of faith and religion. (IFS Spring 2013: 4)

In itself, this is also an implicit recognition that much of the Scottish population is secularized and juxtaposed with their lack of acknowledgement of the Non-religious in the 2011 census, is evidence of unease about the place of religion in modern Scotland. Not only are the contexts in which IFS offers education or training (e.g. schools, local governments or police) understood to be secular, but those who use these spaces are assumed to be secularized. An important fact to consider about IFS' educational endeavours is that there is no discernible presumption that modern Scots are especially familiar with Christianity as a living religion.

There is also a common assumption that the media has an anti-religious bias, though this has been disputed by scholarship on religion in the British media. It is undeniable that some critiques of religion are made on occasion by some journalists, but the media tends to be supportive of and at times deferential to forms of religion perceived to be 'moderate' in contrast to 'fundamentalist' religion. In other words, they are not by and large hostile to the forms of religion which IFS represents. However, the major exception to this rule has been with regards to Muslim communities in Britain who have been the subject of hostility and suspicion (Knott, Poole and Taira 2013: 173–8). Nonetheless, IFS was highly concerned with the set of attitudes which they refer to as militant secularism and is one of the few worldviews to receive sharp and sustained critique:

> A lot has been said recently about a secular Scotland with the suggestion that there is no place for religion apart from the privacy of home and place of worship. In a recent article in a well-known Scottish newspaper,[3] religion is depicted as intolerant and judgemental, excluding and exclusive. (IFS Spring 2013: 12)

Smyth acknowledged that religious groups do exhibit problematic tendencies but argues that this reflects their humanity. Religions are represented in their best form as tolerant, open and welcoming to all people regardless of their beliefs. She was particularly eager to stress the charitable contributions of religious groups to wider society but also called for greater dialogue between religious and Non-religious people. Despite the irritation with anti-religious attitudes, there is a strong desire to demonstrate the value of allowing religions to work within the public sphere to a secular audience:

> Do the detractors of religion know what actually happens within faith communities? Do they know of the work of interfaith relations that bring together people of different faiths to explore differences as well as commonalities? This kind of activity allows people to move beyond tolerance to respect and appreciation of different beliefs and views (ibid).

This also a tacit admission that the Non-religious need to be acknowledged as a population that should be negotiated with, not ignored. In her speech she also recognized the importance of secular governance to ensure that society can incorporate people with different worldviews and norms (IFS Spring 2013: 12).

Indeed, IFS are far more secular than they may at first appear. Even the emphasis on the practical contribution of religious groups to social welfare is an example of this. Unsurprisingly, they are opposed to a model of secularism which shuts them out of public life. However, they have striven to lead by example, not by turning this approach on its head but by advocating a different model of secularism inclusive of all faiths and none. One of the reasons that they do not attack the Non-religious population as a whole is that they are seeking accommodation and sympathy for their position and are likely trying to avoid alienating that entire group. It would be far more desirable for them to distinguish those sympathetic or neutral to religion from those who are hostile to it. Lastly, it is an important part of their ethos that they are among those who bridge divisions rather than deepen them, especially as the division between religious and secular Scotland has been identified as a potential 'new sectarianism' (replacing the old Catholic/Protestant divide, see University of Edinburgh 2014: 2–4).

Common ground

IFS has now participated in several joint activities and dialogues with Non-religious groups, mostly Humanists and Secularists. This next section will focus on a pioneering conference which brought together Catholic, interfaith and Non-religious participants: the first 'Common Ground' conference held in Coatbridge in November 2013, though with some later events hosted by the Scottish Parliament (IFS Spring 2014: 23). This was organized by the Xaverian Missionaries of the United Kingdom and the United States and was held at the Roman Catholic Conforti Institute with which Sister Smyth is affiliated (Xaverian Missionaries of the United Kingdom and United States 2013: 4). Along with representatives of specific groups there were also some notable academics who participated: the historian of religion in Scotland Professor Calum Brown and the theologian Professor Willie Storrar. I will focus on this because it was the first such event and because there is a fairly robust if not complete record of the papers through a publication by the Xaverians: *Common Ground: Conversations among Humanists and Religious Believers* (henceforth *Common Ground).*

As shall become obvious, IFS and many of its leading figures played a key role in this conference. This makes it a pertinent case study for the ways in which interfaith and Non-religious activists have begun the process of co-constructing common norms and language. These are dependent on certain shared assumptions which also reinforce religion/Non-religion (or belief) as equivalent but distinct categories, both of which can be integrated into national space.

The sociologist Colin Campbell distinguished two broad tendencies among Non-religious groups according to their attitudes towards religion: the 'abolition' and 'replacement' schools. The abolitionist stance is anti-religious on principle and engenders critique of religion as a whole, as the key factor upholding perceived injustices or impeding scientific progress. The replacement stance also involves critiquing religions but only to the extent that they run counter to a Non-religious ethical or political system, for example, Humanism or Marxism. This latter approach recognizes laudable aspects of religions, such as their community-building tendencies and does not oppose religion for its own sake. For the latter, their Non-religious identity has *replaced* religion for them, but it does not include a commitment to *abolish* religion for everyone else in all possible forms (Campbell 1971: 37–8, Kasselstrand 2018 cited in Cotter 2020: 42). Stephen LeDrew made a similar distinction between the more uncompromising critiques of religion rooted in appeals to the natural sciences by figures such as T. H. Huxley and those appealing to the social sciences, exemplified by figures such as Karl Marx and Friedrich Engels (LeDrew 2012).

The Non-religious contributors to *Common Ground* definitely represent the replacement or social tendency. In fact, they even express contempt for the avowedly anti-religious strands within their own movement. This has allowed them to make common cause with the IFM, which it must be borne in mind, is only one strand within contemporary religion. This means that these activists may in fact have more in common with each other than many within their own camp. The cultivation of an appropriate socially conscious replacement for religion among the Non-religious has to some extent become an aim of IFS when relating to that population. Constructing distinct but equivalent niches allowed for the institutional representation of seemingly all groups in society, fulfilling one of the key aims of secular-pluralism. This is simply an extension and slight modification of the ways in which different religions have been accommodated but also projects similar assumptions on to what we might term 'organised Non-religion'.

My analysis of the 'common ground' evident from these proceedings can be characterized by the following core values: (1) the importance of *tolerance*, (2) the necessity of *dialogue*, (3) respect for individual *journeys* and (4) the desire to uphold sacralized communitarian *ethics*. Furthermore, they also stress the significance of (5) *inclusivity* and value (6) *integration* into a common (national) society to which all can partake, and all should contribute. I will outline this drawing on examples from the different articles in the volume which are written versions of the papers given at the conference.

These common values are used to unite and define these activists as representatives of segments of the populace. They are also used to differentiate what they understand to be the benign, harmonious forms of religion/Non-religion from those which are exclusionary, hostile and anti-social. There is a distinct tendency to lump together those opposed to this common ground with those who are simply apathetic about these relations, or who are not driven based on their religious identification into joining a community defined by them. This is a convenient equation for these activist groups because it defines a common *other* contrasted with their own commitment, activism and willingness to dialogue.

This conference also reflected the transnational networks in which these groups are embedded, some notable contributors were from the United States and there were some attendees from England as well as Scotland. Nonetheless, the Scottish context of the conference was important and frequently referenced by participants. These tendencies fit with those already observed in interfaith circles where world traditions and a global scope are accorded higher value, but at the same time there is also stress on the need to adapt to local or national contexts. Respecting the importance of local culture and democratic civic-political structures for resident communities is also a principle they hold to as well.

The Non-religious participants included Chris Stedman – Humanist chaplain for Harvard and Yale Universities, Prerna Abbi – member of the Chicago-based Inter Faith Youth Core (IFYC) (now Interfaith America), Jeremy Rodell – chair of the Southwest London Humanists and Gary MacLelland from the Edinburgh Secular Society. The proceedings also include articles from Sister Smyth, Dr Sier and from the American Xaverian Superior Friar Carl Chuddy along with an introduction simply credited to the Xaverian Missionaries. I will now examine the six themes mentioned earlier in turn as listed, drawing on contributions from these participants.

Tolerance

The Xaverians' introduction acknowledges from their Catholic perspective that the Non-religious have the same abilities to search for truth, goodness and beauty as the religious. It describes them as 'precious allies' in the pursuit of peace and human flourishing (Xaverian Missionaries of the United Kingdom and United States 2013: 4). Nonetheless, various contributors discussed the ways in which this has been denied to their community through intolerance and dehumanization. However, contributors recognized the ways in which the others have been impacted by similar intolerance. Speakers were often very astute in their ability to frame their groups' concerns and struggles by highlighting analogies with their interlocutors. Taken together, this underscores the value of tolerance for all. These papers gave space for a limited airing of grievances between religious and Non-religious groups, but were used to construct a shared normative position.

The American Humanist Chaplain Chris Stedman begins by critiquing sensationalist media portrayals of religion which focus more on contentious examples such as the anti-LGBT protests of the then infamous Westboro

Baptist Church rather than the soup kitchens which neighbourhood churches are commonly involved with. He uses this as a jumping off point to contest the equation of atheists with militant anti-religious hostility (Stedman 2013: 9). Similarly, Sier acknowledges the repression of Non-religion in some contexts but concentrates on the persecution of religions:

> Sadly some of the worst atrocities committed against humanity have been motivated by strongly held ideologies, these include massacres that have occurred because of religious beliefs but have equally been perpetuated ... by people holding strong held beliefs that include wiping out a specific religious community or suppressing religion generally. (Sier 2013: 34)

Sier gives particular mention to Arn Chorn Pond, a survivor of the Cambodian genocide committed by the Communist Khmer Rouge in the 1970s who contributed to IFS' Holocaust Memorial Day commemorations in 2014 (IFS Spring 2014: 18–19). She highlights the role that religious groups played in rebuilding communities in the aftermath of atrocities (Sier 2013: 34).

Edinburgh Secular Society's Gary McLelland began his paper by acknowledging the value of Non-religious groups' participation in dialogues with religious groups because it affords them with an opportunity to address stereotypes and discrimination directed at them (McLelland 2013: 50). Smyth refers back to Professor Calum Brown's 'sobering' talk on people who have left religions, particularly those sparked by restrictive and traumatic experiences, such as many LGBT persons brought up in conservative religious households. She invoked the Sri Lankan Catholic theologian Aloysius Pierris, who categorized religions as made up of 'oppressive' and 'liberating' aspects (though there is an implication that this could be extended to Non-religious systems as well). Smyth then proceeds to provide a full-throated critique of some forms of religion:

> This is shameful for those of us who are religious. Much of the tensions between religious and non-religious people is caused by religions being dogmatic and rejecting people who felt they couldn't fit in and some of this feeling had begun at an early age which also shows the importance of good religious education ... Prof. Brown's research showed a significant decline in religious affiliation in the 1960s ... The reason was attributed to the self-realisation of women at the time – another lesson for religion. (Smyth 2013: 42)

I would contend that the examples where some of these contributors focused on the persecution of the other are not simply a case of tolerant moderates commiserating together about the excesses of their hard line brethren. Even the unsurprising condemnations of the persecution of one's own camp served to develop a common identity and construct a shared space demarcated by particular expressions, terminology, references and prescribed behaviour. Arguably, shared symbolism has begun to emerge, the interfaith tree mentioned in previous chapters has been utilized on the document's cover, but the leaves have been stylized into a globe rather than religious symbols. These tendencies were made especially clear by Jeremy Rodell of southwest London Humanists, who discussed the need to build bridges over the 'faith line' between religious and non-religious (drawing on a term coined by the founder of the IFYC/ Interfaith America – Eboo Patel). This introduces a new division between the self-understanding of these moderates in contrast to their hardline brethren even if they are on opposites sides of the line. The tone in this document is sometimes reminiscent of converts to a new religion or ideology discussing how to preach the message to their own communities:

> But the fact that we don't directly reach the hard liners doesn't invalidate the exercise. They can only be reached or perhaps faced down, by more open-minded people from their own belief backgrounds – people on 'our side' of the line. It is by dialogue that we can all become better informed and feel better supported in advocating the interfaith approach within our own communities. (Rodell 2013: 45)

Dialogue

As discussed previously, the interfaith ethos goes far beyond mere tolerance to advocate for the practice of regular dialogue, which has simply been extended to the Non-religious. It is clear that while there is currently a division between 'religious' and 'Non-religious' people, this is not intended to be read as a naturally insurmountable one. This is the gulf that can be bridged for those who are willing to travel across it, but only some on either side show willingness to do so. Smyth argued that dialogue between the religious and Non-religious is vital because of:

> our common humanity and common citizenship, our common concern for the future of our world, our nation and our society. (Smyth 2013: 41–3)

Nonetheless, there is also recognition that this dialogue is in its infancy. Many participants touched on the dearth of institutional and regular opportunities for such dialogue. Friar Chuddy stated that the Xaverians had worked to build a 'safe and deferential space' for this and praised Pope Francis' efforts to build better relations with the Non-religious and the Catholic Church (Chuddy

2013: 36, 40). Dr Sier pointed to the IFM as especially equipped to conduct such dialogues due to their experience hosting dialogues between religions (Sier 2013: 33). As things stand, neither side is attempting to erase the religion/Non-religion binary as such but transform it to their mutual advantage. Though it is possible that relations bridging 'all faiths and none' become more significant, it is unlikely that this will be a total assimilation of either group without remainder. Just as ecumenical movements and intrareligious relations are still significant despite the greater prominence of the IFM, it is likely that these relations will continue to be multi-layered even if they harden into a supra-religion and belief movement in the future.[4]

As noted previously, this common ground and those willing to take a stand upon it have been rhetorically differentiated from the unwilling; whether through hostility or apathy. The trope of 'good religion' and 'bad religion' has simply been widened to include 'good' and 'bad' Non-religion, the yardstick employed here is openness to dialogue. Smyth took the opportunity in her piece to heap praise on Stedman as an influential Humanist chaplain and his promotion of Non-religious engagement with interfaith dialogue. Notably, she compares him favourably with Richard Dawkins as the most famous example of the anti-religious New Atheist movement (Smyth 2013: 41–2). Stedman's paper itself focused on how to include the Non-religious into dialogue written from his own Humanist position but addressed to a religious, especially Christian audience (Stedman 2013: 8–11). The Xaverians' introduction similarly recognized the capacity for dialogue among all human beings along with the equally strong tendency to ignore it (Xaverian Missionaries of the United Kingdom and United States 2013: 4). This was echoed by Friar Chuddy:

> One of the remarks that surfaced consistently in our common ground conference among humanists and religionists was that it seemed easier to find ways to dialogue among religious believers and humanists because we all believed this dialogue was important to undertake and came to the conference for that explicit purpose … That conviction that we all saw so apparent in our conference is in fact not shared at all with many of our colleagues, friends and fellow believers. (Chuddy 2013: 38)

Rodell adds to this by sarcastically disparaging those within all kinds of community 'who know they're right (Rodell 2013: 45)'. This all serves to demonstrate the processes through which a common identity is being constructed by many of these participants. The boundaries around this tentative community are marked by attitudes to dialogue.

Personal journeys

Contributors from all communities also discernibly expressed a shared individualistic and liberal model of religious identity which valorizes the person's choices and efforts to find an identification authentic to them. Any attempt to repress, coerce or coax a person out of their religious identification is cast as oppressive. It logically follows from this that the best judge for how well-fitting any religious or Non-religious identification is the individual themselves. This is also understood in terms of a quest for the tradition and community authentic to them which provide an outward, communal expression for their innermost convictions. This is part of their personal journey and may involve moving between religious communities, from religious to Non-religious or *vice versa*. In many cases, it may not involve movement at all but rather entail deepening appreciation of one's own tradition, especially through dialogue with others.

Sier's upbringing was one common to many Scots: secularized but with a Presbyterian cultural influence. Despite this, she become fascinated with religion in general and found her personal journey led into the Bahá'í Faith. Here she drew specific parallels between her movement into religion to those who moved out of it, acknowledging that this has often involved personal and familial strife. She uses this comparison to underscore the point that for some people, the shift into a religious position can be liberating (Sier 2013: 32–3). In her paper, Smyth acknowledged that the movement away from one's natal position can be both 'liberating' and 'honest (Smyth 2013: 42)', reinforcing the significance of personal authenticity as crucial to understanding both forms of religious identification.

Sacralized communal ethics

Despite the fact that these activists espouse a form of individualism this is balanced with a stress on collective ethics and active involvement in their communities. For example, American interfaith activist Prerna Abbi of IFYC, stated that while she knew she was agnostic from a young age she was still drawn to the communitarian practices of Hinduism. The concept of *Karma Yoga*, the 'path of action' remained significant to her. She also highlighted charitable work as a particularly valuable opportunity for collaboration between religious and Non-religious groups (Abbi 2013: 22–30).

The Xaverians' introduction was especially critical of 'personal spirituality', though this was less for its own sake and more because they associate this with a lack of altruism and wider societal concern (Xaverian Missionaries of the United Kingdom and United States 2013: 6). The condemnation of personal spirituality and emphasis on communitarianism alongside promotion of the voluntaristic, personal view of religion may appear contradictory, but this is not necessarily the case. All parties involved in the conference were activists who have a remit to promote certain agendas, activities and ethical convictions to the public. These seemingly contradictory principles are built into the WRP: a focus on personal beliefs and ethics while at the same time valorizing broad traditions defined by institutionalized communities. To be included in this approach, one must conform to a recognized tradition, but belonging is ideally open to anyone who ascribes to these beliefs and practices. This particular normative pluralism holds that one should be free to find one's authentic community, but among similar kinds of traditions.

All of these activists are representatives of institutionalized groups defined by their religious identification and the promotion of their interests. These actors gain legitimacy from claims that they represent a distinct section of the population which is bolstered by encouraging active membership and identification. It is also in their interest to convince that population that they are parts of well-defined groups with definite characteristics and interests. These communities and their values are all sacred in the Durkheimian sense (2001) to these participants; they are of supreme socio-personal significance or even their most important identity. This is not something we should assume is representative of the publics they purport to speak for.

Inclusivity

Participants at *Common Ground* emphasized the need to strengthen relations between their communities. As highlighted in the account of the development of the IFM, these kinds of relations have depended on making accommodations for all parties involved. This need was particularly stressed by the Non-religious contributors due to their less established status; reiterating the right of Non-religious groups to be present. At the same time, they implicitly reinforced their own prerogative to represent that population through institutionalized groups such as Humanist societies.

Abbi's biographical details state that 'she is particularly passionate about including the voices of the non-religious like herself, in interfaith'. She recounts the difficulties many Non-religious representatives have had in gaining recognition within chaplaincies and other interfaith environments. She also emphasized the need for Non-religious people to form their own communities as well (Abbi 2013: 22). All of this broadly fits with the interfaith agenda which has been to promote greater recognition of religious diversity within the public sphere and simply includes another identification related to religion. Dr Sier ends her own article with a call for the recognition of both sides of the religion question as equals and their protection through legal rights (Sier 2013: 31–4). IFS' efforts to realize this vision will become more evident in the discussion of their relationship with the HSS later in the text.

The theme of inclusivity is also used as a means of addressing perceived inequalities while at the same time resubscribing to a common moral framework. The fact that such appeals are made is an indication that there is recognition that both audiences share those principles and that such appeals are perceived to be effective. For example, Stedman critiqued the sense of 'persecution' of many American Christians, highlighted the persistent prejudice against atheists in the United States and called for the recognition of 'Christian privilege':

> Imagine how you would feel if, instead of hearing President Obama make references to God and Jesus in speeches, he spoke about how what unites us as Americans is that we don't believe in God. (Stedman 2013: 7–11)

McLelland pointed to the fact that Humanists are a minority but acknowledged that interfaith dialogue provided an opportunity to pursue their ends of opposing extremism and oppression. He acknowledged that Non-religious communities could learn much from the IFM:

> As secular humanists, we must not waiver from our responsibility to expose injustice and collusion, yet at the same time, seek to promote a positive and friendly dialogue of compassion and understanding. (McLelland 2013: 50)

Several contributors also reflected on their differing understandings of 'secularism'. McLelland asserted that Secularists had their work cut out for them in explaining the concept in a way that appeared less threatening to the religious (ibid.). Rodell called for more nuanced usages of both 'secularism' and 'interfaith' in order to be inclusive of the religious in the former and inclusive of the Non-religious in the latter (Rodell 2013: 46). This echoes the form of secularism advocated by the philosopher Charles Taylor in which the state and public sphere are differentiated from any specific religious or philosophical position but also in which those positions can be freely expressed (see Taylor 2011b: 47–8). Taylor's work was approvingly invoked by Friar Chuddy in his paper. Chuddy expressed sympathy for the discomfort many Non-religious people may feel with religious influences on public policy. In a thoroughly Taylorian fashion, he called for a balanced approach in which all religious and Non-religious groups should be able to contribute to the public sphere, but a degree of separation needed to be maintained between politics and religion (Chuddy 2013: 35–40).

The integration of the Non-religious envisioned in these discourses does not appear to be limited to dialogues or even liaisons with governments and public bodies. It also involves symbolic and intellectual equivocation between these groups which helps to further legitimate their inclusion. This was conveyed by Smyth where she made a clear effort to relate to and draw on concepts associated with the Non-religious to explain the significance of her own religious worldview. She stated that she could identify as 'humanist' in supporting human rights, 'secularist' in defending religious freedom and even 'agnostic' (but notably not atheist) in relation to the 'unfathomable mystery of God'. She did this to demonstrate her efforts to learn from the 'wisdom and insight of others' (Smyth 2013: 42–3). This is a common rhetorical device in interfaith circles, engaging with different religions by appealing to their key doctrines and intellectual traditions. It is especially important in their efforts to pry the benign core of a tradition from the more malignant manifestations which have accrued to it. Appealing to the presence of the golden rule as in *Values in Harmony* is a key example of this discourse. In this document as we have seen 'good' religions and Non-religions are communal, active, tolerant and socially integrated. It is often the national community into which these groups are implicitly integrated into.

Integration and nation

As mentioned previously, this conference was somewhat international (in a very limited way, with contributors from the United States, England as well as Scotland), but its Scottish location and the prominent role of IFS mean that this 'national' context was significant. This had a discernible influence even on those who had travelled from outwith Scotland. Part of the reason for this is the pervasiveness of national categories globally, which means that despite nationalist stress on difference, rhetoric can be translated or adjusted into another national context with relative ease. While a degree of internationalism or global consciousness is part and parcel of interfaith discourse, so is the sense that different groups should collaborate on equal terms through a common framework for their respective societies. This can mean acting as a global citizen or as a member of a local community at times but for the most part, encouragement of active citizenship and membership of 'society' implies the nation. This is rendered all the more obvious when we consider that legally speaking at the time of writing, there is no such thing as Scottish citizenship because Scotland is not an independent nation. Therefore this is not dictated purely by a pragmatic need to work within the structure of a sovereign state.

Even when interfaith activists are speaking and working globally or universally these are usually forged in a practical sense at a more 'local' level (relative to the global level) at events, shaped by pre-existing conventions of where the 'local' is and how far it extends (e.g. whether we refer to 'here' as Coatridge, Scotland or the UK). Attendees at interfaith events who traverse these presumed boundaries will have cemented their value systems (their 'common ground'), in their home location, though likely through similar influences. Nonetheless, this can be brought into and adapted to a new setting so that the ethos and aims they share with their 'hosts' can be localized to the needs of that society. According to this perspective, interfaith dialogue may be useful everywhere, but it can still be useful here; to help Scottish communities recognize their shared interests for the betterment of their society. This reflects both globalization and the continued prevalence (to the point of invisibility) of most forms of nationalism which are banal, international and assume the equivalence of national communities.

Public engagement in Scotland entails working within its devolved political system but also relating to a public who overwhelmingly consider themselves to form a distinct nation. The fact that some of the proceedings of the conference were held in the Scottish Parliament will have brought this to the fore to a greater extent (Rodell 2013: 46). Notably, this led to some engagement with the civic symbolism and rituals of the nation's legislature. The significance of the Scottish national context was evident from Dr Sier's opening statement:

> It is in the context of wider 'dialogue with other religion and belief groups' that Interfaith Scotland is delighted to engage with humanists, secularists and see this dialogue as playing an important role in ensuring that Scotland as a just and inclusive country that promotes dialogue and civic engagement whether you have or have not religious beliefs. (Sier 2013: 31)

Smyth commented on the fact that while Scotland's interfaith scene has been very successful, dialogue between religious and Non-religious has been lacking. This shows that the ways in which the nation is repeatedly invoked do not have to be done with uncritical pride to be effective. It is *here* that relations must be improved. The fact that she holds up a successful event in London as a model (Smyth 2013: 41) demonstrates both how the nations' borders are reinforced, even though they are part of the same sovereign state (a similar event in Inverness would likely have been relevant for encouraging an audience in Coatbridge, but not an event in London) but also that 'beyond those borders lie other nations' (Anderson 1983: 6). Those other nations may currently be doing better than we Scots at organizing interfaith-Humanist dialogue events. This highlights the ways in which nationalist discourses can even valorize other nations where it is deemed beneficial and also that the nationalist norm is that nations are equal, equivalent to each other.

A parallel remark was made by Rodell, who acknowledged that while Scotland is far less diverse than London in real terms, Scotland appears to be 'way ahead' in the ways in which it has institutionalized interfaith relations. He singled out the Scottish Government's 2011 *Belief in Dialogue* (compiled with significant contributions from IFS and the HSS) for its focus on the issue of how to integrate the Non-religious into interfaith relations. Furthermore, he took the opportunity to reflect on the values inscribed on the mace of the Scottish Parliament – wisdom, justice, compassion, and integrity, which 'no Humanist with disagree with' (Rodell 2013: 44–7). McLelland also praised the Parliament's adoption of the 'Time for Reflection' as an opening of session ritual over the Christian prayers which are still used in Westminster (McLelland 2013: 48–50).

Humanism as a 'belief' tradition

This conference and the interactions that it sheds light on are examples of a wider dynamic whereby Secular-Humanism has been especially elevated into legitimate representatives of the Non-religious. The representation of Humanism within IFS' texts focuses on its institutions, core doctrines and ethical tradition similar to its representation of religions. IFS and the HSS would doubtlessly have had an interest in collaborating and developing some form of relationship. Nonetheless, the relationship that they do have has undeniably been promoted and facilitated by the Scottish Government. This follows the government's agenda of instilling a common Scottish civic identity through these relationships and through shared values.

An important part of this process that we have already touched on was the introduction of the category of 'belief' which has been a means for governments and public bodies in the nations of the UK to classify and relate to Non-religious identities. This category was introduced by the 2010 Equality Act applied across the UK, as a protected characteristic equivalent to religion alongside age, disability, gender reassignment, marriage and civil partnership, pregnancy and maternity, race, sex and sexual orientation. This category of 'belief' allows for Non-religious convictions to be recognized as both equal to and different from religion. However, this equivocation with religion has baked in many (if not all) of the assumed characteristics of religions. For Non-religious identities to qualify as 'beliefs' they are described as 'philosophical' positions but are also taken to be overwhelmingly important to a certain category of person (The Scottish Government 2011: 45, The University of Edinburgh 2014: 6). It is the fact that they are assumed to be sacred to a growing segment of the population which necessitates legal protection, governmental recognition and outreach from analogous groups in the national public sphere.

An interesting feature of this characteristic as elaborated in the legislation is that it protects the 'lack of religion' and the 'lack of belief'. This does show a degree of recognition of the more positive, active and self-conscious forms of religious identification and the more negative, habitual or natal forms they may take. Confusingly though, the wording of the explanation of belief could include religion and becomes somewhat tautological: 'Belief may mean any religious or philosophical belief'. It has been invoked to protect individual's commitment to certain political-ideological convictions e.g. environmentalism, the Labour Party (The University of Edinburgh 2014) and Scottish independence (Davidson 2019). However, it is generally used to refer to Non-religious systems and often specifically to Secular-Humanism (The Scottish Government 2011: 4–6).

While the exact conceptual boundaries between religion and belief have not been clearly articulated, and the lack of belief has been protected, this does not apply to all beliefs that individuals can hold. It may not be clearly articulated, but the concept does not map closely on to more general anthropological or epistemological understandings of 'belief'. The category is explicitly stated to refer exclusively to those for whom this belief is an overriding part of one's identity, which is what is implicitly assumed about religions for their adherents. To reiterate, beliefs have to be sacred in a Durkheimian sense. It is only those who take their religion or belief 'seriously' who necessitate recognition and accommodation by the government and public bodies.

> To be protected, a person must belong to a religion that has a clear structure and belief system … A philosophical belief must satisfy various criteria, including that it is a belief about a weighty and substantial aspect of human life and behaviour – so, for example humanism. (Scottish Government 2011: 45)

This state of affairs is itself a product of the processes of consensus building among religions, interfaith and Non-religious actors with secular authorities.

This consensus stresses the importance of ethics, wisdom traditions and public-communal activism. For governments, it is easy to appreciate why they might offer the most attention to groups whose identity will likely have a profound impact on their welfare. Governments are most likely to be concerned with how these beliefs effect the provision of services, the public pressure believers may exert and their potential voting patterns. It is also much easier for institutions to relate to institutionalized groups with recognized spokespeople along with policy documents, core principles and even revered texts which can be appealed to. It is difficult for them to relate to amorphous, decentralized groups, especially those defined in purely negative terms. This new terminology was enthusiastically adopted by IFS, and they began to make use of this terminology in their training courses for council staff. Relating to 'belief' groups was one of their stated aims: '[t]o support a wider interfaith dialogue with other religion and belief groups' (cited in Sutherland 2018a: 20).

In practice, relating to belief communities means relating to the HSS and the broader Humanist tradition for the most part. The historical development of Non-religious movements is rich and complex. Certain groups were more prevalent in certain periods: 'Ethical Societies' in nineteenth-century Britain and America (see Campbell 1971, Nash 2013), state-sponsored 'Scientific Atheism' in the USSR (see Hormel 2010, Borowik, Ančić and Tyraľa 2013) and 'Rationalism' in contemporary India (see Copeman and Quack 2015). Cultivating novel collective identities and institutions outside religion has given rise to a degree of creativity and experimentation, often limited in appeal and short lived, for example, Dawkins's attempts to popularize the label 'Bright' (Dawkins 2007). It is possible that a new movement will become prominent, such as the London-based Charismatic Christian inspired Sunday Assembly movement (see Mortimer and Prideaux 2018), which has opened a church in Edinburgh (Macaulay 2018, Cotter 2020: 37). Nonetheless, Secular-Humanism has emerged as the pre-eminent organized Non-religious movement in much of the English-speaking world and remains so[5] (Campbell 1971: 89–96, Fowler 1999: 25–30, see also Cimino and Smith 2007, Law 2013, Copson 2015).

Humanism is described as a 'non-theistic ethical life stance' which bases its morality on the welfare of human beings along with science and reason (Fowler 1999: 11). The question is why has Humanism become so dominant, at least in terms of public recognition from governmental, civil and religious bodies? One likely reason for this is the fact that Humanism is first and foremost concerned with providing a system of popular Non-religious ethics not restricted to academic moral philosophy seminars. Humanist groups have also produced volumes of writings, codes and concepts which can readily be equated with those from world religions. Also, in terms of its ethos and practices, they at least outwardly (for many no doubt sincerely) conform to the replacement or social strand within Non-religion; indeed, their practices are modelled on religion (more accurately, low-church Protestant Christianity).

Humanist societies hold meetings for their members, but one of their most notable activities has been their provision of rites of passage (baby naming ceremonies, weddings and funerals) conducted by trained celebrants (Fowler 1999: 283, see Engelke 2014, 2015). These rituals have proven popular with a growing number of the Scots and after Humanist wedding ceremonies were made legally binding in 2005, they overtook the number of Roman Catholic weddings in the country from 2010 (The Scotsman 2011, Kasselstrand 2018: 278 cited in Cotter 2020: 30). In secularizing societies, life-cycle rituals often remain the preserve of the established religions such as the Kirk, for a long period, but it should be borne in mind that attachment to these novel ritual specialists may be just as nominal and circumstantial as it often was with established religion.

As we have noted throughout this book, IFS are an organization of organizations which relate to communities through appointed representatives but also establishes appointed representatives for each of the recognized world religions. For them, it is a natural extension of their modus operandi to relate to the representatives of the HSS, as well as to recognize Humanist groups as representatives of the Non-religious in Scotland and custodians of their tradition. One of the reasons that IFGs can relate to groups such as Humanists is their community-building and active identification as Non-religious reinforces the importance of religion. The question of religious identification is central to both interfaith and Non-religious groups.

The simplest reason why the HSS have become dialogue partners among religious, interfaith and government circles is because they have actively sought out this role. For example, the HSS collaborated with the Kirk on a proposal to change religious observances in non-denominational schools to Time for Reflection, reflecting the practice of the Scottish Parliament (Marshall 2014). The Kirk was historically responsible for providing religious services in non-denominational schools in Scotland. In this case, these two parties found common ground on the conception that schools should introduce children to multiple religions and beliefs; the underlying conviction that they both share is that the question of religion is vital.

These developments conform to longer and broader patterns in the pluralization of Scottish society: the progressive inclusion of non-Presbyterian,

Catholic and non-Christian religions in the public sphere. The recognition and promotion of belief communities makes it easier to justify the prominent position of religions in a secularizing society. This inclusivity demonstrates that all groups have access to a similar level of influence, but this is understood to be relevant only to communities, not loose categories of people. Newer, smaller and less established groups have had to be built up, encouraged and institutionalized to achieve this.

One important text which offers an insight into the forging of a relationship between IFS, HSS and the Scottish Government is *Belief in Dialogue: Religion and Belief Good Practice Guide* (henceforth: *Belief in Dialogue*). This document was created by the Scottish Government's SWGRBR, which was established in 2008 and was chaired by Smyth. Its members included Sier along with other IFS figures along with Ron McLaren of the HSS. It is credited to the Scottish Government but is in effect one produced by IFS, likely with a fair amount of input from HSS. It was launched at the Scottish Storytelling Centre on 8 March 2011 (SIFC August 2011: 2). It is beyond doubt that this working group has greatly encouraged both organizations to relate more closely, and for IFS to begin to reflect much more clearly and openly on the Non-religious.

> This is a very particular kind of guidance document for dialogue. It is one which has the ultimate aim of encouraging constructive dialogue to take place between those who hold religious beliefs and those who hold non-religious beliefs. Such dialogue is vital if we are to live harmoniously together in society. (Scottish Government 2011: 3)

Belief in Dialogue shows how easily many interfaith tropes can be expanded to accommodate belief communities as well. These are the same rhetorical devices analysed in *Common Ground*: acknowledging mutual violence and prejudice but highlighting contributions to society, as well as dividing 'good' from 'bad' manifestations of these traditions. The text criticizes the assumption that the Non-religious are inherently anti-religious, along with stereotypes about religions as intolerant and dogmatic (ibid.: 48). The solution that it proposes to overcome stereotypes that these two groups project onto each other is unsurprisingly more regular dialogue between them (ibid.: 6). It also explicitly defends secularism by specifying what it does not have to entail:

> Secularism is often defined as a doctrine that rejects religion and religious considerations and accepts the complete separation of religion from government. (ibid: 7)

The greater ambitions of the authors of *Belief in Dialogue* and the interlocutors discussed in this chapter contrast starkly with the rather sparse opportunities for dialogue and 'inter-belief' relations in reality. For example, under a section outlining dialogue initiatives by belief groups there is a single entry, the dialogue event held in London mentioned in *Common Ground* (ibid.: 10–12). It should be borne in mind that the conference and text of *Common Ground* came from a Catholic, not Non-religious organization. *Belief in Dialogue* also provides suggested activities for its readers, and one such hypothetical example was a Humanist group visiting a local mosque. It is clear that the desired end is:

> The local Humanist group feel that they have developed a greater understanding of Islam and that a friendship between the two groups has begun, creating more community harmony and respect. (ibid: 24)

This offers an ideal depiction of the relations between religion and belief groups rather than an overview of their existing relations. Notably though, the HSS were involved in the writing of this text (ibid.: 51). When this fact is coupled with many of the recorded speeches by Humanist leaders in *Common Ground*, this would suggest that they concur with this vision, though it is also possible to interpret some of that as strategic enthusiasm directed at influential audiences. It seems likely though, for the most part that this is a sincere desire, but it must be remembered that this reflects the views of active members of communities and largely those of their leaders. Nonetheless, Humanists have been mentioned on more frequent occasions in the newsletter since then and IFS and HSS held a joint dialogue and dinner for Scottish Interfaith Week (SIFW) in 2016. Dr Sier also spoke at the HSS' monthly gathering in February 2017 (IFS 2017: 14).

To a large degree this representation is based on self-selection; those able and willing to engage in dialogue are noticed by other communities, organizations and authorities. It also depends on the ability to fit into the kind of niches that have previously been carved out for others. Inclusion is shaped therefore by pre-existing categories and expectations and by the actual relationships between groups. However, once that niche has been filled and accepted by other parties, these representatives are now treated as the voice of 'their' people, now a slight majority of Scots. These spaces are defined and dominated by activists, but this can obscure the fact that even those who have simply registered as Humanist to make use of their services, let alone active members, represent a small segment of that demographic (Cotter 2020: 40). Even the growing popularity of Humanist rituals arguably reflects the declining position of the Kirk as much as it does Humanism itself.

The ways in which IFS relates to and represents Humanism is not confined to the HSS as an organization but also as a belief tradition, a philosophical-ethical system perceived to rightly belong to the Non-religious population but one all too often left unclaimed by them. This is most evident in *Values in Harmony* in which a section of this text was devoted to Humanism, and which was compiled by members of the HSS. This type of representation closely resembles the essentialist approach to religions discussed in previous chapters. The introduction to the document as a whole takes pains to present the Non-religious as a 'community':

> The *Humanist Society of Scotland* is one such representative of wider society, otherwise also known as *Secular* society or the *non-religious community*. Humanists base their moral principles on a rational approach to life, underpinned by shared human values and respect for all others … although, not deriving their moral and ethical positions from any 'higher authority' such as God, by virtue of their common humanity Humanists share the same values in common with Faith communities that promote good relationships, and naturally this includes the *Golden Rule* [*sic*]. (SIFC 2011: 10)

A statement from the Dalai Lama is offered to lend authority to its claim that the Non-religious carry the same 'spiritual qualities' as the religious embodied in the values of love, compassion, patience, tolerance, forgiveness and humility (SIFC 2011: 11). A series of quotes are provided at the end of the introduction to substantiate the assertion that these groups converge on the same basic morals.

> Humanism is ethical. It affirms the worth, dignity and autonomy of the individual … and Humanists have a duty of care to all of humanity including future generations [*sic*]. (SIFC 2011: 12)

The introduction within the Humanist section sets out the core characteristics of their belief system, the basis of which is reason and empathy for fellow human beings. A desire for greater Humanist representation but also for deeper relationships with religious groups can also be discerned. However, it does advance explicit criticisms of perceived religious privileges and oppressive tendencies: '[t]o this end, humanists aim to co-operate with people of all faiths and none, to achieve a caring free society, but deplore any religious adherence that harms or disadvantages others (SIFC 2011: 46)'. The introduction goes on to explain that the label Humanism is not interchangeable with atheism and describes it as a distinct, systematic conceptual, moral and ritual system:

> Humanism provides a moral framework for a life free from superstition and
> supernatural beliefs, and holds that this life is the only one we have. Although
> ... Humanism is more than just a simple denial of religious belief ... Humanists
> demand equal opportunities for all, irrespective of age, disability, race, creed,
> gender or sexual orientation. (SIFC 2011: 46)

Like a church or other institutional religious group, Humanist representatives
can point to official policies and doctrines which they have enshrined. The
text highlights the six points of the Humanist Declaration which was adapted
at their World Congress in 2002. Though this was only introduced in 2002,
it is described as the culmination of a historic lineage of 'free thought', which
has striven to balance individual freedom and social responsibility (ibid.: 47).
This demonstrates the degree to which Humanism has in-built features which
make it relatable to the WRP. Furthermore, the section describes Humanism
in similarly universalistic terms: 'Humanism can be a way of life for everyone,
everywhere (ibid.: 48)'. The text also provides insight into the ways in which
the more 'replacement' or 'social' strands of organized Non-religion recognize
the value of certain aspects of religion and advocate tailoring them to their
needs: 'Humanism ... is a response to the widespread demand for an alternative
to dogmatic religion' (ibid.).

The introduction to the Humanist section closes by reflecting on balancing
the need for human creativity along with science. It is followed by an anonymous
poem titled 'Community', which ruminates on humanity and nature (ibid). The
last section of *Values* reflecting on the different sections of the document as a
whole and their importance for modern Scotland, also reveals the changing
ways in which the Non-religious are approached by actors in Scottish public life.
It is revealed with alarm that while 68 per cent of the focus group participants
who consulted on the document, knew that the Golden Rule was shared by
religions, only 47 per cent knew that it was shared with 'non-religious, that is,
Secular Humanism' (ibid.: 82). Similarly, many of the young people who made
up two out of five of the focus groups, asserted that religions did not engender
social harmony. For the document's authors, this revealed the importance
of developing relations between religion and belief communities, as well as
addressing stereotypes, especially among youth: 'notwithstanding the need
to respect differences, Religion and Beliefs communities should be raising
awareness of their shared commonality' (ibid.).

The final section of *Values* also stresses the benefit for young people to
belong to some kind of group and tradition because they can be dealt with

through institutional channels and because of the moral guidance they offer. As Humanism became better established and gained more recognition, it was increasingly treated as an equivalent dialogue partner for the world religions at least in interfaith and governmental circles.

Conclusion

In contemporary Scotland, the Non-religious (those who have identified themselves as such) are now a majority of the population. This fact has meant that actors such as Interfaith Scotland and the nation's government have found it necessary to acknowledge, relate to and include them to varying degrees. This loose self-identified category has increasingly been reified as a 'belief' community, people defined by a shared belief in a worldview counter to 'religion' which is of deep socio-personal significance to them regardless of whether this applies to many 'Non-religious' Scots. This can be distinguished from the kind of secularism which has taken root in Scottish politics, the public sphere and society which is differentiated even from the question of religion.

The Non-religious, especially organized Non-religious groups such as the HSS, on the other hand, are not differentiated from the question of religion, they are defined by it. The remit of the government and to a more limited degree IFS, is to represent the Scottish population and therefore developing closer relations with these groups has helped to fulfil that. This chapter traced the increasing engagement of IFS with the Non-religious, the construction of 'common ground' and the inclusion of Humanism as a belief tradition. In some of the earlier sources, the Non-religious were only depicted in implicit, negative ways not as a group in themselves but simply as the conceptual shadow of religion. Though they were somewhat more discernible as the source of possible stereotypes about religions and even as proponents of a militant, anti-religious secularism. These depictions demonstrate an awareness that the Non-Religious are an increasingly normalized, influential and potentially dominant force. However, when IFS asserts the importance of representing religions in Scottish secular public life and allowing them to vocalize their interests, it draws attention to the need to represent the Non-religious in turn to tamp down critiques of religious privilege.

To achieve these ends, it has been necessary to find actors within that segment of the population with whom sufficient common ground could be laid down, and this has largely entailed the Humanists. This dialogue between IFS and Humanists can be traced back to the SWGRBR established in 2008 but was further cemented and disseminated through texts such as *Belief in Dialogue* and *Values in Harmony*. The means of representing Humanism follow an established historical pattern in which an abstract, historic global tradition is stressed to provide representatives of specific institutional groups with legitimacy on behalf of their people. This has depended on the presence or construction of analogous institutional, philosophical, moral, universalistic and timeless traditions but which also allow them to fit into a common secular national framework.

However, this construction of the Non-religious is still fairly undeveloped in comparison to religious groups. Nonetheless, this is not unprecedented either. More established groups such as the Christian churches, government and IFM in Scotland have played a role in facilitating greater social engagement of less established religious minority communities in tandem with leaders of those communities. Indeed, it is the leadership of the HSS and their allies in the government and IFS who are pushing for their people to become more active and self-conscious, including doubtlessly many nominal Humanists. An important reason why Humanism has been encouraged to play this role is that they have actively modelled themselves on some of the ritual and communal aspects of religions and because they offer a replacement for religion on those terms. This replacement can and has been reconciled to the continuing existence of religions and participation in public life rather than its abolition. For the Scottish Government at least, this encourages the integration of this segment of the population into one nation of many faiths and beliefs.

6

'The Country in which we live': Interfaith Scotland's representation of Scottishness, the independence referendum and its aftermath

Introduction

The previous chapter focused on Interfaith Scotland's (IFS) changing relationship with Non-religious Scots. The organisation now increasingly includes representations of the Non-religious, namely Humanists, in their materials and frequently works alongside them. This allows IFS to claim to much more comprehensively relate to the Scottish population. However, the processes of this widening inclusion were based on an established formula: focusing on selected spokespeople from institutionalised groups as well as systems of doctrines and ethics. This chapter will analyse how IFS represents the Scottish people in a more general sense through their political system, civil institutions, stipulated national values and culture while also advocating on behalf of specific religious groups. How do IFS relate to this common national identity while emphasising the importance of religious pluralism and multiculturalism? How do they construct Scotland as one nation of many faiths?

In this chapter I will analyse their representation of Scottish nationality by focusing on three elements in particular: *cultural heritage, secularism and civic-identity*. I will show how IFS have made use of different aspects of Scottish cultural heritage, tailoring them to be inclusive but still recognisable as expressions of those traditions. Secondly, IFS' representation of nationhood reflects a form of secularism which further differentiates religion from national identity. Their own role in the devolved public sphere further intensifies a shift from a strong association between 'Scottishness' and Presbyterianism, to a nation of many religions and beliefs. This is a form of secularism which is religiously inclusive, allowing for religious participation in the public sphere but reinforcing the overarching authority of the secular nation. These conditions ensure that it is difficult for any group to dominate but also offers incentives for them to conform as well. The organisation does not only represent nationality in terms of broad cultural tropes but also depicts the different communities as having a stake in the Scottish political system and civil society. They promote a common civic identity, encourage active involvement in that system, and 'citizenship' of sorts which is bound up with a set of shared democratic norms.

Before moving on to analysing those central concepts, I will briefly re-introduce my concept of 'civic-cultural nationalism' and Michael Billig's concept of 'banal nationalism'. Scottish culture, secularism and the civic institutions of the nation's public sphere have been continuous parts of the social environment in which IFS has developed. However, a specific historic event, the build up to and aftermath of the 2014 referendum on independence will be central to this chapter. This is because it brought the question of Scotland's nationhood and future into sharper relief, highlighting how these dynamics effect groups such as IFS but also how they can shed light on these events.

Civic-Cultural Nationalism

As discussed previously, a widespread typology applied to nationalism is to divide forms of nationalism into 'civic' and 'ethnic' types, drawing attention to the ways that national belonging are marked out. Prototypically, membership of a 'civic' nation is dependent on factors such as citizenship, participation in legal and political systems, territorial residence and espousal of key values associated with the nation, e.g. freedom, equality, democracy etc. The other side of this binary model is 'ethnic nationalism', but which also often lumps in 'genealogical' as well as 'cultural' nationalism. According to this typology, these forms of nationalism determine nationality through ancestry, ethnicity, race or (markedly) cultural features such as language, customs or religion (Smith 1986: 134, Özkirimli 2005: 22–8, 2010: 35–6, Sutherland 2017a: 11, 2017b: 75–7).

However, this was deemed to be an unhelpful dichotomy because it separates out factors which are important to varying degrees in all national projects. Furthermore, the grouping together of factors such as 'race', 'ethnicity', 'religion' and 'culture' was considered dubious. 'Culture' for example is not synonymous with 'ancestry' or 'race' and the work of the anthropologist Frederik Barth and contributors to his volume have shown that ethnic boundaries are often permeable rather than fixed (Barth 1969).

The civic institutional nationalism of countries such as the USA and France are also deeply 'cultural.' They assume common language, inherited symbolism, myths and collective memories related to a specific people and landscape (Smith 1986: 134). In more subtle ways, culture in the broader sense permeates all of these institutions because they are part of a cultural context in which they are meaningful, understood and accepted by the population. Even the most civic and pluralist nation involves symbolism such as flags, depends on a conception of citizenry and on an understanding of the role of institutions like courts, parliaments, and presidents.

Nonetheless, the typology does draw attention to the differing emphases nationalist movements, actors and traditions may place on certain elements over others. To the extent that it is possible to identify some forms of nationalism as more 'civic' or 'ethnic', this should always be understood as a spectrum in which some cases express more or less of these features. Indeed, these characteristics also differ from questions of openness or exclusivity (though all nations depend on limited boundaries to an extent), whether cultural components of national identity are implicit or explicit: are they compatible with pluralism, hybridity or multiculturalism? The case of IFS provides ample evidence that they have been rendered compatible in various ways, though that pluralism is highly structured and limited. Nonetheless, as the accounts of IFS' activities should have conveyed, they are nothing if not cultural. They are certainly not concerned purely with the civic aspects of life in modern Scotland.

To analyse IFS' reinforcement of Scottish national identity I have coined the term 'civic-cultural' nationalism. This is because in their literature there is a thorough mixture of both elements and because they are an unmistakably pluralist and pro-multicultural organisation. IFS' national discourses simply do not fit the label 'ethnic nationalism', but at the same time their relationship to national identity is if anything primarily cultural. This is because of their frequent use of symbols or cultural tropes, their seemingly 'apolitical' (non-partisan) stance and also because their primary activities is hosting culture-laden events. Their pluralism in fact underscores the value of sharing and therefore expressing one's culture and the value of cultural distinctiveness. Their role is one caught between the more 'civic' realm of the devolved government and the cultural sentiments diffused among the population because they have interests in relating to both.

Banal Nationalism

All social identities, including national and religious ones, depend on inducement and continuous refreshment in the minds of their population. This is achieved by reminders such as symbols, media, and everyday discourse. As acknowledged previously, 'nationalism' is most commonly identified with its most militant, forthright and striking expressions through explicitly nationalist political parties or movements, rallies etc. It is most visible when mobilised during national crises or campaigns for specific goals e.g. independence or unification. However, this level of active and passionate involvement is not durable for much of the population, but nonetheless national identities and sentiments do not seem to evaporate following these events (Billig 1995: 8).

According to Michael Billig, nations retain their relevance because in a world of nations people are periodically reminded that this is how the world is divided and they are part of one nation among many. These reminders take the form of the permeation of symbolism but also casual references to the nation in the discourses of everyday life which often have little explicitly to do with nationality (ibid: 8, 11). Periodic national events of various kinds can aid in this process, but not every day can be St Andrew's Day or Burns' Night. This is why Billig coined the phrase 'banal nationalism' for this more diffuse, every day, and sedate expression of nationalism. As Billig explained, this kind of nationalism is embodied in the flag lying unnoticed in a public building rather than the one being fervently waved (ibid: 5–7). A crucial interest of this book is the way that nationalism is embedded widely in societies. Organisation such as IFS help to document the everyday, ongoing development of nationalism precisely because they are somewhat tangential to them and their role may go unnoticed, especially because their involvement may seem counter-intuitive. Representing national identity may not be IFS' most overt concern but their desire to help remake Scotland into an inclusive nation means that they contribute to the continuous process of making a Scottish nation.

Interfaith and Cultural Heritage – New
Patterns in an Old Style

The wide consumption and reproduction of common cultural symbols and tropes among the Scottish population has meant that they can be adapted to different political and social agendas. However, the diffusion and relatively long establishment of this cultural nationalism makes it difficult to monopolise. While the act of naming or labelling as 'Scottish' and 'national' have a considerable power to reinforce identity these are more effectively anchored by association with sensory stimulation: notably images, but also music, song, poetry, dance, cuisine etc. Specific cultural symbols, practices and paraphernalia help to focus and make tangible more abstract sentiments.

IFS draws from this pool of symbolism to convey their identification with Scotland, appeal to shared experiences, exert influences and underscore their rights within the public sphere. The refabrication of these innocuous cultural products may not seem important, and they (and even expressions of national identity in general) are rarely front and centre in IFS' messaging. However, the incorporation and recontextualization of these symbols aid in the analysis of social change by focusing on the ways in which inherited culture is re-orientated. Appeals to the naturalised cultural community are ideal for helping to naturalise newer groups, practices, and norms. This process was charted in earlier chapters through examples such as the diversification of aspects of the Christian heritage of Scotland as pertaining to 'people of faith.' Speaking to the cultural identity of much of the population may influence the wider public more than appeals to political and civic institutions which are more the preserve of elites, though appealing to these powerful groups has been important too.

The most readily reproduced symbol is unsurprisingly the national flag – the saltire. IFS logo is a stylised reproduction of the saltire which simultaneously symbolises the organisation but also links it with the nation. The saltire is an especially interesting symbol because it is in a sense both 'religious' and 'secular.' It represents the country's national saint who is the apostle Andrew and the x-shaped cross on which he was reportedly crucified but his long association with Scotland has meant that it is now largely perceived as a secular national symbol first and foremost. St Andrew's Day on the 30th of November is also historically a national celebration in Scotland but it has been somewhat eclipsed by Burns' Night on the 25th of January.

A variation of the saltire is also used by the Muslim Council of Scotland[1] and at one time by the Humanist Society Scotland (see SIFC 2011: 46), which was made possible by its secularisation. However, its religious origins are far from obscure, it is common knowledge that Andrew is a saint and that crosses are Christian derived symbols. This is testament to the fact that truly ubiquitous symbols can be victims of their own success in losing some of their original meanings; prior efforts to fuse distinct identities e.g. 'Christian' and 'Scot' may simply transfer ownership from one to the other. This means that this borrowed (or inherited) symbolism does not inhibit the development of new relationships between nationality and religion. For IFS though it is perhaps doubly useful because of, rather than in spite of, this duality. The religious ambiguity of the saltire can reinforce secular-pluralism but also underscores the historic importance of religion to the nation.

As mentioned in the introduction, Scottish Inter Faith Week (SIFW) was for a long time held in the week of St Andrew's Day, though it has generally been held the week before for several years now. It is significant that they chose not to bring it into line with UN Interfaith Harmony Week which is held in February (SIFC February 2011: 9).[2] The Religious Leaders Forum (RLF) also expressed enthusiastic support for making St Andrew's Day into a public holiday but stipulated that it should also reflect the country's diversity:

> [they] agreed that while it was desirable that Scotland should have a national holiday, it should reflect the faith and multicultural nature of Scottish society. This could be an opportunity for all citizens, of all faiths and none, to learn more about what it means to be Scottish (ACTS n.d: 19).

IFS participates in the Scottish Parliament's cross-party group on St Andrew's Day, they put together a multicultural and multireligious celebration of St Andrew's Day held at the Parliament in 2022 featuring Hindu music and a poem by the Makar[3] (IFS Spring 2023: 7). This reflects a mindset that seeks to balance expressions of common nationhood with respect for the different cultural, religious and belief communities within Scotland. This is one example of the ways in which Scottish traditional culture and pluralism are arguably mutually employed to inform and support the other. There are countless examples in the accounts from the literature which present a hybridity between traditional Scottish culture and ethno-religious diversity. Interfaith events have included 'curry and ceilidh' nights (IFS Spring 2015: 9) hosted 'Scottish-Indian fusion' dancers (IFS Spring 2014: 2), or reported on the Indian-spiced haggis Burn's lunch organised by the Sikh Sanjog (IFS Spring 2021: 36) all of which embody multicultural Scotland through performance and sensory stimulation.

In documenting and commenting on these events, the literature of IFS is not simply important as a record of the interfaith movement (IFM), as worthy of study as in its own right as that is. It is invaluable as offering accounts of broader societal change, especially the forging, dissemination and embodiment of new norms and practices from below. It also provides insight into how these grassroots events are reincorporated into larger frameworks, in this case the national interfaith association. The actors on the ground in these sources and these texts themselves, along with politicians and other public figures represented, are part of a chorus which largely harmonise on the expounding of these worldviews. The fact that IFS will often recontextualise other discourses which they deem compatible provides a unique vantage point to view these processes in action.

For example, an Episcopal church in Aberdeen made an agreement with a local mosque to allow Muslim worshippers to pray within church grounds due to lack of space within the mosque (See Brittain 2016). This event could have remained local and could have been classified as a bilateral relationship between neighbouring congregations. Instead, this was interpreted and presented as of national significance and reflecting religious pluralism more broadly. It is also a good example of the ways in which multiple different actors' words and deeds are recontextualised to construct a narrative.

Then First Minister Alex Salmond was reported as characterising this as: "different strands of Scotland's tartan coming together to celebrate the diversity of our nation and the values we share" (SIFC February 2011: 9). This statement was incorporated into the newsletter's account of this event alongside quotations from the local Imam. Tartan is a particularly versatile image because it is one of the most famous and evocative aspects of Scottish culture but also because it encapsulates the idea of unity in diversity perfectly. There are further insights which can be gleaned from analysing these fairly innocuous comments because its wording is well chosen for its purpose of instilling a common identity by suggesting embodied movement. In Salmond's statement, Scots from different communities are offered a model scenario of how to "come together", to accept pluralism, to "celebrate the diversity" contained within "our nation" which also reflects "values we share." Interestingly, in recent decades many minority communities have created their own unique tartans which have been given official recognition: Buddhist (SIFC August 2011: 7), Chinese,[4] Jewish (McCall 2016), Muslim,[5] Sikh[6] and Pagan.[7] It is common practice in Scotland to wear tartan affiliated with one's specific clan or family, but this is a way of providing an alternative for many Scots from an ethnic or religious minority community.

Other trappings of Scottish traditional culture have been depicted at interfaith events across the country: fiddle music (e.g. SIFC August 2009: 2), Clàrsach (a large harp) (IFS 2017: 9), ceilidhs (traditional dances) (e.g. SIFC

March 2012: 10), bagpiping (e.g. SIFC January 2009: 3), Gaelic songs (SIFC February 2011: 2), Scots language poetry (usually Burns e.g. SIFC 2010 March 2010: 9) and Burns suppers (IFS 2016: 13). As we have seen these elements are either presented alongside or blended with elements from many cultures.

IFS events are always simultaneously 'local' and 'national', because of where specifically they are held and their framing as an event of Scotland's national interfaith association. These serve an integrative role in binding local IFGs to IFS (though they are autonomous from each other) and binding members of different religious communities into an interfaith space defined in local-national terms. IFGs frequently work with newly established immigrants and asylum seekers who would often find themselves isolated. Interfaith Glasgow was especially active in this regard, holding a weekend club for asylum seekers and people new to the city, including teaching 'Glesgae slang' to "help newcomers better understand Scottish culture and feel more at home in Glasgow (IFS 2016: 13)." This statement is a good illustration of the fact that while 'local' and 'national' can be quite separate spheres in some cases, they are probably more often thoroughly blended in the minds of many. Interfaith Glasgow have held talks on the history of immigration to Glasgow, which help to place recent migrants into a broader context which normalises pluralism.

Another important means of grounding interfaith discourses in the national space has been to evoke the actual Scottish landscape itself. Romantic nationalism is often associated with idealised artistic depictions of national landscapes and Scotland, especially the Highlands, is prototypical in this regard. One example of this are the paintings of Highland landscapes from a document produced with the Scottish NHS *Reflections of Life* (2011). We have discussed in previous chapters how much of the built Christian heritage of the nation, especially sites like Iona have been paired with newer religious sites belonging to minorities, especially the Buddhist monastery of Samyé Ling and Holy Isle (though also recognising the Callanish standing stones as legitimately connected to Paganism). Alongside these major sites of religious tourism, local places of worship are also included (SIFC August 2009: 9) to create a sort of plural sacred landscape through interfaith pilgrimages which render interfaith engagement into an embodied, contextual and ritual practice. Evoking the landscape or nature can also reinforce their commitment to environmentalism both globally and locally (e.g. SIFC Youth Committee n.d., SIFC September 2010: 6, IFS 2016: 6).

Secularism

Representing diverse religious communities in Scotland is one IFS' most important goals. As we explored in the previous chapter, they have built bridges with Non-religious groups such as the Humanists but also maintain a distinction from them. They have also vociferously opposed any perceived 'militant' or anti-religious secularism (IFS Summer 2013: 12) and explicitly called for the official recognition of religions within any future Scottish political arrangement (IFS Summer 2014: 6–7) whether independent or within the Union. However, this can obscure the fact that they are much more secularist in orientation than they appear to be.

A reason for this potential confusion is the fact that there have been many forms of secularism, including different normative models and ways that secularism has developed in practice in different contexts. The form of secularism most readily identifiable as 'militant' is French-style secularism or *Laïcité* (also Laicism), or rather its strictest interpretations which is exemplified by France itself (see Fernando 2014, Bacquet 2015) and until recently by Turkey (See Soysal, Özçürümez & Diner 2015). This model advocates for the enforcement of strong walls between religion and not only the state but also takes a dim view of expressions of religion in the public sphere. Laicism developed in relation to a particular understanding of religion: the power and prestige of the Catholic Church in pre-Revolutionary France. In contemporary France however, restrictions on religious expression in the public sphere have effected religious minorities whose practices include wearing religious garb (e.g. turbans, kippah or hijabs) to a much greater extent. This is partially because these norms are derived from relations with Christianity and most forms of Christianity do not prescribe any kind of religious dress for lay people. Furthermore, the practice of secularism can become embroiled with the prejudices of the society in which it is found, this strict interpretation of Laicism has exacerbated tensions with the French Muslim community, especially with the ban on 'the veil' (burqas and niqab) in 2011 (See Fernando 2014, Bacquet 2015: 114).

The type of secularism predominant in the UK is quite different. While there are advocates of what might be called a more 'muscular' kind of secularism, conditions would have to shift considerably before that could be implemented. There is no specific label for this kind of secularism, but it could be dubbed the Northwestern European model. It is predominant in the nations of the UK, many former British colonies such as Canada, Australia, New Zealand along with the Scandinavian nations. These countries combine an established church with a thoroughly secularised public culture: electoral politics, national identity and participation in the public sphere are clearly differentiated from religion. Political divisions such as 'left' and 'right' or support for independence or Union, largely cut across religious affiliations. Furthermore, religion is rarely used as a means of appealing to voters unlike the US for example.

Arguably, this kind of secularism turns the American model of secularism on its head because the US combines a staunch official secularism, strictly prohibiting any kind of established religion, with a strong religious influence on electoral politics (see Chapter 7). Nonetheless an important feature of this system, especially as it has been practiced in the UK, is that it does not place official barriers against religious groups expressing their interests or views within the public sphere. The very coexistence of the secularity of public life in the UK with the existence of national churches appear to actually work in the favour of religious groups, especially smaller groups. This is because it renders them less threatening but also means that including them in civic spaces can be justified as a fair extension of the status quo.

The German social theorist Jürgen Habermas who introduced the concept of the public sphere as a discursive space between the domestic and governmental domains argued that this was an essential feature of modern liberal-democratic systems. Habermas held that the public sphere intrinsically intensified secularisation but reassessed his position later in his career, holding that religious influences could be communicated in the public sphere without becoming wholly secularised. However, he still held fast to his position that by and large religious messages had to be 'translated' into secular language to be effectively conveyed to a wide range of citizens (Habermas 2011: 25–7).

The Canadian philosopher Charles Taylor challenged this position. He presented secularism as neutral on the question of religion but also neutral to any moral position or worldview other than those that make public exchange possible e.g. the democratic system, constitutions, laws, civil rights etc. Taylor acknowledged that many religious discourses may not be influential outside of their own context or may no longer be as effective (e.g. appeals to Calvinism in modern Scotland) but others such as basic Christian concepts would be perfectly intelligible to a secularised audience without much translation. Nonetheless, even Taylor's model of secularism necessitates that the governmental and public realms are differentiated from any religion (or belief) and should not be monopolised by any specific group (Taylor 2011b: 34–5).

This is a form of secularism which would appeal to IFS because it is inclusive of religion but also emphasises diversity. Taylor's work was referenced at the Common Ground conference discussed in the previous chapter (Xaverian Missionaries of the United Kingdom and United States 2013: 46). This Taylorian secularism fits the developing relationship between religion and devolved governance in Scotland quite well. The gradual shift away from recognising the pre-eminence of the Church of Scotland, Protestantism or even an ecumenical Christianity towards an interfaith and belief model would exemplify this. The institutionalisation of practices such as Time for Reflection in both parliament (Bonney 2013) and in schools (Fraser 2013) and prominence of groups such as IFS shows how even a minimal, symbolic Presbyterian hegemony no longer typifies modern Scotland. Instead, a variety of religious and Non-religious groups have been included in public discourse and consulted by secular authorities; further differentiating Scottish civic, political and cultural life from religious identification. This kind of secularism is for the most part implicitly nationalist, it is the nation into which these groups are incorporated, and which is the basis of this communal life – a role once played by religion (Anderson 1983: 10–12, Greenfeld 1996: 171–4). This fusion between religious pluralism and secularism arguably further intensifies secularisation because imposing a broad religious agenda is much more difficult under these conditions but also because the only authoritative nationwide institution is the government itself.

The Religious Leaders Forum

The ultimately secular characteristics of normative religious pluralism and the IFM is especially evident from the Religious Leaders Forum (RLF). As previously described, the RLF is technically distinct from IFS but administered by them, and brings together religious leaders from communities across Scotland to discuss issues related to religious representation. The RLF also plays a similar role to IFS, acting as an institutional bridge between diverse religious communities and institutional public bodies, especially the government. Their utility for secular authorities stem from their status as a gathering of representatives with recognised authority to speak on behalf of their respective communities. This entails that when they gather, collaborate and especially when they produce consensus views, they can be claimed to speak for much of the nation. There is evidence that they do to some extent view themselves as playing this role, one that the Church of Scotland traditionally claimed for itself. The Bahá'í representative Allan Forsyth remarked in the newsletter that they have a "shared commitment to serve Scotland" (SIFC August 2009: 11).

The RLF also recently commemorated their 20 year anniversary by holding a gathering on the isle of Iona and travelled there with a BBC film crew, visiting the local school. They used this as an opportunity to draft a 'statement of commitment':[8]

> We, representatives of the Scottish Religious Leaders' Forum, meeting on the holy and historic island of Iona, mark this…by restating our commitment to work together.
>
> We share this land of Scotland with people of diverse cultures, religions and beliefs. (IFS Autumn 2022: 12–13)

These leaders are people who have relevant connections who can play a significant role in mediating wider influences or pressure exerted by government or civil authorities within their communities. In turn, they can use the access they have been granted to push for their concerns and interests within the secular public sphere as well as among their colleagues in the RLF itself. For example, when the RLF spoke out against persecution of Bahá'ís in Iran (IFS Spring 2015: 13) this was certainly due to the influence of the Faith's representatives. Allowing specific groups to express views and help to shape policy of concern to their community may be desirable for the government, at least when their interests do not clash with each other, much of the public or politicians. This unity in diversity allows for each group to find its own voice on specific matters while also conveying a greater influence as a diverse chorus. The very fact that they can produce consensus positions, while downplaying the ways they have been shaped by common discourses, adds to their authority.

However, these characteristics also point to the ways that they are more limited than they may first appear. Their diversity does in fact mean that their ability to call for specific policies which might exert great pressure on the government is hampered. They are more likely to be divided on political questions as they are on theological or religious ones. It is the former which could potentially alienate them from political factions among politicians and among the public at large. For example, Christian churches have long been as internally divided on questions such as same sex marriage. The Catholic Church continues to oppose same-sex marriage while the Religious Society of Friends ('Quakers') conducted homosexual marriage ceremonies before these were made legally binding in any of the UK nations (See Cranmer 2015), and the Church of Scotland is still deeply divided on the issue (Carrell 2011).

This is one reason that it appears unlikely that IFGs will be able to act as any kind of rival authority or counterweight to secular governments in a way that religions often have historically. In some respects, the secularity of the IFM is encouraged by greater diversification because they cannot appeal to shared theologies, scriptures, or practices. This contrasts with ecumenical movements within religious traditions or collaborations between closely related religious traditions e.g. Abrahamic religions (at least on some matters). This is why content produced by IFGs may not always appear especially 'religious' (or 'theological') but generally reinforce support for broad shared ethics: pluralism, altruism, a civic mindedness, good (local, national, and global) citizenship and care for the environment. None of these positions are truly apolitical of course, but in modern Scotland mostly uncontentious enough to be safely non-partisan.

It is quite likely that the views that they express are perfectly sincere. This is testament to the ways that broad liberal-pluralist values have circulated, have been internalised by different actors, and blended with different traditions. At the same time, they have reinforced the authority of the secular nation and its elected government. One of their political interventions was to call for St Andrew's Day to be made a public holiday. Unsurprisingly, they have shared interests in the treatment of religion within any future Scottish political arrangement and called for the official recognition of religion if Scotland becomes independent. They were founded to respond to national and international events with a diversity of voices which they have done but are somewhat limited in what they can say. In some ways their role is symbolic and authoritative rather than direct. As one statement put it, "they symbolise the inclusive and dynamic nature of Scottish society" (IFS Spring 2015: 13). The RLF are an example of the ways that the separation of the religious and political spheres especially empowers the latter, while the former carries some traditional authority, it is the latter which governs.

The advancement of secularisation which this process represents was in some respects anticipated by the changing relationship between Scottish nationalism and the Catholic Church. Many Scottish Catholics were historically suspicious of the SNP and historically tended to support Labour (Ritchie 2009). In the 1990s the relationship changed and the leader of the Scottish Catholic Church Cardinal Tom Winning recognised the SNP as a legitimate form of civic-nationalism. Historic political associations between electoral politics and sectarian identities also broke down as Catholic populations became more integrated and exposed to the same developing secular-pluralist norms as the Protestant and other populations. Notably, this was the same period in which the Catholic Church and the main Protestant churches in Scotland and elsewhere were developing a friendlier ecumenical relationship. These slow but significant shifts in the relationship between Catholicism and Scottish nationalism meant that when the SNP government was elected by landslide in 2011 and expressed their desire to legalise same-sex marriage, church leaders could not use their relations with the SNP to stop them. This is despite the considerable pressure church leaders tried to exert on politicians and lay Catholic which provided ineffective (Braiden & Dinwood 2011, Gordon 2011).

These examples illustrate the forms that successful religious influences take in secular-pluralist societies. They must conform to the dominant normative framework in society at large and be ideologically supported by the government or other powerful actors. While that very pluralist system ensures that many voices can indeed be heard to an extent, it is only some which are amplified. These voices tend to be the ones that are already influential, but especially those that conform to the prevailing ideology. The fact that each group presents itself as espousing values in harmony further legitimates and reinforces this adherence to the prevailing status quo. It still leaves space for groups to communicate their specific needs but framing these needs in secular-pluralist terms or as unobjectionable to that system means they are more likely to be heard. On the surface the system is Taylorian, but in practice it conforms to the later Habermasian concept of translation. However, groups such as IFS, IFGs, the RLF act as gatekeepers or mediators who have exerted power over the ways that religious discourses reach secular authorities or the forms that religious pluralism takes in the national public sphere.

Civic Identity and Interfaith Corporatism

Developing relationships with groups such as IFS, as well as religious and belief communities allows the government to influence different segments of the population and understand their needs. By entering into voluntaristic relationships with third party representatives they can exert a subtle form of indirect influence among different communities without threatening their autonomy. The type of power employed in these relationships can be characterised as 'soft' power: the use of persuasion and influence rather than force (which would include laws and their enforcement) (See Heywood 2002: 11, McLean and McMillan 2003: 431–4). IFGs are ideally placed to use soft power among diverse religious communities to encourage values, attitudes or actions considered desirable by governments.

As discussed at length in previous chapters, documents such as *Values in Harmony* and *Belief in Dialogue* encourage acceptance of common morals rooted in the golden rule, discourage insularity, and promote close relationships between religion/belief groups explicitly identified with segments of the population (most strikingly in the Humanist case). These texts involved collaboration between IFS and the Scottish Government, especially *Belief in Dialogue* produced by the Working Group (SWGRBR). *Values in Harmony* also carries a foreword by a government minister and an explicit critique of 'mosaic multiculturalism (SIFC 2011: 5–8).'

While *Values* in particular stresses universalism and pluralism it does also tacitly encourage identification with the nation, something which is more evident in *Belief in Dialogue*. Many religions and belief communities are encouraged to integrate into the overarching Scottish nation but not expected to assimilate without remainder. Indeed, assimilationism would by its very nature not fit into the pluralist vision of the nation proffered by these documents. Whether clerical or lay, members of these communities are cast as bearers of distinct traditions which are equally profound and benign influences on society. It should also be noted though that it is also true that conceptions of Scottish nationhood are reshaped through these processes as much as component communities adapt to it.

While *Values* sets out the ideal form of pluralism in a more abstract and general sense, *Belief in Dialogue* practically elaborates on how these relationships should be established and maintained at the grassroots level. In this context the link with secular civic-cultural nationalism is made clearer. For example, it is explicitly stated that specific religions or belief groups should not impose their views on (Scottish) society as a whole (Scottish Government 2011: 6). Tensions and bad relations between these communities are compared to illnesses within a human body (ibid: 8–10), implying an organic view of Scottish society, but also that dialogue is the antidote to these societal ailments. This is summarised thus: "[a]ll the inhabitants of Scotland are interconnected in a way that makes them interdependent" (ibid: 9). This sentiment was echoed by the statement of Allan Forsyth, the Baháʼí representative at the RLF:

> I have been struck by the common affection that everyone around the table has for the country in which we live and the desire to help make Scotland a better place. (SIFC 2009: 11)

As established in earlier chapters of the book, IFS have encouraged a proactive attitude among their constituents towards the public sphere and devolved political system of Scotland, along with cultural nationalism. This is undeniably political, but not partisan, and in some ways less banal than their engagement with Scottish traditional culture because it is activist in nature. The older SIFC newsletter also used to all carry the following statement on its front cover:

> [w]e commit ourselves in a spirit of friendship and co-operation to work together as people of faith for a just and inclusive Scotland (e.g. SIFC March 2012: 1).

There is a discernible sense in much of their literature that they are represent Scotland as a whole and not simply interfaith or religious groups who happen to reside there, especially within international circles. IFS is a member of IFNUK but is independent of them just as local Scottish IFGs are independent of IFS. However, IFS also specifically represents Scotland at the annual four nations meetings with the national interfaith associations of Wales and Northern Ireland, while England is represented by IFNUK (IFS September 2012: 3). This scenario provides a curious mirror to the current devolutionary settlement with devolved administrations set up for the smaller nations of the UK while Westminster functions as the parliament of England and the UK. This would appear to reflect a recognition of the distinctiveness of these national contexts within interfaith circles and not merely that they relate to different governments, laws, and populations.

These national labels are not simply applied to organisations in the literature though, but also individual activists in conjunction with the stress on their religious identity. This is especially evident through their coverage of international interfaith events such as the Parliament of World Religions in Melbourne in 2010. In Pramila Kaur's report on the conference she writes that "there were a few Scottish faces at the Parliament including Di Williams the Chaplain at Edinburgh University, Rabbi David Rose and Donald Reid" (SIFC March 2010: 11). These are occasions to express belonging to Scotland while also promoting pluralism and helping to reconcile these tendencies.

This reinforcement of national identity alongside religious and interfaith identity is even more pronounced when visitors to Scotland are profiled. One striking example of this was when the Inverness and Skye interfaith groups organised a joint picnic in Whin Park in Inverness. The newsletter describes how they welcomed a tourist couple from Saudi Arabia who had been harassed by local drunks. It is reported that "the picnic had restored their faith in Scottish hospitality and friendship" (SIFC August 2009: 1). The focus of this statement is of course the values of hospitality, friendship as well as tolerance, but a desire to foster a good image of Scotland and the Scots is also evident. In this understanding, it is the role of the Scots of many backgrounds and faiths, but nonetheless differentiated from non-Scots who carry the burden of making up for their countryfolks' uncouth behaviour. While universalistic norms are important here, at no point do they render the couple 'Scottish' nor the offending drunks 'un-Scottish.'

As I have outlined in this chapter, much of IFS' understanding of its public remit involve working closely with the Scottish Government which has influenced their relationship to a broader national identity. The Scottish Inter Faith Council (SIFC) was founded in 1999 in the same year as the establishment of the Scottish Parliament with the explicit aim of representing religious groups within the novel framework of devolution (e.g. IFS n.d: 5). The development of SIFC/IFS can be viewed as part of the wider devolutionary process, as an example of the cultivation of a distinctive civil society and public sphere surrounding this emergent Scottish political system. On the occasion of their 20th anniversary the newsletter expressed their historic position in the following terms:

> The founding of a national interfaith organisation coincided with the re-convening of the Scottish Parliament. This was not a coincidence as it was the faith communities of Scotland who decided it was critical to have a national interfaith organisation that would be able to demonstrate in the 'new Scotland' that we are a multi-faith nation and this is something to celebrate and build on. (IFS Autumn 2019: 1)

The newsletter described the context of the time as invoking a new sense in what it meant to be Scottish but at the same time there was a worry, especially among non-Christians that religious freedom could be restricted in a changing system (ibid: 3). One of IFS primary activities is to organise public interfaith events, especially SIFW which have become part of the calendar of Scottish civil society. Their role in organising Holocaust Memorial Day (HMD) on behalf of the nation between 2012–2022 brought them into even greater public significance.

IFS and local IFGs are sought out by governments and civic authorities for various reasons. The most obvious one is based on their primary purpose, to act as representative bodies for different religious groups and because they offer the kinds of public events described above. A common related role for them is to act as consultants on matters pertaining to religious diversity as subject matter experts. In relation to this they have frequently been brought into provide training courses for government staff, the NHS, the police, colleges, and universities (IFS Summer 2014: 3) as well as voluntary sector workers (IFS 2013–2014: 16–17).

The fact that interfaith events have become part of the visible routines of civic life at local and national levels demonstrates interfaith groups' close intertwinement with the political class. Important politicians have often been guests of honour at interfaith events from the Lord Provost of Stirling (SIFC January 2009: 4) to the First Minister on several occasions (e.g. IFS Spring 2015: 19). These events have been hosted by local councils such as Falkirk City Chambers (SIFC August 2009: 2) to the Scottish Parliament itself (e.g. IFS Spring 2015: 22), while IFS have employed their own Parliamentary Officer with a devoted section of the newsletter (IFS 2016: 5). In 2015 then FM Nicola Sturgeon hosted an 'interfaith summit' at Bute House – the First Minister's official residence in Edinburgh, attended by members of IFS, the RLF, Interfaith Glasgow and Edinburgh Inter Faith Association (EIFA). According to the reports in the newsletter, Dr Sier used this as an opportunity to draw attention to the work of IFGs and called for further governmental support. She also highlighted the fact that Scotland was viewed as a 'leader', or model for other countries in interfaith circles and that continuing to do so will "keep our country safe, open and tolerant" (IFS 2016: 4). Sturgeon also commented:

> Interfaith work and the contribution of faith groups is essential in transforming lives and building a stronger, fairer and equal Scotland. By working together with all communities I want to see a safer, stronger and more inclusive society, one which we are all able to fully contribute and benefit from. (ibid.)

This has become an annual summit between IFS, those other IFGs and the FM (IFS Spring 2019: 3) IFS have also collaborated with Police Scotland in planning events for school visits (SIFC August 2009: 8), a youth conference (SIFC August 2011: 11) and used their global interfaith links to allow Police Scotland to attend an interfaith conference in New York City (IFS Summer 2013: 5). As previously noted, they have provided both training and materials for staff of the Scottish NHS to provide better treatment to patients of multiple religion and belief traditions along with inspirational content for the latter. IFS and other interfaith activists have been appealed to as subject-matter experts or as technical specialists of a kind who can provide training, resources and legitimacy to governments and public bodies.

The question remains, why would these secular authorities expend energy in relating closely to them if different communities obey the law and pay their taxes? One obvious reason is electoral, they represent blocks of voters whose specific concerns could be translated into support for certain parties and politicians. Nonetheless, this does not account for the depth or regularity of these relationships. Given that Scottish politicians were able to resist pressure from powerful churches or factions within them, it does not seem likely that they relate to IFGs, small religious groups or the HSS for electoral clout alone.

This could be explained by the French Poststructuralist philosopher Michael Foucault's concept of governmentality. According to Foucault modern governments as systems (not simply specific parties and politicians) are dependent on securing the broader welfare of their populations for legitimacy. To achieve this complicated goal in a society characterised by liberal individual rights; authorities have utilised, encouraged, sponsored, and even created entire fields of expertise in the public sphere which are separate from the government itself e.g. health, education etc. According to this understanding, a plethora of specialised or technical disciplines have garnered a distinct authority through their delivery of public services without necessitating direct government control of the lives of citizens (Chamberlain 2014).

To a limited extent the work of many IFGs and their public presentation of their role, has begun to resemble governmentality. Key examples of this include their training courses, consultations, and dissemination of knowledge about religions to the public through their texts. One of the suggested projects for IFGs in *Belief in Dialogue* is to work towards specific goals on behalf of local or national governments (Scottish Government 2011: 42). Ann Davies, a representative of the RSF who worked with IFS revealed that interfaith activists are frequently consulted on proposed legislation in the Scottish Parliament (IFS Summer 2013: 11). Another suggested role for IFGs in *Belief in Dialogue* is providing a public consultation on religious forms of animal slaughter (The Scottish Government 2011: 23). The Crown Office and Procurator Fiscal Services (COPFS)[9] included representatives of IFS into their Equality Advisory Group to comment on policies and discuss the impact of hate crimes on religious communities. IFS also brought COPFS officials to different places of worship to meet members of their congregations (SIFC February 2011: 11).

These technical and representative roles are important, but as I have argued IFS also play a significant role in helping to legitimate and channel desired attitudes, behaviours, and norms among the population. This is achieved through their public events and general educational texts to a limited extent, but also their engagement with schools, the NHS etc. IFS also have their own youth committee and youth conference which alongside engagement with schools and universities help to instil these values among Scotland's youth. They have recently established a National Youth Advisory Board (IFS Spring 2023: 3). IFS and local IFGs have aided schools in organising 'interfaith days (IFS Spring 2013: 4),' while schoolchildren are often involved in interfaith events, especially HMD (e.g. IFS Spring 2013: 12).

IFS has developed a multi-layered role for themselves: voices of religiously diverse Scotland, moral educators, models of good pluralist citizenship and technical experts in religion as well as in the practice of organising pluralism. Developing and maintaining this role and image also depends on reinforcing the model of religions as essentially benign, tolerant, pluralist and even secularist. To achieve this, it has also been useful for religions to be intelligible to the public, political and media. They do provide greater details about religions and reject stereotypical or negative portrayals of them but this aim is more easily achieved when their portrayals conforms to some extent to primed expectations. These expectations have been shaped by the wide and long-term influence of the WRP but strategic essentialism also carries further benefits for these parties. The fact that 'religions' are presented as systematic traditions which can be pinned down to leaders, texts and doctrines which can be sought out, will likely be reassuring to these audiences. Religions can thus also be portrayed as fundamentally moral systems which can be reconciled to secular-pluralism. They are also globe spanning, universal, and timeless entities which do not conflict with the limited and temporal authority of national democracies.

The critiques of religious isolationism in *Values* can be interpreted partially as a rejection of alternative, transnational sources of authority and community; albeit only to the extent that they lead to disengagement from national society. This was echoed in a description of the aims of *Belief in Dialogue* in the newsletter: "to make Scotland a country where all feel at home and all will feel valued for the contribution they have to make to the common good (SIFC August 2011: 2)." This statement encapsulates the marriage of pluralism and civic nationalism rather well. For the IFM, greater civic engagement among members of different religions will also likely encourage interfaith engagement in addition. In the foreword to this document, the same minister who contributed to *Values* (Fergus Ewing MSP) asserts:

> I believe in a Scotland built on the basic values of mutual trust, respect and understanding. A Scotland where everyone regardless of background, can live and raise their families in peace and fulfil potential by contributing what they can to the society we all share…Dialogue…helps us all find common ground… [and] live harmoniously together as a society (The Scottish Government 2011: 3).

In her introduction to *Belief in Dialogue*, Smyth states that Scotland affirms the importance of "social cohesion, justice and equality." She described how devolution instigated a renewed political engagement and sense of national identity among many Scots but also underscored the need to ensure that all can participate and have their voices heard. Interfaith dialogue has a unique role to play in this, in reducing "moments of tension which threaten to disrupt stability and undermine community cohesion (ibid: 4)." This encourages the conception of Scotland as one nation of many faiths and beliefs; as people with common rights, interests and responsibilities bound to their country; who can draw on the ancient, transnational wisdom of their traditions. Similar themes were evident in the commentary on the planting of a tree to commemorate the ten-year anniversary of IFS in 2009:

> [t]he tree acts as a reminder to Scotland's diverse faith communities of the need to be unified in their common goal of living and working for the good of Scotland. (SIFC March 2010: 10)

IFS' role in the Scottish public sphere and relations with governments and other civic institutions can be characterised as part of a kind of corporatism. This term refers to the inclusion of non-governmental representative bodies and interest groups into the processes of governance related to their area of concern; most commonly trade unions and industry groups (Heywood 2002: 275–81, Hague & Harrop 2004: 177–8). Religious groups have been sometimes included in this way, most notably in Germany through a federal ministry (see Spohn 2015). The role of the Kirk in non-denominational schools and incorporation of Catholic schools into the Scottish education system could also be viewed in this way. Corporatism should not be mistaken for totalitarianism which refers to a one-party dictatorship where institutions in society are fused with state and party. In corporatist systems both governmental and non-governmental actors are independent of each other but work through official channels through which they can discuss and devise policy. A key example of this is of course SWGRBR.

Scottish Values

As the above statements indicate, both IFS and the government suggest that modern Scottish society is bound up with certain values not simply that they advocate for them; though they have recognised that it has fallen short of them as well. Broadcasting these purported 'Scottish values' has been part and parcel of their efforts to represent and reconstruct Scottish society according to their normative image. One example encountered in an earlier chapter was the ways in which interfaith activists at the *Common Ground* conference made several references to the words on the mace of the Scottish Parliament: 'wisdom', 'justice', 'compassion', and 'integrity' (SIFC January 2009: 3). More recently during the opening of the FFWBU Peace Embassy in Glasgow, Dr Sier highlighted the fact that IFS was founded at the same time as the Scottish Parliament and described how the organisation's values aligned with those on the mace (IFS Spring 2023: 13). These are universalistic values par excellence, but ones here literally fused into the symbolism of the most important institution of Scottish national politics.

It has also been important for them to highlight the consequences of abandoning values such as tolerance, compassion, and the inclusive liberal-pluralist ethic. Holocaust Memorial Day (HMD) as mentioned previously commemorates the victims of racial, ethnic, religious and political genocides. This does not just include the Nazi Holocaust but many other genocides. HMD events are almost always attended by local and national politicians and in 2015 its key events were hosted at the Scottish Parliament (SIFC Spring 2015: 22). HMD events focus on educating the public about the experiences of the victims of atrocities, the ways that intolerance paved the way for them and examples of people who resisted these campaigns or provided relief for the effected communities. The husband of Dr Maureen Sier, Nick Sier's own grandparents were murdered in Auschwitz which Dr Sier reflected in relation to these commemorations:

> we thought of all Nick's murdered relatives and thanked God that Scotland was a country committed to never forgetting, and committed to building a society where bigotry, prejudice, extremism and hatred is constantly challenged. (IFS Spring 2015: 21)

Educating the public about genocide and upholding universalistic liberal-pluralist values is certainly the primary aim and effect of these commemorations. Nonetheless, these discourses also serve to reinforce the sense of a national community as an entity which must continue to secure these principles and guard against the growth of intolerance and bigotry within its borders. The nation is described in terms akin to a person: it thinks, feels, and acts. Scotland "remembered" these atrocities and in doing so, it "welcomed" survivors who had travelled from other nations to attend these events happening across Scotland (IFS Spring 2016: 27). This language closely fits Anderson's concept of 'simultaneity' as a crucial component of the ways that nations are imagined. He drew attention to the importance of many nationals who live in different parts of the land acting in analogous ways, especially where this is self-conscious. He gave the example of people reading the same newspaper on a daily basis, this is especially apt with a national newspaper which writes for an imagined national audience (Anderson 1983: 34–5). In the case of Sier's commentary, it is her writing which brings to mind the acts of different people in different local communities, in a way that renders these statements plausible. This is an especially useful concept made even more powerful in conjunction with Billig's point about the continuous daily reminders of the nation (and other nations).

Ultimate Sovereignty and Independence

Interfaith Scotland's expression of civic-cultural nationalism and understanding of its own role as an active but also neutral conduit for public engagement was especially evident during the 2014 referendum on independence. As described earlier, the referendum was held on the 18th of September 2014 with a majority of 55 per cent voting against independence with 44 per cent voting in favour of independence. Throughout this process IFS used this as a means of encouraging political consciousness and participation among its constituencies but without endorsing either a pro-independence or anti-independence position. This was the same neutral stance held by the major churches in Scotland.

The reasons for this neutral position are fairly clear, they would risk dividing their own membership and could potentially alienate politicians from either side regardless of the result. It is important to realise that the question of independence no longer corresponds to party preferences among the electorate. If it ever did. The SNP continued to dominate the Scottish Parliament and formed the largest party among Scottish MPs at Westminster despite the electoral rejection of independence in 2014. On the other hand, I would also contend that the primary reason for IFS' neutrality is the fact that they view themselves as supra-political, part of the public and civic structure attached to the Scottish political system but aloof from partisan politics or the ideological affiliations which inform it. Instead, they view themselves as a moral influence on that system and in a certain way represent the whole nation, not political factions within it.

Though Scotland did not form an independent state, IFS' representation of the nation is not simply cultural but reflected in the civil society revolving around the devolved government. They may have no official or constitutional role, but they have become part of the informal traditions which living political systems develop (especially in the case of the UK because of the lack of a written, codified constitution). They have arguably become part of what the English political scientist Walter Bagehot termed the 'dignified' rather than 'efficient' parts of a political system (Bagehot 1963 cited in Kingdom 1991: 32). They are part of the symbolic and ritual life of Scottish democracy and ironically as we have established above, secular in Taylor's sense. As mentioned above, the RLF called for religion to be officially recognised in any post-referendum constitutional arrangement. As the introduction to their statement in the newsletter put it:

> The statement paints a bigger picture than the binary 'yes' or 'no' of the referendum debate and…will help navigate the relationship between the state and faith communities for future generations. (IFS Summer 2014: 6)

While they did not take either side on the referendum, that did not hinder them from claiming the referendum process itself as a point of national pride due to its peaceful and democratic nature. They could transcend this binary division of the population between supporters of independence and the Union, but also reinforce a common national identity in reaffirming the health of Scottish democracy. This can also be viewed through the lens of Anderson's simultaneity, the act of people across Scotland voting together in the referendum can be brought to mind as Scots exercised their self-determination or ultimate sovereignty. A particularly powerful example of this is a reflection by a young Scots-Pakistani Muslim interfaith activist Zaf Ziza in the newsletter who writes about his visit to a church and conversation with an elderly couple on the day of the referendum:

> as we talked about the Referendum I felt a sense of shared emotion. We all felt the gravity of our place in Scottish society, on the eve of such a huge decision… [they] spoke passionately about their history, their political choices, and their belief in a fairer and more equal society. (IFS Spring 2015: 27)

During the months leading up to the referendum IFS used its publications to disseminate information about the process. It outlined the Scottish Government's white paper (draft legislation) proposing the referendum to the parliament (IFS Spring 2014: 6). It covered debates hosted by local IFGs (IFS Spring 2014: 8). This had been on the horizon for several years and two years beforehand Roseanna Cunningham MSP, a Scottish Government minister was also allotted space in the newsletter to outline the process of the referendum. She was also responding to a public consultation: 'Your Scotland, Your Referendum':

> [w]e are considering our future in a peaceful and inclusive way to find the best system of government for the people of Scotland to bring fairness and prosperity…the referendum on independence will allow the people of Scotland the chance to shape their future, the Scottish Government is determined to listen to society as a whole….

> We want to know your views and now is the time to get involved and make your opinions heard. Faith groups are such a vital and meaningful part of civic society and I urge all readers to…join the discussion, put forward your vision and help build a better Scotland. (SIFC March 2012: 11)

As ever, IFS was a useful source of information about events happening in interfaith circles in local communities across the country. One such event called 'listening lugs (Scots: 'ears')' was held at the Conforti institute organised by an artistic collective called the 'the bus party' who asked members of the public to reflect on "what kind of Scotland do you want?" The event was rich with invocations of Scottish culture including bagpiping but also poems and stories from the artists. Attendees were asked to write down their wishes for the future of Scotland on a scroll which the bus party had taken to communities nationwide. The artists also each performed a piece reflecting on Scotland as 'home'. The event also included a lecture by the theologian Professor Willie Storrar, who noted that the responses hoped for things like greater equality and care for the environment rather than greater wealth (IFS Spring 2014: 4–5).

Conclusion

Reconstructing Scotland into the homeland of many religions, beliefs and cultures has involved adding to and sometimes reframing its national identity. This national identity is composed of both identifiably 'cultural' and 'civic' elements. This broader Scottish nationalism found widely among the population has not been successfully monopolised by any specific political project, even if it is by no means apolitical. It is this nationalism which IFS have had to appeal to when helping shape the kind of Scotland that they and their constituents want to live in, whilst also finding a secure, neutral place with which to withstand the rival political forces which develop from that broader nationalism.

IFS focuses much of its attention on groups within the population, emphasises global bonds and universalistic norms; but this should not distract from their reinforcement of a territorially bound sense of nationhood. The implicit conception that emerges from their literature is of a single, unified nation which is simultaneously composed of multiple religious, belief, cultural and ethnic communities. While they profess no preference for how that nation should be governed or (for the most part) how its constitutional arrangement should operate, there is a definite sense that the nation is ultimately sovereign, possessing an intrinsic right to self-determination however it may decide to use that right. IFS have also played a part in the further secularisation of Scottish public life especially because of this neutral position, further differentiating it from any specific religious identification. With considerable care, IFS and their allies have been able to grasp the thistle for their own purposes. At the same time, they are themselves only one part of the processes which reinforce national identification for Scots on a daily basis along with many other institutions and groups outside of the overtly political world of governments and parties.

7

From Scotland to the world: The study of the global interfaith movement, religious pluralism and nationalism

The interfaith movement in the contemporary world

This monograph has traced the origins and development of the interfaith movement (IFM) globally, examined the case of Interfaith Scotland (IFS) in detail as well as reflected on the study of this topic. As noted previously, the IFM began as a highly international movement through the 1893 Chicago Parliament of World Religions and the interfaith groups (IFGs) established in its wake (Pederson 2004: 80–5, Brodeur 2005: 43–4, Halafoff 2013: 2, Hedges 2021: 327, McCarthy 2007: 16, Howard 2021: 4). Subsequently, a range of local, regional and national IFGs proliferated, though they were also a product of community activism and the diversification of local ecumenical councils (Pederson 2004: 80). The modern IFM was characterized as a fusion of these international and local forces.

Interfaith activists have also consistently if broadly, aligned themselves with progressive positions (Halafoff 2013: 3, 121, McCarthy 2007: 56), disavowing religious exclusivism but usually distancing themselves from perennialist claims that religions are interchangeable or should blend into one (Halafoff 2013: 116–7, McCarthy 2007: 42). Though, the analysis of their reliance on the world religions paradigm (WRP) showed that they hold major religious traditions to be fundamentally equivalent partners. Indeed, this position of equality in diversity (or at least plurality) fits the rationale of interfaith practices quite closely: to represent and learn from each religion through dialogue and to pursue common interests. This has included the exploration of theological and philosophical questions in pursuit of common insights, but these are purportedly gained by consulting representatives and texts from different traditions. The appeals to different practitioners and religions are important to these endeavours too, there is not assumed to be a singular truth so pervasive that it does not require approach through plural paths. Frequently though, IFGs address more practical issues at the local level: religious discrimination, racism, poverty but also environmentalism (Halafoff 2013: 3). Tackling Islamophobia, religious prejudice and hostility to religion became a much greater focus of IFGs at all levels, with the rise of reactionary politics across the world.

As things currently stand, the IFM is a global and localized movement which is increasingly influential with religions leaders, policymakers and ordinary citizens. Despite this, there is still much work to be done to analyse these developments more critically, especially regarding the ways in which IFGs have been effected by the reality of power relations. Further research on the relationships between IFGs and national communities is required; to highlight that these are dynamic, ongoing projects rather than the mere background environments in which they operate.

Interfaith, religious pluralism and nationalism at a glance

As outlined in the introduction, the contemporary world is marked by globalization and diversification. Transnational migration has been one of the most important parts of these processes, the movement of peoples and their cultures (including religions see Tweed 2006, Dawson 2016a: 1–3, 6) into other territories, which greatly affects the 'host' societies which receive them. At the same time, global flows of commerce and cultural exchange have been greatly facilitated by ease of travel, the expansion of multinational companies (MNCs) and especially by faster communications technology (Dawson 2016a: 1, 17). The internet has become even more pervasive since the 2010s with the development of social media platforms such as Facebook, Instagram, YouTube and X (formerly Twitter). These media have exposed people across the world to a much greater range of influences.

The interlinked character of the contemporary world has to some extent encouraged more global or transnational consciousness in some, it has also made many people more aware of their specific local or national contexts in new ways. These forces have produced a range of responses from enthusiastic acceptance of globalization to backlash, especially given the economic dislocation and cultural erasure which it can be associated with. The recent spread of COVID-19 throughout the world and the imposition of lockdowns which followed exemplified this perfectly. It highlighted the integration of global society but also that internal and external borders (and boundaries) are still significant and could be reasserted by governments and communities. The different policies pursued by authorities and effects among different communities to the crisis show that they still have power in a globalized world.

Nonetheless, these changes long predated the pandemic and having developed over the last handful of decades have garnered a range of responses. One of these responses has been to embrace this diversity and cultivate a normative pluralism which recognizes that society is made up of multiple cultures and religions. The IFM is a movement which has emerged within normative religious pluralism which takes that further: institutionalizing religious dialogue and cooperation over shared concerns considered to benefit broader publics. At the same time, this has accompanied the re-emergence of exclusionary religious politics which would be called 'fundamentalist' (Dawson 2016a: 2, Halafoff 2013: 58). Simultaneously, more belligerent, exclusionary or supremacist forms of nationalism have appeared to resurge which proffer culturally homogenous models of the nation (Dawson 2016a: 15), sometimes drawing on religious traditions as a kind of 'religious nationalism' (see Armstrong 1997, Grosby 2018, Jaffrelot 2011, Jakelić 2014, Rieffer 2003, Sutherland 2017a: 4–5, Van der Veer 2013).

Sometimes cases of religious nationalism can be understood as religious forces attempting to monopolize the nation to further promote the position of that religion. Conversely, sometimes religion is used as an exclusionary cultural marker, one which would alienate minorities of different religions but is not necessarily otherwise a reflection of a confessional position (Jaffrelot 2011, Sutherland 2017a: 4–5). An example of this would be the attempts by the European far-right to appeal to the heritage of European countries to alienate Muslim immigrants (Koenig and Knöbl 2015a: 6). The degree to which these traditionalist challenges should be viewed as 'parochial', separate from or even unequivocally hostile to the globalizing world, should not be overestimated. The actions of Islamic State fighters to obliterate borders within the territories of their universal caliphate should help to underscore this. The global networks or links fused by Islamist groups, conservative Evangelicals, anti-liberal nationalists such as Vladimir Putin, Viktor Orban or Steve Bannon, as well as online movements such as the 'alt-right' have been important. Nationalism in its multiple forms is still a pervasive, global and in certain ways universalistic ideology (Anderson 1983: 6–7, Billig 1995: 4–7, 13–14, Sutherland 2017a: 14–16).

The tension between globalization and the apparent resurgence of specific, non-universal identities is often painted in simplified and moralistic terms as two camps arranged against one another: 'cosmopolitans' and anti-cosmopolitans'[1] (e.g. Halafoff 2013: 30, 75). Globalizing forces appear to stir up reflections on and renewed agitation on behalf of localized identities. This challenges the normative model which naturalizes competition between secular, universalistic economic ideologies as the only legitimate form of politics. Instead, there has been an increasing power and visibility of what is often derisively referred to as 'identity politics', but whose proponents are generally progressive (Dawson 2016a: 11) rather than reactionary or even necessarily anti-globalization. This has included quests for greater recognition and self-determination by many groups within societies: racial and ethnic minorities, women and LGBT groups. It has also involved a resurgence of many national movements for autonomy and independence, such as Scotland and Catalonia.

The point is that globalization, the increasing interchange of cultures and peoples, has not led to any kind of straightforward teleological fusion into a singular global society or shedding of all specific particular identities. It has not rendered local or national conditions, political systems or boundaries irrelevant; they continue to mediate the effects of these global flows. Undeniably, nation-states and other localized authorities have had their authorities opened to greater challenge and have had no choice but to try to manage these flows. Both globalization and the political-cultural significance of different groups and locations have to be taken into account to understand international movements such as the IFM. This is because these changes unsurprisingly do not simply wash away local conditions nor leave them perfectly intact, rather they provide new opportunities for hybridity. Scholars should allow that this hybridity may not be confined to claiming both the identity of one's parents' homeland and the land of one's birth, along with religious and other neatly classified identity slots. Rather, these forms of hybridity may defy the conventional distinctions between categories such as 'global', 'local', 'national' as well as 'religious' and 'secular', arranging them in new patterns we are as yet unfamiliar with (Dawson 2016a: 8).

Exclusionary projects depend on appealing to and galvanizing their constituencies, but in some instances have rejected their characterization as wholly exclusive, merely as protecting the heritage or autonomy of their society. For example, Hindu nationalists have often claimed that they are simply protecting the common Hindu culture of India and not restricting religious freedom (see Bhatt 2001, Doniger and Nussbaum 2015, Ramaswamy 2010). Similarly, the most inclusive projects do necessitate the maintenance of some forms of boundary, even accepting universalistic norms and practices require some kind of adaptation. Even the most liberal forms of nationalism involves the reinforcement of some kind of national identity and boundaries, usually with some specific cultural referents. Interfaith projects meanwhile depend on particular ways of representing religions and insist on a distinct status for them, differentiated from other groups in society. Furthermore, IFGs have to work alongside and relate to different kinds of cultural groups; they have to work among populations defined in local, regional and national terms. Lastly, they have to relate to governments and other authoritative civic institutions who legitimate themselves according to these identities.

Wha's Like Us?[2] How interfaith Scotland exemplifies transnational trends

I hope it will have become clearer to the reader through the overview of the IFM and the case study of IFS; this data exemplifies much broader patterns within the development of interfaith and religious representation. IFS is just one among many examples of a national IFG which relates closely to governments and which is imbricated with (formal) politics, albeit indirectly. Practices such as using IFGs as consultative bodies to help design policies and as quasi-official representative groups have become common practice in many societies.

Furthermore, the manner in which pluralism has been confined, usually according to the WRP, as well as made accessible and understandable to governments, media and publics is also far from unique. IFS is certainly not alone in promoting a kind of civic-cultural nationalism as well which renders religious pluralism and multiculturalism compatible with the official nationalism of civil society and the broader nationalism of the population. The fact that IFGs are in the business of encouraging civic engagement and representing religions within the public sphere, but rarely wish to enter the political fray itself has encouraged similar stances. They frequently valorize the political system but rarely become more openly partisan unless they have to. In turn this ensures that they have usually acquiesced to a form of secularism with which they are comfortable. They promote recognition of the timeless, universal authority of religions but also concede the limited, territorial sovereignty of national political systems. In the Scottish context, cultural nationalism may seem fairly live, but IFGs are generally in the business of cultural recognition and culture sharing, so this is far from unique. Interfaith engagement with national identity generally takes on a more broad, cultural form concerned with the sentiments, identities and ways of the people that they represent.

As I have stated on several occasions, normative pluralism is just one response to religious diversity, but it is the one promoted by the IFM wherever it can influence political conditions. Nonetheless, even societies in which more exclusionary relationships between religion and nationality have become ascendant, there are often undercurrents which promote pluralism as a more authentic reflection of the nation's society and heritage (see later in the text).

Scotland is often treated as a society of only parochial interest. It may seem to be of little relevance, especially to larger established nation-states, especially those outside of the UK and Ireland, or similar stateless nations such as Catalonia or Québec (see Guibernau 1999, Anderson and Keil 2016). Nonetheless, despite its relatively progressive leaning, IFS' pursuit of pluralism is limited and defined by nationalism in a way which is fairly commonplace. The importance of nationalism and the politics of culture may be closer to the surface in Scotland than it traditionally has been in some societies. Nonetheless, the relationship between interfaith dialogue and the construction of nationhood and national space has often been underappreciated.

In the following sections, I will show how these trends are exemplified in three other national contexts: (1) India, (2) the United States and (3) the UK framed as a 'national' context. The latter example is to show how national identity is constructed by actors such as politicians, media, members of the public and indeed scholars. It is these agents who imbue these things with the necessary significance, nothing is intrinsically so. The UK may be commonly recognized as a 'plurinational' state by the fact that it is made up of one larger 'nation' and several smaller ones (but commonly identified with the former). However, because the UK operates in a world of nation-states it is commonly treated as a nation, especially when the English heartlands are involved and the 'Celtic fringes' are left out or largely ignored. This analysis will commence with a discussion of the IFM in India.

Comparative study 1: India

While interfaith dialogue can be characterized as a primarily western phenomenon, people from India, and Indian religions have been crucial to its development. The presence and contribution of the Hindu religious leader Swami Vivekananda (1863–1902) among others, encouraged western liberal Christians to take Hinduism, Buddhism and other Asian religions and their practitioners more seriously. Though by 1893 this was informed by centuries of prior contact between British colonial officials and European scholars with Hindu intellectuals. Translations of religious texts such as the Vedas and Upanishads into European languages were made available through the work of scholars such as Max Müller and the *Sacred Books of the East* series.

India is a country with a diverse religious, as well as ethno-linguistic demography. A large majority, 79.8 per cent of the population are Hindu, but this can obscure the many different traditions and religious practices classified under this label. Muslims are the largest minority group at 14.2 per cent but there are also smaller but still sizeable populations of Christians 2.3 per cent, Sikhs 1.72 per cent, Jains, Buddhists, Parsis, Baháʼís and others[3] (Kim and Singh 2016: 49). Interfaith activists often highlight the country's diversity to legitimate their work and give it wider appeal to the point of reinforcing a kind of 'Indian exceptionalism' (Fahy and Bock 2018: 6, 22–3).

IFGs have been present in the country since the early years of the IFM and have proliferated at national, state and local levels (Fahy and Bock 2018: 24–5). Interfaith activists in India can appeal to a long history of religious coexistence, tolerance and interreligious relationships, from the edicts proclaimed by the Buddhist Mauryan Emperor Ashoka (304–232 B.C.E.) on religious tolerance to the wide-ranging religious interests and hybridity promoted by the Muslim Mughal Emperor Akbar (1542–1605) (Fahy and Bock 2018: 22). The modern, independent Indian state (1947) and its constitution (1950) established a religiously inclusive secular republic through its iconic independence leaders Mohandas K. Gandhi (1869–1948) and the first Prime Minister, Jawaharlal Nehru (1889–1964) (Kim and Singh 2016: 51, Swamy 2016: 25). Interfaith activists also commonly invoke these secular foundations of the state as fundamental to the flourishing of a multi-religious society (Swamy 2016: 34, 98).

Many IFGs in India have an especially active Christian membership and were often founded by Christians despite forming a fairly small minority on a national level, albeit with longstanding international links and resources (Fahy and Bock 2018: 24, Swamy 2016: 23). This is not a wholly unique situation, the Baháʼí community in Scotland is a tiny minority but is very prominent in interfaith circles, as they are in the United States (McCarthy 2007: 88). Other minorities are well-represented in the Indian IFM as well, for example, Sikhs, Parsis, Buddhists, Jews and so forth (Fahy and Bock 2018: 25). The significance of Christians to the Indian IFM seems to reflect a desire among Christians to reach out and make connections with Hindus, because Hinduism is the tradition of the majority with strong links to Indian cultures[4] but this has not been evenly reciprocated (Swamy 2016: 25–6, 32, 99). It is also the case that the concept of religion in general and especially the WRP reflects a western, Christian-influenced approach (Fahy and Bock 2018: 31–2, Swamy 2016: 8, 33–4, 153–4), which further explains the overrepresentation of Christians. This is one way in which the Indian IFM has perhaps somewhat surprisingly similar history and characteristics to its western counterparts.

Muthuraj Swamy's critical ethnographic study of the work of IFGs in the Kanyakumari district of the southern coast of the south-eastern state of Tamil Nadu, exhaustively demonstrates their reliance on the WRP. Swamy highlighted their tendency to appeal to scriptural sources such as the Upanishads, which in the case of many ordinary Hindus especially, have little relevance to lived religious practices (Swamy 2016: 33–4, 98–99, 153–4, 165). He also illustrates interfaith activists' reliance on their own programmes and models for conducting interfaith relations, contrasted with the scant attention paid to the interreligious relations between ordinary Hindus, Muslims and Christians in the district, as well as the complexity of their identities (Swamy 2016: 3, 58–9, 61, 102–4, 168). The core practice and emphasis of interfaith relations in India, as elsewhere, is dialogue which is touted as key to solving religious conflicts and other social ills, while the less grandiose, localized means of diffusing conflicts practiced in the villages of Kanyakumari are ignored (Swamy 2016: 3, 146–53, 163, 171).

Fahy and Bock also made similar observations through ethnographic work in Delhi that the interfaith scene centred around dialogue and idealized representations of religious traditions fairly removed from everyday religious practice (2018: 6). The IFM has carved out a niche for itself among the liberal, educated elite strata of Indian society and circulates among that milieu (Fahy and Bock 2018: 25–6, Swamy 2016: 9, 58). Interfaith activists tend to be older, overwhelmingly male religious leaders and they tend to avoid concrete, national issues such as Hindu-Muslim tensions or the persistence of caste discrimination in favour of broad, global concerns such as world peace (Fahy and Bock 2018: 28–31). There are many initiatives to encourage Indian citizens to engage with interfaith relations at the grassroots level, and while they may participate in interfaith events, the long-term impact of these seems limited. India has been politically transformed in recent decades by the ascendancy of Hindu nationalism or Hindutva (Sanskrit 'Hindu-ness'), especially the Bharatiya Janata Party (BJP) under Prime Minister Narendra Modi.

Hindutva have been a rising force since the 1980s and have sometimes presented themselves in more moderate terms as advocating for Hindu identity as the basis of Indian national identity, inclusive of other religions. In general, they have promoted Hindu supremacy as well as discrimination and violence, especially against Muslims (see Bhatt 2001, Doniger and Nussbaum 2015, Ramaswamy 2010). Since Modi assumed office in 2014 the secular-pluralist foundations of modern Indian democracy have been eroded (Kim and Singh 2016: 49). While secular milieu, secularist parties such as Congress and IFGs continue to operate throughout the country, they have not been effective at countering the Hindu right. While interfaith activists have condemned Hindu nationalism (Swamy 2016: 39, 100–1), they have still tended to present a non-partisan stance and maintain independence from the state (Fahy and Bock 2018: 6, 31).

Comparative study 2: The United States

The United States is another country whose size and diversity vastly dwarf that of Scotland. Diane Eck famously described the modern America as having become the world's most diverse country[5] (Eck 2001 cited in McCarthy 2007: 2). Interfaith activists have appealed to the fact that the national motto was for a long time *E Pluribus Unum* ('Out of Many One') as reflecting a distinctly American pluralist ethos (Lewis and Cantor 2018: xi, McCarthy 2007: 2). It is also renowned for its distinctive secular configuration in which any kind of established or official religion is strictly prohibited by the constitution (Lewis and Cantor 2018: xiii, Patel 2018: 4). This applies to the official identification of the nation itself (Patel 2018: 5), all levels of government but also generally by extension to public institutions, for example, public (state) schools (McCarthy 2007: 71–2). Nonetheless, by western standards the United States is also notably devout, with higher levels of Christian belief and practice than most other western countries (McCarthy 2007: 2, 52, Patel 2018: 7). Furthermore, religion has never been excluded from participation in the public sphere, open religious pressure on policymakers and expression of religious sentiment by politicians are commonplace (Hertzke 2016: 156, McCarthy 2007: 53–4), which would be unusual and controversial in Scotland.

A vocal and powerful conservative Christian Evangelical movement, sometimes in alliance[6] with conservative Catholics and some Orthodox Jews, has successfully pushed political agendas based on religious doctrines back into the public square (McCarthy 2007: 56–7, 65). This includes opposition to abortion, same-sex marriage, transgender rights, the promotion of religious prayer in schools and fusion between Christianity and American national identity. This movement which rose to prominence in the 1970s has especially been able to mould the conservative Republican Party in its own image since the election of President Reagan. This contrasts markedly with the largely secularity of most conservative parties in other western nations, even if they are often sympathetic to religious traditions and values.

Another key feature of the American context is a long tradition of exceptionalism which is caked in religious language, though it also draws on the fact that the United States was fairly novel as one of the modern world's earliest modern constitutional republics. The idea that America is singled out by providence or described as having been chosen by God predates the formation of the United States as an independent secular state in 1776. English Puritans refused to conform to the Church of England and who settled in the Massachusetts colony over a hundred years before independence regarded America as a 'promised land' and themselves as a 'new Israel.' This was also channelled into the concept of 'manifest destiny', the idea that white Americans had been divinely ordained to claim and settle throughout the entire continent. This can also be discerned in the contemporary discourse of American exceptionalism which arose during the Cold War, and that the United States has a special role in the world to guarantee freedom, security and spread democracy (Cauthen 2004, Bellah 1992).

One aspect of American secularism and public religiosity which is quite distinct is what the American sociologist Robert Bellah identified as 'civil religion.' This is a broad, non-denominational and not specifically Christian invocation of God and divine providence by national leaders such as the president, which form part of quasi-official discourse. These are usually reassuring references to the ways in which God guides and protects the nation (Bellah 2005). The United States may be characterized by Eck as the world's most diverse nation, but it still has a Christian and specifically Protestant majority. Historically, the cross-denominational Protestant identity of the nation was taken for granted. However, in the early twentieth century there were efforts to be more inclusive, but this largely meant inclusive of Catholics and Jews and was nonetheless based on Protestant foundations (Halafoff 2013: 36, Lewis and Cantor 2018: xiv, McCarthy 2007: 4, Patel 2018: 25, 34).

The United States is also an excellent example of a nation where the IFM has flowered in multiple different forms and at different levels: national, state and locality (McCarthy 2007: 85–7). America, specifically Chicago is after all the birthplace of this movement and contemporary religious pluralist thought generally. Nonetheless, despite its vast size and huge population, its much greater diversity in terms of religion, ethnicity and indeed IFGs; similar themes and issues can be detected in the United States as found in the Scottish context.

The American IFM largely appeals to broadly inclusive, even progressive or at least liberal forms of religion and does not generally attract the large Evangelical[7] or Pentecostal movements in the country, nor many Black-led churches (McCarthy 2007: 67, 94–5, 108–9). Most 'mainline' forms of religion have found representation with many of the nation's IFGs, but they have also struggled to include groups which lack strong institutional leadership, including some newly established diasporic religious communities, for example, Muslims, Hindus and so forth. (McCarthy 2007: 88, 93, 106–8). The inclusion of Pagan and similar new religious movements also proved controversial in some American IFGs, especially at the local level, but they have become more accepted over time. IFGs have also struggled to include decentralized groups (McCarthy 2007: 88–9, 93). As in India, there is a considerable tension between the needs of grassroots engagement, especially charitable endeavours that many local IFGs engage in and the desire to explore philosophical questions with different religious representatives (McCarthy 2007: 85–6, 100, 105, 113–4). Furthermore, the fragile alliances between different religious groups mean that truly controversial issues are rarely broached (McCarthy 2007: 102, 111–2, 118–9) as noted with the Scotland's Religious Leaders Forum (RLF).

Interfaith representation in America is an important part of the further diversification of religion in the public sphere, expanding on the normalization of the triune 'Judeo-Christian' religions. It also appeals to the broader-secular pluralism of many of the eighteenth-century 'Founding Fathers' (not to be confused with the 'Pilgrim Fathers') who wrote the constitution. However, this involves competing with a more exclusionary white Christian vision of the nation championed by the former president and leading Republican Presidential candidate Donald Trump. Nonetheless, interfaith activists such as Eboo Patel, founder of Interfaith America, formerly the Inter Faith Youth Core (IFYC) established in Chicago in 1999 (Halafoff 2013: 58), have cultivated a strong relationship between a liberal-pluralist American nationalism and interfaith dialogue (Patel 2018: 3, 25, 27). These appeals to the nation have not consisted only of appeals to the past or certain traditions as in Scotland or India, but a strong sense of codified national values (certainly compared to the fairly broad appeals to values in the Scottish context).

Comparative study 3: The United Kingdom as a distinct 'national' context

The UK is arguably an especially complicated case to bring into comparative consideration here, not only because it contains four 'constituent nations' with distinct identities, institutions and cultures, but also because one of those nations is the case at the heart of this book. Nonetheless, this is a useful example because it highlights the situational and constructed character of nationhood; the fact that it is dependent on the claims, perspectives and expressions of agents in their social environment and on media. It is also a workable comparison because while the UK does include Scotland at the time of writing, future independence or not, Scotland is a small, peripheral and distinctive nation within it. Scotland's devolved politics, distinct identity and position within the Union make it somewhat unrepresentative. Perhaps it would have been more useful to compare Scotland directly with England, to gauge how IFGs operate in the centre rather than the periphery of the UK, but this would be more complex than it might first appear.

It would be much more straightforward to compare Scotland (population: 5,480,000) with the other two small nations within the Union: Wales (3,105,000) and Northern Ireland (1,905,000) or perhaps the independent Republic of Ireland because of their size and the prominence of national cultures in their self-presentation. England is a more complicated case because it makes up over 80 per cent of the population of the UK at 56,536,000 (ONS 2022a: 3) and is home to the largest cities: Manchester, Liverpool, Leeds and the capital city, London. Also, 'English' identity in both institutional and cultural terms can be difficult to separate from 'British' identity (notably the collective label is not 'Ukanian', see Nairn 1977).

'English', 'British' and the 'UK' are often treated as interchangeable in England itself and globally. The fact that one of these broader categories, British, technically does not refer to Northern Ireland, is telling. Scottish and Welsh people generally identify strongly with their nationality, and where they do identify as British, usually clearly differentiate them. Northern Ireland is complex because it is home to two different communities; one identified as 'Nationalist', 'Catholic' and 'Irish', the other identified as 'Loyalist', 'Protestant' and 'British' (or sometimes identified with 'Ulster').[8] This is contrasted with the fact that in England many people identify first and foremost as British and conceive of their country primarily as the UK (see Bond and Rosie 2010).

Furthermore, in terms of international discourse and not merely formal diplomatic contexts, the UK is commonly presented as a nation compared with other nations in comparative studies which often draw primarily or entirely on data from England. Whether the UK is imagined as a national context may depend on the intended audience as much as the writer. Part of the reason is that referring in much detail to Scotland, Wales and especially to Northern Ireland requires more work because of the complexities of their governance, cultural identities and legal systems. This may make them appear to be minefields best circumvented when the desire is to offer simple comparisons with other nation-states.

As mentioned previously, Scotland has a distinct legal system, as does Northern Ireland (inherited from pre-partition Ireland), and Wales has the same legal system as England ('England and Wales') but some different laws. Devolution established separate parliaments for Scotland (Holyrood), Wales (the *Senedd*) and Northern Ireland (Stormont) but the UK Parliament (Westminster) continues to legislate for the UK as a whole and for England specifically. There are other UK-wide institutions, but these are also quite often concerned most of all with England because it is the bulk of the population and because the other nations tend to develop their own equivalents.

As with all other cases under consideration, there are a variety of local IFGs in many areas, sometimes several in the same city as is the case in of London (Fahy and Bock 2018) or Leeds (Dawson and Prideaux 2018). There are three national IFGs in the UK: one for Scotland of course (IFS), one for Wales[9] (Inter Faith Wales) and one for Northern Ireland (Northern Ireland Interfaith Forum,[10] and there are multiple regional groups for different parts of England but no specific national one.[11] Instead, England is represented by the UK-wide Interfaith Network for the UK (IFN or IFNUK) founded in 1987 with over 200 member groups (Dawson 2016b: 141, Fahy and Bock 2018: 50, IFNUK 2007: 6, Pearce 2012).

The basic conditions outlined in the Scottish case are also evident with regards to much of the UK. It is defined by a residual cultural Christian influence and established Christianities, most prominently the Church of England (Anglican), the head of which is the UK's monarch: King Charles III. The Church of England and its clergy continues to play an especially prominent role in the organization of local IFGs in England (Dawson and Prideaux 2018: 369, 371), which differs from the more backseat role of the Kirk in interfaith relations in Scotland. Christians continue to form the majority of the population, but at the same time Christian identification has declined, non-religious identification has grown and the culture is highly secularized (see Parsons 1993a).[12]

The UK became increasingly diverse through immigration from the empire and then Commonwealth beginning in the nineteenth century but increasing after the Second World War during a labour shortage. Further waves of immigration during the 1960s and 1970s brought many practitioners of non-Christian religions, especially from South Asian backgrounds to the UK, joining the Jewish community which had established itself in the seventeenth century and greatly expanded during the nineteenth century through Jewish immigration from central and eastern Europe (see Englander 1993). This same period encouraged many younger people in the UK to explore newly arrived and new religious movements as well as alternative religious or spiritual milieu. The Church of England has like the Church of Scotland, presented itself as *primes inter pares* in Christian ecumenical and interfaith relations as Judaism, Islam (see Wolffe 1993), Hinduism (see Thomas 1993a), Sikhism (see Thomas 1993b), Buddhism, Jainism, and new and alternative religions (see Parsons 1993b) became ingrained parts of the UK religious landscape.

However, while this demographic history is evidently reflected at the Scottish level as well, focusing on the UK as a whole offers a somewhat different picture from the Scottish one.[13] This is because Scotland (National Records of Scotland 2024), along with Wales[14] and Northern Ireland (NISRA 2012: 13, 19), are less diverse than England as a whole if broken down by nation. The disparity in levels of religious diversity is far more striking if England is broken down into regions. It is also the case that the more urban industrial and financial centres of the south, midlands and large urban settlements of the north of England (e.g. Manchester, Liverpool, Leeds) attracted more immigrants, and usually earlier than other areas of the north and west (ONS 2022b: 3–6). London is unsurprisingly much more diverse, and due to the fact that it has experienced high immigration levels, it is one of the most religious places in the UK but only 49 per cent Christian. The population of London is 15 per cent Muslim, 5 per cent Hindu, 2 per cent Jewish, 1 per cent Buddhist and 1 per cent Sikh (Fahy and Bock 2018: 49, ONS 2022b: 5). Religious minorities have also formed their own networks, such as the Muslim Council of Britain (MCB) to organize themselves and engage in relations with other religions, the public and governments (see Birt 2005).

The interfaith scene in the UK grew out of the Christian ecumenical movement and the development of bilateral Judeo-Christian relations (Fahy and Bock 2018: 49). Initially, the UK IFM was concerned with theological dialogue (Fahy and Bock 2018: 53) but have also concerned themselves with practical concerns in their community (Fahy and Bock 2018: 59–60). Like IFS,

IFNUK has also developed a strong working relationship with the government and similarly has struggled with the inclusion of more controversial religious groups, also including Pagans but has grown to include them to a greater extent over time to the point of granting full membership to many NRMs (Dawson 2016b: 133).

As in the other cases though, even in London, IFGs have largely been unable to attract Evangelical and Charismatic Christians or many Orthodox Jewish congregations (Fahy and Bock 2018: 54, 61). Humanist participation in interfaith events has also become commonplace throughout the UK and most interfaith events are advertised as for "all faiths and none" (Fahy and Bock 2018: 56). As discussed in a previous chapter, a pioneering dialogue event was held in London between interfaith and Humanist activists which was held up as exemplary during the *Common Ground* conference in Scotland (Xaverian Missionaries of the United Kingdom and United States 2013: 41).

IFNUK has also been committed to broad liberal, inclusive and multicultural positions. These norms complemented the attitude of the government during the early New Labour period under Tony Blair in 1997. This was also a period of renegotiation of what national identity meant in the twenty-first century with a positive view of globalization, multiculturalism and European integration (Dawson 2016b: 137–8). It was even complemented by a cultural agenda, subverting and appropriating British identity through new culture, 'Britpop' and 'Cool Britannia'.

However, following 9/11 and the London bombings on 7 July 2005 ('7/7') community cohesion, namely security and deradicalization concerns, led to greater state pressures on minorities, especially Muslims, towards conformity and demonstrations of loyalty. This was a period of backlash among both politicians and the public to conceptions of multiculturalism, often inaccurately characterizing it in terms of separatism, 'silo' or 'mosaic multiculturalism.' This was a far-fetched depiction of the multiculturalist discourse in the UK before 9/11, to the point of caricature. While relations with IFGs continued, there was more pressure to promote strong integration, if not necessarily assimilation (Dawson 2016b: 139–40, 145, Halafoff 2013: 80). However, this encouraged the state to officially sponsor IFNUK, which it has did annually from 2001 (Dawson 2016b: 143) until this was cancelled in January 2024 (Sherwood 2024). While the Scottish material discussed in previous chapters presents multiculturalism as viewed much more positively, including by the Scottish Government, this reflects the contrast drawn strategically or sincerely between Scotland as progressive in relation to Westminster's policies. Nonetheless, while a softer integrationism not assimilationism is undeniably promoted in Scotland, as mentioned previously, the concept of mosaic multiculturalism was singled out for special critique (SIFC 2011: 8).

Following the election of Prime Minister David Cameron in 2010, and the beginning of thirteen years of Conservative government, the idea that the UK should be understood as a 'Christian country' was promoted, and the government preferred to delegate funding decisions for religious matters to the Church of England where possible (Dawson 2016b: 147). Funding for regional faith forums was cut and funding for IFNUK itself was drastically reduced (Dawson 2016b: 146). The same government did continue to meet with IFGs and religious minorities as well as legalize same-sex marriage, despite criticisms from conservative church leaders who do not have the same clout as either the Indian Hindu or American Christian right.

IFNUK continued to weather these changes in priority, engagement and national image successfully but adopted the same largely apolitical or non-partisan stance as we have seen in the other cases, despite its concern for refugees and representation of immigrant communities (Fahy and Bock 2018: 60). However, IFNUK's funding was suddenly cut by the Conservative Communities Secretary Michael Gove on 19 January of 2024 because a member of the MCB was appointed as one of their trustees. The UK government has longstanding antipathy and a policy of non-engagement with the MCB due to their criticisms of the State of Israel (Sherwood 2024) as well as the invasions of Afghanistan and Iraq (Birt 2005). This does highlight that despite similar socio-cultural conditions, the policies and outlooks of different UK and devolved governments have an immense impact on the institutional representation of religious pluralism. However, there are reasons to hold that governments' power to influence the self-understandings and norms of their society is quite limited, once these have been disseminated among the population at large and have become part of everyday life.

Despite all of this, the different ways in which religion in the modern UK is framed by successive governments can obscure the fact that the public sphere is largely secular and pluralist because politics is still divorced from religious affiliation and is open to multiple groups. The existence of multiple religious groups, recognition of their rights and routine relationships forming part of the public sphere has largely remained characteristic of the contemporary UK. In spite of the exclusionary nationalism associated with Brexit (Fahy and Bock 2018: 52), as well as the importance of extreme anti-immigration rhetoric and policies, this has not so far shown many signs of turning the UK back into a homogenously Christian society or one in which other groups lack voice or recognition within the public sphere.

Glocalization, power and representation

Throughout this exploration of the global interfaith movement and IFS as a specific Scottish national group in comparison with the Indian, American and broader UK contexts; it has been evident that the IFM has always had to adapt to local conditions and recognize the peculiarities of where they are. This is what sociologists term 'glocalisation' (Robertson 1995 cited in Dawson 2016a: 20), the recognition that globalizing forces are never unmediated, and that they are adaptive to local conditions as well as influential upon them. There are certainly many important parallels that highlight the common interfaith ethos and modus operandi among IFGs. Compared to many global movements, IFGs can at times seem quite intent on reproducing the same structures without reflection on whether these suit the society in question or whether their aims and ethos would be better served by drawing on local practices or categories (Fahy and Bock 2018: 8, Swamy 2016). Failure to embrace glocalization and the insulation of the sphere of religion from wider society can help to explain why they have often been unable to resist the rise of competing, exclusionary movements more rooted in those societies' mores and self-images.

Nonetheless, IFGs demonstrably have had to adapt. While their internal processes and representation of religions have been quite similar, their appeals to national cultures' as well as the differing agendas of national governments seem more adaptive. They have sometimes been quite successful in helping to drive the public representation of religion in a pluralist direction and played a part in reconstructing national identity as inclusive of multiple religions. In some societies, or some niches within those societies, they have made interfaith engagements a routine part of the activities of both religious groups (McCarthy 2007: 90–1) and secular civil institutions. Nonetheless, the degree to which this is successful still depends to a large extent on the will of more powerful agents, especially governments and more dominant religious groups.

Fundamentally, the IFM across the world is built on the ethos that religions essentially have much in common, that they should relate to each other closely and that they have common interests. This also entails that they should learn from each other through dialogue and that they should collaborate on common projects in pursuit of their shared interests but also for the good of the society at large whether that is a city or region, a nation or humanity in general. In turn, they have been involved in helping to re-imagine and re-substantiate those societies through reconfiguring relations and representations of their constituent communities. The interfaith ethos builds on normative religious pluralism which holds diversity to be good and healthy but rendered more concrete and specific through their discourses and practices, as well as the deliberate effort to include multiple religious groups. Nonetheless, the IFM does not otherwise promote specific doctrines or theology beyond the fact that it is generally not theologically exclusivist (McCarthy 2007: 120–3).

They do also frequently recognize that religions can be associated with harmful things but nonetheless hold to the idea that the essence of religions is good (Fahy and Bock 2018: 65–6, Halafoff 2013: 59, Swamy 2016: 114). Similarly, interfaith activists tend to deny that religions are identical but nonetheless hold to the conception that they partake in a common essential nature. Fixing the harmful and anti-social aspects of religion and exploring this common nature of religion in a non-assimilationist fashion can in their view, be achieved through dialogue and regular relations. IFGs which differ in their scale, composition and location usually also prioritize a world religions approach: stressing broader religious affiliations, scriptural sources (Fahy and Bock 2018: 32, 66), doctrines and the most universal as well as ethically concerned elements of those religions.

However, the working out of interfaith relations necessitates dealing with the fraught politics of representation. In practice, this has tended to favour the recognized leadership of a tradition and the most organized, coherent, systematic presentations of a given community (Fahy and Bock 2018: 69). It has meant that religious groups that are controversial, on the fringes of a tradition or NRMs have had to struggle to gain access. While these groups often have been able to gain access and acceptance within interfaith circles eventually, this is a demonstration of the inevitable limitations of this kind of structured and limited pluralism.

This makes it even less likely for non-structured or non-cohesive kinds of religion or spirituality such as much of the alternative, holistic, new age or mind-body-spirit milieu to find a place within IFGs[15] (unless they are already also affiliated with a tradition). Nonetheless, as I have stated earlier, persons from these alternative milieu and interfaith circles tend to share a similar conception of established world religions as interfaith activists. It is as likely that IFGs do not tend to attract these people much more than they actively discourage them. Similarly, more conservative, exclusionary or 'fundamentalist' groups are rarely members of IFGs (Fahy and Bock 2018: 54, Halafoff 2013: 121); this appears generally to be mutually reinforcing as interfaith circles are bound by their own norms (e.g. that all religions have value) and practices (e.g. banning or frowning upon proselytizing) which would put them at odds with many traditionalist or revivalist conservative religious groups.

It is important to reiterate the point that in no way do IFGs represent the contemporary diversity of religious beliefs and practice in the societies they operate in, neither proportionately nor comprehensively. This would almost certainly not be a reasonable expectation of them, but it is easy for casual observers, such as their secular partners who know little about religion, to view them as all-representative. Exactly who is represented in interfaith circles and how they are represented is ultimately the decision of agents. However, it is also shaped by the unavoidable tension between a desire to represent multiple religious groups on equal terms, a desire to retain existing membership (Fahy and Bock 2018: 61) as well as to avoid alienating influential partners in secular civil society, especially governments.

The IFM as a form of normative religious pluralism is also generally quite secular because it differentiates the public sphere from domination by any one group. Nonetheless, they have had to adapt to the different forms and uses of religious identity and secularity, whether relatively inclusive or relatively exclusive. In general, it is fair to say that they have been able to continue to operate and even relate to governments promoting a more assimilationist or exclusionary agenda without appearing to contradict their principles. Nonetheless, the generally apolitical role that IFGs have adopted and the diversity within their own membership means that they have not been well placed to act as social critics because their critiques are generally broad and permeate little beyond those external agents who opt to work with them.

Despite their global reach, their universalistic outlook and their treatment of religions as *sui generis*, even apolitical (Fahy and Bock 2018: 60), IFGs have had to adapt to and relate with other dynamic social forces. One of the most important if often underappreciated examples, is with nationalism. This is because it is nationalism, as understood in this book, which binds the overarching political and cultural identity of place and people and channels the circulation of authority and power between the political class and the population at large. This is a process that interfaith groups could not help but get caught in, but also one which they have actively contributed to in Scotland, and elsewhere.

8

Conclusion

The limitations of pluralism and the pervasiveness of nationalism

This book has highlighted the role that Interfaith Scotland (IFS) has played in constructing a specific kind of normative religious pluralism in Scotland, which has been shown to resemble parallel processes in other nations fairly closely. The most obvious role that they have played is promoting what I have termed 'the interfaith ethos'. This is based on the assumption that religions have a unique status within societies and an essential nature. For this reason, religions are depicted as having much in common, much to learn from one another and much to give to society as a whole. That essential core of religions is held to be benign, even if malignant practices or attitudes can accrue to them, these can be excised through the act of opening oneself to the wisdom of others in dialogue which can restore one's own practice to its more irenic state. This is why interfaith pluralism is marked not by competition but by collaboration in pursuit of the common good and polyvalent truth.

In interfaith understanding, religion and ethics are understood to be universal in reach, and IFGs promote a degree of internationalism and global consciousness related to issues such as peacebuilding, environmentalism and eradicating poverty. Nonetheless, this ethos and these concerns are always adapted for specific national, regional or local frameworks. Their recognition of the power of these territorial forms of belonging and the authority of the governments or other parts of civil society has the effect of reinforcing the legitimacy of the latter. These frameworks delimit, territorialize, glocalize, embed and hybridize these universal principles which diminishes the risk that they will obliterate them. At the same time, it is also likely that this international movement's descent to the ground would not land effectively without allies and local references to help direct it. The continuing power and pervasiveness of nations and other bounded groups in a globalizing world is why IFGs have not simply relied on purely global networks and references. To have influence they had to work with, recognize and appeal to national and similarly localized stakeholders. The meeting of interfaith and nationalism both reinforce a kind of secularism because the promotion of normative pluralism differentiates the identity and governance of society from any specific religious position, and nationalism has elevated the nation to the status of an overarching imminent frame into which different religions can fit.

The pluralism promoted by IFS, among others, is limited and structured in multiple ways, including through its territorial ties. As this monograph has outlined at length, it is also limited and structured by their model of religion, especially the WRP. This has meant that religious diversity is represented largely through major religious traditions treated as holistic entities rather than overarching categories for groups of people which have developed over time. These world religions are those which are dominant in certain parts of the world: Christianity, Islam, Buddhism and Hinduism. In addition, religions which have become more widely accepted such as the Bahá' í Faith or which have longevity and connections to larger traditions, for example, Judaism and Sikhism, have also been given a similar status. Religions in IFS' representations are generally essentialized as codified, doctrinal, scripture-based, philosophical and ethical traditions which are universal entities, unlike tangible, local or even national religious groups.

The book has examined the ways in which this limited pluralism is reinforced and institutionalized by IFS and other groups in Scotland. It has also touched on similar practices in the wider UK, American and Indian contexts to point to parallel dynamics in other national contexts. IFGs continuously reinforce the message of dialogue and commonality among religions throughout their literature and at their events. The WRP is more specifically reproduced through the ways in which their documents are broken down by broad religious traditions, often with little references to internal differences or the peculiarities of the Scottish context. The scripturalist focus of interfaith is especially evident from the frequent use of these in the literature to lend authority to practices and norms, but also with the underlying assumption that these are key to understanding a given religion. This has been reproduced even for groups who lack any kind of canon, for example, Pagans, 'Believers not Belongers' and so forth. Interfaith Scotland's membership also cements the role of religious leadership because the organization is exclusively made up of institutionalized groups and because of their involvement with the Religious Leaders Forum (RLF). IFS' administration and publication of this group have helped to bridge the leadership of multiple religions with political and civic leaders, the media and the public. Nonetheless, members are classified by broad religious affiliation, and that newer religious movements such as the SPF were given a second tier of membership until 2022 and had to lobby to gain membership. Nonetheless, since they have gained membership, they have been consistently presented in the style of a world religion, as a universal tradition with principles and core authoritative texts.

These processes reflect aspects of the socio-historical context of the contemporary world and are much wider than IFS or even the IFM in general. The construction and dissemination of the world religions paradigm, transnational migrations and the changing power dynamic between traditional religions and secularizing societies are hugely important. IFGs have faced a definite need to accommodate the interests of both established and emergent religious groups, adapt to the political environments without alienating members as well as appeal to publics and governments without compromising their values. For the most part, all of the actors in question are not viewed as simply having made any of these categories to order. Instead, they are understood as having inherited and internalized assumptions and categorization schemes circulating in their societies. Conversely, like old clothes from a charity shop, these are inherited and restrictive to some extent, but also selected and combined according to taste or need and then worn in the course of their activities. By this I mean that while agents make choices in these processes; once they have internalized these social norms, assumptions and categories, they become part of the background of quite different lives, agendas and activities. These conditions may restrict and define agents but only by so much.

As I have stressed repeatedly, the relationship between the IFM as well as pluralism more generally, and nationalism has been underappreciated by scholars. Despite predictions of its demise, nationalism remains as potent and pervasive a discourse in the contemporary world as it ever was. Nonetheless, it bears repeating that the concept of nationalism I am referring to is not necessarily, or even largely belligerent, intolerant or chauvinistic let alone supremacist. I have not even confined its application to political projects to establish or maintain the unity of, achieve independence or gain autonomy for a putative national community. Rather, I have discussed the common ideological underpinnings of these projects; the concept of nations as communities with a legitimate claim to self-determination and which holds that these frameworks to be authoritative, even sacred. Highly divergent national projects within the same nation have been built on these foundations. There are certainly many forms of nationalism that do not have any affinity with the interfaith ethos and working IFGs, at all. Nonetheless, the nationalist ethos is ultimately a vision of human diversity, albeit packaged and limited by certain norms and assumptions. It is perhaps unsurprising then that in some of its forms, often normalized to the point of not being noticed as such, some nationalisms have fit with other normative expressions of diversity quite easily, for example, multiculturalism and interfaith dialogue.

IFGs in the pursuit of their goals, have had to relate not only to religions but also to other types of collective identity and ideological forces in society, such as political movements and authorities of various kinds. The legitimacy of many of these entities depends on claims to represent a population and in the cases of national governments to represent the nation into which religious groups are expected to fit harmoniously and securely. National symbolism and discourses are pervasive throughout social environments across the world because the nation-state is the predominant political unit. That predominance has also generated rival, sometimes pacified or quasi-accommodated stateless nations with influence in specific territories. While this can be a fraught environment to work in sometimes, for the most part this is encountered as a banal part of everyday life, which has the effect of reinforcing that national identification of place and people. This is one of the reasons that the pervasiveness of nationalism and its' effects on progressive and internationalist movements is often ignored. This scenario effects the ways in which IFGs must communicate their messages and with the audiences they cultivate.

While an IFG may not see eye to eye with what is often referred to as 'ethnic' nationalism, they can generally be seen to operate with conceptions of 'civic' nationalism. Generally, the view that religions should have a stake in and say over the specific society they operate within (frequently implicitly and often explicitly the nation), and also that they should contribute to its common good is widespread. The fact that IFGs are generally in the business of promoting culture sharing, including the expression of ethnic heritages but also the sensory and aesthetic aspects of religions (one clear way they do not purely follow the most abstract forms of the WRP), means that appeals to national culture reconciled to pluralism, have been useful and fit their milieu very well.

The core case study of this book is a very good example of this. It was established how IFS' literature constructs a common sense of Scottish nationhood often depicted through its most famous cultural tropes, to which many communities can belong while keeping their identities intact. They were observed to encourage a sense of attachment to the devolved political system and the exercise of the right of the Scottish people to self-determination during the 2014 referendum process. They have developed a close relationship with the devolved Scottish Government and sought to gain a wider influence to secure the position of religion in any future Scottish society and ensure that smaller religious communities can access the ear of government. It is increasingly IFS and the RLF who represent religion and its recognized place within the secular Scottish nation, not the traditionally dominant Christian churches.

In reaching out for some comparative examples, it was noted how Indian interfaith activists appealed to the country's diverse religious history and the foundations of the modern republic to validate their approach in a country increasingly defined by exclusionary nationalism. Nonetheless, these appeals can be understood as a rival national project rather than as a contest between nationalism and universalism or cosmopolitanism. American interfaith writers for their part have been eager to invoke American values and the ethos of the Enlightenment Founding Fathers along with the constitution. The appeal to these national myths and norms, along with appeals to the conception of America as the world's most religiously diverse country are similar attempts to ground interfaith in the soil of that nation but also compete with the exclusionary religious nationalism of their opponents.

The UK is a thornier example in certain respects because it lacks a clear national narrative and is not in fact understood by many of its inhabitants to form a single nation. Nonetheless, in turning to this case we saw how IFNUK have tried and succeeded in helping to implant a conception of religious diversity at the highest levels of society despite their own travails with the UK government. The cultural secularization of the UK means that attempts to create an exclusionary Christian nationalism have limited appeal even during a time where questions of national identity and sovereignty were heating up. The fact that the UK still has a complicated established church-state dynamic related to the monarchy means ironically that it is difficult to argue that Christian traditions have been sidelined or shut out of the public sphere, and even appeals to cultural Christian nationalism are unlikely to have the effect of seriously undermining pluralism, in the manner of the Indian Hindu right or the American Christian right.

Why interfaith and interfaith Scotland matter

As things currently stand, interfaith relations is an area that has received far too little attention in religious studies, at least outside of interreligious/interfaith studies which is quite distinct from the priorities and approaches of critical RS. While IRS/IFS is an undeniably lively and complex field, it has a distinct agenda, methodology and normative position. It has struggled to maintain much distance from the interfaith movement itself. Similarly, Interfaith Scotland (IFS) has received almost no attention at all aside from my own doctoral thesis and a couple of my articles.

This absence of RS scholarship on the IFM is a large gap for our field because it means that RS scholars have failed to note the manner in which this movement influences the changing relationship between religion, politics and society in many parts of the world. Interfaith groups (IFGs) have developed their own routine activities, ethos and agendas adapted for different contexts. IFGs are largely independent of one another, but they share the same roots and retain close family features.

The interfaith movement is a distinct social movement and an area of human life worthy of study by scholars of religion, given that they permeated from the high level of government meetings to informal conversations over refreshments in a local community centre or congregation. It is a mistake to treat these relationships as some purely casual meeting though, they must be studied as a socially constructed set of norms, spaces, institutions, practices and worldview like any analogous phenomenon. Even if, for many high-ranking religious officials interfaith engagements may be one more obligation or date on the calendar which does not reflect their primary identity or role, the fact that it is a regular event should encourage study of the institutions and actors which make that possible.

IFGs are important for scholarship above all because of their role, shared with many others in renegotiating the place of religion in societies and the ways in which that place is understood. This is a particular example of the process many critical scholars of religion have observed whereby 'religion' has become a shared category over and above specific religious identities. Similarly, the point that religion is far from *sui generis* or self-contained but is enmeshed with other factors in society has nonetheless not thoroughly been applied to the IFM. Having made an attempt to do so here, I hope that I have shown how that has revealed surprising connections, such as the common links with nationalism. Interfaith sources are also under-utilized resources which record and exemplify these societal and indeed global changes, often relatively speaking from the bottom up. They also diversify the types of sources scholars would rely on such as governmental, media and more conventional religious publications.

Interfaith Scotland is a particularly instructive case study despite the seemingly niche profile of the organization and niche profile of Scotland itself.

It is a clear example of how an IFG has developed a close working relationship with government and a broader nationalism. This may be easier to observe in Scotland due to its small size and because the issue of national identity is often close to the surface in stateless nations, especially those divided on the question of independence. At the same time, Scotland is quite analogous to many other countries in the west which have moved from a Christian to a secular-pluralist society rapidly.

A call for further scholarship

As the above-mentioned section has alluded to, there is a pressing need for further scholarship on interfaith relations across disciplines, methods and approaches in the non-confessional study of religion which will complement the broader work of the field. The flowering of IFGs throughout the world would be particularly suitable for ethnographies but more critical histories of the movement and the kind of study I have offered here: analyses of their expansive media and popular literature, including much online content. My view is that these texts may serve the same purpose as parish newsletters and missionary writings have for the history of Christianity, in helping to understand the lived reality and locally embedded workings of a still emerging, nascent force in a period of intense social change.

Interfaith relations is an area ripe for further exploration through many issues, many of which I have barely touched on. The complicated and intricate power relations in IFGs is an issue that will require an approach from multiple perspectives for years to come, and the relationship with nationalism will also likely be an especially fruitful one for empirical focus. The manner in which interfaith representation relates to race, class, gender, LGBT groups and the relationship between the global north and global south are issues which I have only touched on but will likely be especially vital if the call for greater scholarship is answered. Interfaith groups are certainly not going anywhere soon and I feel that it is not hyperbole to state that the scholarship on this area is truly in its infancy. It is hoped that this book has made a small contribution to this emerging area within the critical, social scientific study of religion.

Notes

1

1 This key argument and the bulk of my research on Interfaith Scotland was undertaken for my unpublished doctoral thesis (Sutherland 2018a) but also disseminated in a few publications (see Sutherland 2017b, 2017c, 2018b). On religion and national identity in contemporary Scotland (see Sutherland 2019).

2 To the extent that interfaith groups are male dominated, IFS is a definite exception to this. The founder and director are both women, and they do have high female and ethnic minority representation. In the newsletter they highlighted that 80 per cent of their staff are female and their governing board is 60 per cent female (IFS Autumn 2019: 4).

3 I do not regard these terms as interchangeable, but these categories and the scholarship on them are not easy to separate (and it is unclear how useful that would be here).

4 There is a dearth of work focusing on either sexuality or class as distinct issues in this field, I have not encountered any studies dedicated to them as such.

5 The first edition of the Wiley-Blackwell Companion to Inter-Religious Dialogue edited by Catherine Cornille was also published that year. See Cornille (2020) for the current edition.

6 An unfortunate acronym given the subject of this book, but it will usually be coupled with IRS and I have tried to keep things as clear as possible.

7 Notably, this book is woefully under cited in the field of IRS/IFS, with no acknowledgement in any of the major readers and monographs which have been published recently, with the laudable exception of Hedges (2021).

8 On the insider/outsider distinction see McCutcheon 1999.

9 Equivalent to a speaker in other legislatures.

10 https://interfaithscotland.org/about-us/who-we-are, last accessed 23 January 2024.

11 https://interfaithscotland.org/get-involved/become-a-friend last accessed 23 January 2024.

12 https://interfaithscotland.org/about-us/who-we-are#1532794844502-bbf3543b-a0ea last accessed 23 January 2024.

13 https://interfaithscotland.org/about-us/who-we-are#1532794915396-2fb584ad-2f4a, last accessed 21 May 2024.

14 With the partial exception of the Religious Leaders Forum (RLF), which they administer.

15 https://www.interfaith.org.uk/involved/groups, last accessed 23 January 2024.

16 https://interfaithscotland.org/local-interfaith-groups, last accessed 23 January 2024.

17 Procurator Fiscal are the Scots Law equivalent of prosecutors in other legal systems.

18 https://scottishinterfaithweek.org/, last accessed 23 January 2024.

19 https://www.youtube.com/@InterfaithScotland/videos, last accessed 23 January 2024.

20 https://interfaithscotland.org/resources/publications, last accessed 23 January 2024.

21 https://interfaithscotland.org/news/newsletters, last accessed 23 January 2024.

22 There was likely some pressure exerted in maintaining the boundaries of Christianity in relation to non-mainstream Christian religions such as LDS and FFWPU, see Chapter 3.

23 See Chapter 5 for an extensive overview of this term.

24 See https://interfaithscotland.org/resources/publications, last accessed 31 January 2024.

25 Emic concepts and categories are those in general use among a population, while etic concepts and categories are specialized terms or models imposed for analytical purposes. This distinction is similar but not identical to the insider/outsider one which pertains more to specific groups and their boundaries (Jensen 1993: 124, McCutcheon 2001: 63–4).

2

1 https://www.oikoum ene.org/about-the-wcc, last accessed 31 January 2024.

2 The common and somewhat puzzling use of the phrase 'interfaith encounters', even in academic sources demonstrate how an assumption of innocuity is reinforced often against the grain of analyses of IFGs' development and inner workings.

3 I have also been influenced by the 'culturalist approach' within media studies which attempt to balance focus on environmental conditions and the structures of media themselves while asserting that audiences are not simply passive consumers but express agency in their reception. As the IFM and audiences for its media are usually activists or at least participants invited to dialogue, this is especially astute (see Morgan 2008: 3–4). Ultimately, this position can be traced to the foundational sociologist Max Weber's argument that while concepts were not independent from socio-economic conditions, they could play an important role in reshaping agents' practices and potentially whole societies in turn rather than simply being ephemeral. He argued in fact that Calvinist conceptions of work for its own sake

('the Protestant Ethic') influenced business practices and encouraged the rise of modern capitalism (Weber 2002).

4 I deem it possible, even commonplace, for actors to pursue collective rather than individual interests, which should demonstrate that I do not take them to be purely self-motivated. No doubt unsurprisingly, I also do not consider individuals or their interests to be perfectly autonomous but also socially produced (see Mitchell 2011).

5 See https://www.tartanregister.gov.uk/index, last accessed 31 January 2024.

6 Though, Bangladesh was part of Pakistan until 1971.

7 This pattern of the rejection of traditional Presbyterian upbringing and exploration of new and alternative religious or spiritual beliefs had antecedents earlier in the twentieth century (see Sutcliffe 2010).

8 The census was delayed for a year due to the pandemic. The statistics related to religion, ethnicity, language and national identity were only released in May 2024.

9 https://www.bbc.co.uk/news/special/elect ion2 011/overview/html/scotland.stm, last accessed 24 January 2024.

10 https://www.bbc.co.uk/news/events/scotland-decides/results, last accessed 24 January 2024.

11 http://www.bbc.co.uk/news/elect ion/2015/results, last accessed 24 January 2024.

12 See https://www.bbc.com/news/politics/eu_referendum/results, last accessed 31 January 2024.

3

1 Action of Churches Together Scotland is the primary ecumenical body in Scotland, representing most churches in the country; it is both part of and the Scottish equivalent of Churches Together Britain and Ireland, in parallels to the relationship between IFS and IFNUK.

2 https://www.oikoum ene.org/about-the-wcc, last accessed 31 January 2024.

3 https://interfaithscotland.org/about-us/who-we-are#153279 4915 396-2fb58 4ad-2f4a, last accessed 31 January 2024, http://www.acts-scotl and.org/about-us/about-acts, last accessed 31 January 2024.

4 https://www.edinburghinterfaith.com/about, last accessed 31 January 2024.

5 https://interfaithscotland.org/about-us/who-we-are#153279 4915 396-2fb58 4ad-2f4a, last accessed 28 May 2024.

6 https://interfaithscotland.org/about-us/who-we-are#153279 4915 396-2fb584ad-2f4a, last accessed 28 May 2024.

7 See Gay (2013) for an appreciative Christian theological response to this.

4

1 https://www.ons.gov.uk/peoplepopulat ionandcommunity/culturalidentity/religion/
   bulletins/religionenglandandwales/census2 021#religion-in-england-and-wales, last
   accessed 31 January 2024.
2 https://interfaithscotland.org/about-us/who-we-are#153279 4844502-bbf3543b-
   a0ea, last accessed 23 January 2024, Maureen Sier personal communication
   18 November 2015.
3 This term is taken from Mandair and Dressler (2011).
4 This term was coined by the sociologist of religion Grace Davie (1994).
5 Abdul Bahá (1844–1921) and Shoghi Effendi (1897–1957) were the successors, as
   well as son and grandson, respectively of Bahá'ulláh (Bowker 1997 5, 894–5).
6 Deities and other superhuman beings such as Buddhas and Boddhisattvas are part
   of most Buddhist traditions. It is 'non-theistic' in the sense that its soteriology does
   not depend on deities. This is seemingly recognized by *The Guide* with its use of the
   phrase *creator* gods (IFS n.d.: 6–7).
7 On Muslims in Scotland see Saeed, Blair and Forbes (1999), Maan (2008, 2014),
   Kidd and Jamieson (2011), Bonino (2015, 2017).
8 https://hindutempleofscotland.org/about-temple, last accessed 31 January 2024.
9 An aniconic representation of the Hindu deity Shiva as a pillar-like object (Bowker
   1997: 580–1).

5

1 Ignoring or dismissing agents' self-identifications would of course be highly
   questionable and is not something I endorse. Nonetheless, we could perhaps
   describe this population as 'secularized', among whom religious beliefs and
   observances having lost their traditional significance.
2 This is the motto found at the top of every issue of the newsletter.
3 It is possible she is referring to an article in *The Herald* which argued the following
   about secularism 'religion should not be banned or persecuted, but it [secularism] is
   to ask that it be relegated to the purely personal realm' (Goring 2013).
4 Though Dundee Inter Faith Group has recently changed their name to Faith and
   Belief (Dundee) to reflect the participation of local Humanists, which exemplifies
   the fact that things can be different at the local level but also that future trajectories
   are unclear (see IFS Spring 2021: 17).
5 It also needs to be stated that the scholarship on Humanism suffers from many of
   the same issues as the study of interfaith groups. There is a considerable dearth of

critical scholarship with the laudable exceptions of Matthew Engelke's ethnographic studies. It is also an area dominated almost completely by insiders to the movement.

6

1 https://mcscotland.org/, last accessed 31 January 2024.
2 https://www.un.org/en/observances/interfaith-harmony-week, last accessed 8 May 2024.
3 The equivalent of a poet laureate from the Scots language word for poet.
4 https://www.tartanregister.gov.uk/tartanDetails?ref=636, last accessed 31 January 2024.
5 https://islamictartan.com/, last accessed 1 January 2024.
6 https://www.tartanregister.gov.uk/tartanDetails?ref=3785, last accessed 31 January 2024.
7 https://scottishpf.org/spf-tartan/, last accessed 31 January 2024.
8 An image of this was reproduced in the newsletter, it is stamped with a new symbol they have adopted which combines a stylised version of the saltire with a kind of Celtic-knot design reminiscent of *The Book of Kells*.
9 Procurator Fiscal is the Scots Law equivalent of a prosecutor in other legal systems.

7

1 When 'anti-cosmopolitan' includes very transnational and universalistic groups it is unclear how the concept of 'cosmopolitan' could be a useful analytical category, rather than simply a general expression of sympathy or condemnation.
2 From a traditional Scots toast: *here's tae us, wha's like us? Gey few and they're aw deid.* (here's to us, who is like us? Damn few and they are all dead) (see Fernandez 2000: 125).
3 https://www.census2011.co.in/religion.php, last accessed 26 January 2024.
4 This is leaving aside debates about the unity and antiquity/modernity of Hinduism (see King 1999).
5 It is still a nation with a clear Christian majority, 70.6 per cent Christian, including 25.4 per cent Evangelical, 20.8 per cent Catholic and 14.7 per cent 'mainline Protestant.' The Non-religious ('Nones') make up 22.8 per cent and 5.9 per cent identifying with a non-Christian religious identity, including Jewish at 1.9 per cent and Muslim at 0.9 per cent https://www.pewresearch.org/religion/religious-landsc ape-study/ (last accessed 28 January 2024).

6 McCarthy provides a thorough study of what could be termed conservative or illiberal IFGs (2007). Though they are edge cases of a sort, I do not refer to them as 'interfaith' because these are groups which have built temporary alliances around political goals but do not appear to promote close interreligious relations as ends in themselves. In short, they are not examples of the movement I am concerned with, but they are important parts of the environment within which American IFGs operate.

7 On interfaith groups and Evangelicals see Larson and Shady 2018.

8 The common identification between Northern Ireland and the historic province of Ulster is controversial because the latter includes some counties in the Republic of Ireland.

9 See https://interfaithwales.co.uk/, last accessed 27 January 2024.

10 See http://inter fait hni.org/ last accessed 27 January 2024.

11 https://www.interfaith.org.uk/involved/groups, last accessed 23 January 2024.

12 Though Northern Ireland is a partial exception to this with 82.80 per cent Christian (see NISRA 2012: 19).

13 Discussing demography in the UK is complicated by the fact that separate censuses are carried out in Scotland and Northern Ireland from the one carried out for England and Wales (together). This means that data is not gathered at the UK level, but neither is it completely broken down by the four nations.

14 https://www.gov.wales/ethnic-group-national-identity-language-and-religion-wales-census-2021-html, last accessed 27 January 2024.

15 Though in Norway, the national interfaith council has an 'Alternative Network' as a member (Leirvik 2005: 4, 2014b: 159).

References

Abbi, P. (2013). 'A Secular Hindu Speaks of the Importance of Interfaith Cooperation', in Xaverian Missionaries of the United Kingdom and United States (eds) *Common Ground: Conversations among Humanists and Religious Believers*, 21–30. Coatbridge: Xaverian Missionaries of the United Kingdom and United States.

Action of Churches Together – Scotland (ACTS). (n.d.). *CAIRing for Scotland: The Churches Contribution to Interfaith Relations in Scotland*. Alloa: Action of Churches Together Scotland.

Adamson, J., Ramsay, K., and Craig, M. (1984). *Stella: The Story of Stella Jane Reekie 1922–1982*. Glasgow: South Park Press.

Allocco, A. L., Claussen, G. D., and Pennington, B. K. (2018). 'Constructing Interreligious Studies: Thinking Critically About Interfaith Studies and the Interfaith Movement', in E. Patel, J. H. Peace and N. J. Silverman (eds), *Interreligious/Interfaith Studies: Defining a New Field*, 36–48. Boston: Beacon Press.

Anderson, B. (1983). *Imagined Communities: Reflections on the Origin and Spread of Nationalism*. London: Verso.

Anderson, P., and Keil, S. (2016). 'Minority Nationalism and the European Union: The Cases of Scotland and Catalonia', *L'Europe en Formation*, (1), 40–57.

Armstrong, J. (1997). 'Religious Nationalism and Collective Violence', *Nations and Nationalism* 3 (4): 597–606.

Asad, T. (1990). 'Multiculturalism and Identity in the Wake of the Rushdie Affair', *Politics and Society* 18 (4): 455–80.

Asad, T. (1993). *Genealogies of Religion: Discipline and Reasons of Power in Christianity and Islam*. Baltimore: Johns Hopkins University Press.

Asad, T. (2003). *Formations of the Secular: Christianity, Islam and Modernity*. Stanford: Stanford University Press.

Ascherson, N. (2002). *Stone Voices: The Search for Scotland*. London: Granta.

Azam, I. (2015). 'Why I Believe There Is a Difference between Scottish Muslims and the Rest of the UK When It Comes to Radical Islam', *The Sunday Herald* February, 1.

Bacquet, S. (2015). 'Religious Symbols and the Making of Contemporary Religious Identities', in R. Sandberg (ed.), *Religion and Legal Pluralism*, 113–32. Farnham: Ashgate.

Barker, E. (1989). *New Religious Movements: A Practical Introduction*. London: HMSO.

Barth, F. (1998). 'Introduction', in F. Barth (ed.), *Ethnic Groups and Boundaries: The Social Organization of Cultural Difference*, 1–39. Long Grove: Waveland Press. .

Bell, E. (2018). 'Education and Social Mobility of Chinese Families in Scotland', in T. M. Devine and A. McCarthy (eds), *New Scots: Scotland's Immigrant Communities Since 1945*, 150–75. Edinburgh: Edinburgh University Press.

Bellah, R. (1992). *The Broken Covenant: American Civil Religion in Time of Trial.* Chicago: Chicago University Press.

Bellah, R. (2005). 'Civil Religion in America', *Daedalus* 134 (4): 40–55.

Berger, P. (1969). *The Sacred Canopy: Elements of a Sociological Theory of Religion.* London: Doubleday.

Bhatt, C. (2001). *Hindu Nationalism: Origins, Ideologies and Modern Myths.* Oxford: Berg.

Billig, M. (1995). *Banal Nationalism.* London: Sage Publications.

Birt, J. (2005). 'Lobbying and Marching: British Muslims and the State', in T. Abbas (ed.), *Muslim Britain: Communities under Pressure*, 92–106. London: Zed.

Bond, R., and Rosie, M. (2010). 'National Identities and Attitudes to Constitutional Change in the Post-Devolution UK: A Four Territories Comparison', *Regional and Federal Studies*, 20 (1): 83–105.

Bonino, S. (2015). 'Scottish Muslims Through a Decade of Change: Wounded by the Stigma, Healed by Islam, Rescued by Scotland', *Scottish Affairs* 24 (1): 78–105

Bonino, S. (2017). *Muslims in Scotland: The Making of Community in a Post-9/11 World.* Edinburgh: Edinburgh University Press.

Bonino, S. (2018). 'The Migration and Settlement of Pakistanis and Indians', in T. M. Devine and A. McCarthy (eds), *New Scots: Scotland's Immigrant Communities Since 1945*, 75–103. Edinburgh: Edinburgh University Press.

Bonney, N. (2013). 'Established Religion, Parliamentary Devolution and the New State Religion in the UK', *Parliamentary Affairs* 66(2): 425–42.

Borowik, I., Ančić, B., and Tyraľa, R. (2013). 'Central and Eastern Europe', in S. Bullivant and M. Ruse (eds), *The Oxford Handbook of Atheism*, 622–7. Oxford: Oxford University Press.

Bowker, J. (1997). *The Oxford Dictionary of World Religions.* Oxford: Oxford University Press.

Braiden, G., and Dinwood, R. (2011). 'Bishop Steps Up Attack on Gay Marriage', *The Herald*, 8 October.

Brittain, C. (2016). 'Partnership not Dialogue: Lent and Ramadan Under the Same Roof', *Ecclesial Practices* 3: 190–209.

Brodeur, P. (2005). 'From the Margins to the Centers of Power: The Increasing Relevance of the Global Interfaith Movement', *Crosscurrents* Spring : 42–53.

Broun, D. (1998). 'Defining Scotland and the Scots Before the Wars of Independence', in D. Broun, R. J. Finlay and M. Lynch (eds), *Image and Identity: The Making and Re-Making of Scotland Through the Ages*, 4–17. Edinburgh: John Donald.

Broun, D. (2002). 'The Church and the Origins of Scottish Independence in the Twelfth Century', *Records of the Scottish Church History Society* 31(1): 1–35.

Brown, C.G. (1997). *Religion and Society in Scotland since 1707*. Edinburgh: Edinburgh University Press.

Bruce, S. (1985). *No Pope of Rome: Anti-Catholicism in Modern Scotland*. Edinburgh: Mainstream Publishing.

Bruce, S. (2014). *Scottish Gods: Religion in Modern Scotland, 1900–2012*. Edinburgh: Edinburgh University Press.

Bruce, S., Glendinning, T., Paterson, I., and Rosie, M. (eds) (2004). *Sectarianism in Scotland*. Edinburgh: Edinburgh University Press.

Bullivant, S., and Lee, L. (2012). 'Interdisciplinary Studies of Non-Religion and Secularity: The State of the Union', *Journal of Contemporary Religion* 27 (1): 19–27.

Calhoun, C. (2007). *Nations Matter: Culture, History and the Cosmopolitan Dream*. London: Routledge.

Calhoun, C., Juergensmeyer, M., and van Antwerpen, J. (2011). 'Introduction', in C. Calhoun, M. Juergensmeyer and J. van Antwerpen (eds), *Rethinking Secularism*, 75–91 Oxford: Oxford University Press.

Cameron, E. A. (1998). 'Embracing the Past: The Highlands in Nineteenth Century Scotland', in D. Broun, R. J. Finlay, M. Lynch. (eds) *Image and Identity: The Making and Re-Making of Scotland Through the Ages*, 195–219. Edinburgh: John Donald Publishers.

Campbell, C. (1971). *Towards a Sociology of Irreligion*. London: MacMillan.

Capps, W. H. (2000). *Religious Studies: The Making of a Discipline*. Minneapolis: Fortress Press.

Carrell, S. (2011). 'Gay Clergy Row Threatens Mass Resignations from Church of Scotland', *The Guardian*, 14 November.

Casanova, J. (2011). 'The Secular, Secularizations, Secularisms', in C. Calhoun, M. Juergensmeyer and J. van Antwerpen (eds), *Rethinking Secularism*, 54–74. Oxford: Oxford University Press.

Cauthen, B. (2004). 'Covenant and Continuity: Ethno-Symbolism and the Myth of Divine Election', *Nations and Nationalism* 10 (1/2): 19–33.

Cavanaugh, W. T. (2011). 'The Myth of Religious Violence', in A. R. Murphy (ed.), *The Blackwell Companion to Religion and Violence*, 23–33. Oxford: Blackwell.

Chamberlain, J. M. (2014). 'Governmentality', in B. A. Arrigo (ed.), *Encyclopaedia of Criminal Justice Ethics*, 395–7. Thousand Oaks: Sage.

Chatterjee, P. (1986). *Nationalism and the Colonial World: A Derivative Discourse*. Minneapolis: University of Minneapolis Press.

Chatterjee, P. (1993). *The Nation and Its Fragments: Colonial and Postcolonial Histories*. Princeton: Princeton University Press.

Chidester, D. (2014). *Empire of Religion: Imperialism and Comparative Religion*. Chicago: Chicago University Press.

Cheruvallil-Contractor, S., Hooley, T., Moore, N., Purdam, K., and Weller, P. (2013). 'Researching the Non-Religious: Methods and Methodological Issues, Challenges and Controversies', in A. Day, G. Vincett and C. R. Cotter. (eds), *Social Identities Between the Sacred and the Secular*, 173–90. Farnham: Ashgate.

Chryssides, G. (1998). *The Elements of Unitarianism*. Rockport: Element Books.

Chryssides, G. (2012). 'Can the Moonies Keep on Shining?', *The Telegraph* 3 September.

Chuddy SX, Fr. C. (2013). 'Common Ground: Conversations Among Humanists and Religious Believers', in Xaverian Missionaries of the United Kingdom and United States (eds), *Common Ground: Conversations among Humanists and Religious Believers*, 35–40. Coatbridge: Xaverian Missionaries of the United Kingdom and United States.

Clifton, C., and Harvey, G. (eds) (2004). *The Paganism Reader*, 1st edn. London: Routledge.

Cimino, R., and Smith, C. 2007. 'Secular Humanism and Atheism Beyond Progressive Secularism', *Sociology of Religion* 68 (4): 407–24.

Cohen, A. (1996). 'Personal Nationalism: A Scottish View of Some Rites, Rights and Wrongs', *American Ethnologist* 23(4): 802–15.

Cohen, A. (2000). 'Peripheral Vision: Nationalism, National Identity and the Objective Correlative in Scotland', in A. Cohen (ed.), *Signifying Identities: Anthropological Perspectives on Boundaries and Contested Values*, 145–69. London: Routledge..

Cohn-Sherbock, D. (2001). *Interfaith Theology: A Reader*. Oxford: Oneworld.

Cook, J., and McCool, M. (2024). 'John Swinney Sworn In As Scotland's First Minister' at https://www.bbc.co.uk/news/uk-scotland-scotland-politics-68973772 (accessed 27 May 2024).

Cornille, C. (ed.) (2020). *The Wiley-Blackwell Companion to Inter-Religious Dialogue*. Chichester: John Wiley.

Copeman, J., and Quack, J. (2015). 'Godless People and Dead Bodies: Materiality and the Morality of Atheist Materialism' *Social Analysis* 59 (2): 40–61.

Copson, A. (2015). 'What Is Humanism?', in A. Copson and A. C. Grayling (eds), *The Wiley Blackwell Handbook of Humanism*, 1–33. Chichester: John Wiley.

Cotter, C.R. (2011). 'Consciousness Raising: The Critique, Agenda, and Inherent Precariousness of Contemporary Anglophone Atheism.' *International Journal for the Study of Religions* 2 (1): 77–103.

Cotter, C. R. (2020). *The Critical Study of Non-Religion: Discourse, Identification and Locality*. London: Bloomsbury.

Cotter, C. R., and Robertson, D. G. (2016). 'Introduction', in C. R. Cotter and D. G. Robertson (eds), *After World Religions: Reconstructing Religious Studies*, 1–20. London: Routledge.

Cotter, C. R., Quadrio, P., and Tuckett, J. (eds) (2017). *New Atheism: Critical Perspectives and Contemporary Debates*. Dordrecht: Springer.

Cowan, E. J. (1998). 'Identity, Freedom and The Declaration of Arbroath', in D. Broun, R. J. Finlay, M. Lynch (eds) *Image and Identity: The Making and Re-Making of Scotland Through the Ages*, 38–68. Edinburgh: John Donald Publishers.

Cox, J. L. (2007). *From Primitive to Indigenous: The Academic Study of Indigenous Religions*. Farnham: Ashgate.

Cranmer, F. (2015). 'Quakers and the Campaign for Same-Sex Marriage', in R. Sandberg (ed.), *Religion and Legal Pluralism*, 67–88. Farnham: Ashgate.

Dandelion, P. (2008). *The Quakers: A Very Short Introduction*. Oxford: Oxford University Press.

Dawkins, R. (2007). *The God Delusion*. London: Black Swan.

Dawson, A. (2016a). 'The Politics and Practice of Religious Diversity: National Contexts, Global Issues', in A. Dawson (ed.), *The Politics and Practice of Religious Diversity: National Contexts, Global Issues*, 1–26. Abingdon: Routledge.

Dawson, A. (2016b). 'Religious Diversity and the Shifting Sands of Prioritisation: Reflections on the UK Context', in A. Dawson (ed.), *The Politics and Practice of Religious Diversity: National Contexts, Global Issues*, 133–52. Abingdon: Routledge.

Dawson, A., and Prideaux, M. (2018). 'Interfaith Activity and the Governance of Religious Diversity in the United Kingdom', *Social Compass* 65(3): 363–77.

Davidson, J. (2019). 'Judge Upholds Ruling that Belief in Independence is Protected under Equality Law like Religion', *Holyrood*, 11 March. https://www.holyrood.com/news/view,judge-upholds-ruling-that-belief-in-independence-is-protected-under-equality-law-like-religion_10014.htm.

Davie, G. (1994). *Religion in Britain since 1945: Believing Without Belonging* London: Blackwell.

Day, A., Vincett, G., and Cotter, C. R. (2013). 'What Lies Between: Exploring the Depths of Social Identities between the Sacred and Secular', in A. Day, G. Vincett and C. R. Cotter (eds), *Social Identities between the Sacred and the Secular*, 1–6 Farnham: Ashgate.

Del Vecchio, K., and Silverman, N. J. (2018). 'Learning from the Field: Six Themes from Interfaith/Interreligious Studies Curricula'. in E. Patel, J. H. Peace and N. J. Silverman (eds), *Interreligious/Interfaith Studies: Defining A New Field*, 49–59 Boston: Beacon Press.

Devine, T. M. (ed.) (2000). *Scotland's Shame? Bigotry and Sectarianism in Modern Scotland*. Edinburgh: Mainstream Publishing.

Devine, T. M. (2012). *The Scottish Nation: A Modern History*. London: Penguin.

Devine, T. M., and McCarthy, A. (2018). Introduction: The Historical and Contemporary Context of Immigration to Scotland Since 1945', in T. M. Devine and A. McCarthy (eds), *New Scots: Scotland's Immigrant Communities Since 1945*, 1–20. Edinburgh: Edinburgh University Press.

Doniger, W., and Nussbaum, M. C. (eds) (2015). *Pluralism and Democracy in India: Debating the Hindu Right*. Oxford: Oxford University Press.

Dunbar, S. D. (1998). 'The Place of Interreligious Dialogue in the Academic Study of Religion', *Journal of Ecumenical Studies* 35, (3–4): 455–69.

Dunne, T., and Brian, C. Schmidt. (2005). 'Realism', in J. Baylis and S. Smith (eds), *The Globalization of World Politics: An Introduction to International Relations*, 3rd edn. 161–84. Oxford: Oxford University Press.

Durkheim, É. (2001 [1912]) *The Elementary Forms of the Religious Life*. Oxford: Oxford University Press.

Edwards, O. D. (2012). 'Modern Scottish Catholicism', *Scottish Church History Society* 41(1): 133–55.

Eide, E. (2010). 'Strategic Essentialism and Ethnification: Hand in Glove?', *Nordicom Review* 31 (2): 63–78.

Engelke, M. (2014). 'Christianity and the Anthropology of Secular Humanism', *Current Anthropology* 55 (S10): S292–301.

Engelke, M. (2015). 'The Coffin Question: Death and Materiality in Humanist Funerals', *Material Religion* 11 (1): 26–48.

Englander, D. (1993). 'Integrated but Insecure: A Portrait of Anglo-Jewry at the Close of the Twentieth Century', in G. Parsons (ed.), *The Growth of Religious Diversity: Britain from 1945 Volume I: Traditions*, 95–132. London: Routledge.

Eriksen, T. H. (2002). *Ethnicity and Nationalism: Anthropological Perspectives*. London: Pluto Press.

Evans, N. J., and McCarthy, A. (2018). ''New' Jews in Scotland Since 1945', in T. M. Devine and A. McCarthy (eds), *New Scots: Scotland's Immigrant Communities Since 1945*, 50–74. Edinburgh: Edinburgh University Press.

Fahy, J., and Bock J. J. (2018). 'Beyond Dialogue? Interfaith Engagement in Delhi, Doha and London', Woolf Institute and Georgetown University in Qatar.

Fernandez, J. W. (2000). 'Peripheral Wisdom', in A. Cohen (ed.), *Signifying Identities: Anthropological Perspectives on Boundaries and Contested Values*, 117–44. London: Routledge.

Fernando, M. L. (2014). *The Republic Unsettled: Muslim French and the Contradictions of Secularism*. London: Duke University Press.

Finlay, R. (1998). 'Caledonia or North Britain? Scottish Identity in the Eighteenth Century', in D. Broun, R. J. Finlay and M. Lynch (eds), *Image and Identity: The Making and Re-Making of Scotland Through the Ages*, 143–56. Edinburgh: John Donald Publishers.

Fitzgerald, T. (1997). 'A Critique of "Religion" as a Cross-Cultural Category', *Method and Theory in the Study of Religion* 9/2: 91–110.

Fitzgerald, T. (2000). *The Ideology of Religious Studies*. Oxford: Oxford University Press.

Fletcher, J. H. (2018). 'The Promising Practices of Antiracist Approaches to Interfaith Studies', in E. Patel, J. H. Peace and N. J. Silverman (eds), *Interreligious/Interfaith Studies: Defining A New Field*, 137–46. Boston: Beacon Press.

Fowler, J. (1999). *Humanism: Beliefs and Practices*. Brighton: Sussex Academic Press.

Fraser, S. (2013). 'Not Just "Three Rs" – There's Religion Too', *The Scotsman*, 26 July.

Gadamer, H. G. (1984). 'The Hermeneutics of Suspicion', *Man and World* 17: 313–23.

Gay, D. (2013). *Honey from the Lion: Christianity and the Ethics of Nationalism.* London: SCM Press.

Gellner, E. (1983). *Nations and Nationalism.* Oxford: Blackwell Publishing.

Geoghan, P. (2013). 'Sectarianism still forms a divide', *The Scotsman*, 19 December.

Goldblatt, J. (2022). 'Scotsman Obituaries: Frank Whaling, Founder of Edinburgh Interfaith Association', *The Scotsman*, 14 December.

Gordon, T. (2011). 'The Real Battleground between the SNP and the Catholic Church… Gay Marriage', *The Herald*, 8 October.

Goring, R. (2013). 'Religion Should Be Relegated to the Private and Personal Realm', *The Herald*, 17 June.

Greenfeld, L. (1996). 'The Modern Religion?', *Critical Review* 10 (2): 169–91.

Grosby, S. (2018). 'Nationality and Religion', *Nations and Nationalism* 24 (2): 258–70.

Grung, A. H. (2020). 'Interreligious or Transreligious?', in H. Gustafson (ed.), *Interreligious Studies: Dispatches from an Emerging Field*, 58–66. Waco: Baylor University Press.

Grung, A. H. (2022). 'Interreligious Studies and Gender: Critical Perspectives', in L. Mosher (ed.), *The Georgetown Companion to Interreligious Studies*, 168–75. Washington, DC: Georgetown University Press.

Guibernau, M. (1999). *Nations without States: Political Communities in a Global Age.* Cambridge: Polity Press.

Gustafson, H. (2020a). 'Introduction', in H. Gustafson (ed.), *Interreligious Studies: Dispatches from an Emerging Field*, 1–14. Waco, Texas: Baylor University Press.

Gustafson, H. (2020b). 'The Vitality of Lived Religions Approach', in H. Gustafson (ed.), *Interreligious Studies: Dispatches from an Emerging Field*, 91–7. Waco: Baylor University Press.

Gustafson, H. (2022). 'Sparring with Spider Silk: Models for the Relationship between Interreligious Studies and the Interfaith Movement', in L. Mosher (ed.), *The Georgetown Companion to Interreligious Studies*, 32–40. Washington, DC: Georgetown University Press.

Gustafson, H. (2023). *Everyday Wisdom: Interreligious Studies in a Pluralistic World.* Minneapolis: Fortress Press.

Habermas, J. (2011). 'The Political: The Rational Meaning of a Questionable Inheritance', in E. Mendietta and J. Vanantwerpen (eds), *The Power of Religion in the Public Sphere*, 15–33. New York: Colombia University Press.

Hague, R., and Harrop, M. (2004). *Comparative Government and Politics: An Introduction.* Basingstoke: Palgrave MacMillan.

Halafoff, A. (2013). *The Multifaith Movement: Global Risks and Cosmopolitan Solutions.* London: Springer.

Halafoff, A. (2016). 'Multifaith Relations and Religious Diversity in Australia: Multifaith Relations and Religious Instruction in the State of Victoria', in A. Dawson (ed.), *The*

Politics and Practice of Religious Diversity: National Contexts, Global Issues, 101–17. Abingdon: Routledge.

Halliday, F. (2005). 'Nationalism', in J. Baylis and S. Smith (eds), *The Globalization of World Politics: An Introduction to International Relations*, 3rd edn. 521–38. Oxford: Oxford University Press.

Hearn, J. (2006). *Rethinking Nationalism: A Critical Introduction*. Basingstoke: Palgrave MacMillan.

Hedges, P. (2010). *Controversies in Interreligious Dialogue and the Theology of Religions*. London: SCM Press.

Hedges, P. (2012). 'Interreligious Studies', in A. Runehov and L. Oviedo (eds), *Encyclopedia of Science and Religion*, 1076–80. New York: Springer.

Hedges, P. (2014). 'Interreligious Studies: A New Direction in the Study of Religion?', *Bulletin of the British Association for the Study of Religion* November: 13–14.

Hedges, P. (2019). 'The Secular Realm as Interfaith Space: Discourse and Practice in Contemporary Multicultural Nation-States', *Religion* 10(9): 498; https://doi.org/10.3390/rel10090498.

Hedges, P. (2021). *Understanding Religion: Theories and Methods for Studying Religiously Diverse Societies*. Oakland: University of California Press.

Hertzke, A. D. (2016). 'The Globalization of Religious Advocacy', in A. Dawson *The Politics and Practice of Religious Diversity: National Contexts, Global Issues*, 155–73. Abingdon: Routledge.

Heywood, A. (2002). *Politics*. Basingstoke: Palgrave Macmillan.

Hormel, L. M. (2010). 'Atheism and Secularity in the Former Soviet Union', in P. Zuckerman (ed.), *Atheism and Secularity – Volume 2: Global Expressions*. 45–71 Santa Barbara: Praeger.

Horsfield, P. (2008). 'Media', in D. Morgan (ed.), *Key Words in Religion, Media and Culture*, 111–22. London: Routledge.

Howard, T. A (2021). *The Faiths of Others: A History of Interreligious Dialogue*. London: Yale University Press

Hutchinson, J., and Smith, A. D. (eds). (1994). *Nationalism*. Oxford: Oxford University Press.

Ichijo, A. (2012). 'Entrenchment of Unionist Nationalism: Devolution and the Discourse of National Identity in Scotland', *National Identities* 14 (1): 23–37.

Interfaith Network for the United Kingdom (IFNUK). (2007). *20 Years: Milestones on the Journey Together Towards Greater Inter Faith Understanding and Cooperation*. London: Inter-Faith Network for the UK.

Interfaith Scotland and Interfaith Glasgow (2019). *Interfaith Chaplaincy Research Project March 2018-May 2018* Glasgow: Interfaith Scotland.

Interfaith Scotland. (n.d.). *A Guide to Faith Communities in Scotland*. Glasgow: Interfaith Scotland.

Interfaith Scotland. (n.d.) *Guidelines for Inclusive Civic Events*. Glasgow: Interfaith Scotland.

Interfaith Scotland. (n.d.) *Untold Stories: Women of Faith: Suffrage, Peace and Human Rights* Glasgow: Interfaith Scotland.

Interfaith Scotland *Newsletter* September 2012: Issue 22: Glasgow: Interfaith Scotland.

Interfaith Scotland *Newsletter* Spring 2013: Issue 23: Glasgow: Interfaith Scotland.

Interfaith Scotland *Newsletter* Summer 2013: Issue 24: Glasgow: Interfaith Scotland.

Interfaith Scotland *Newsletter* Spring 2014: Issue 25: Glasgow: Interfaith Scotland.

Interfaith Scotland *Newsletter* Summer 2014: Issue 26 Glasgow: Interfaith Scotland.

Interfaith Scotland *Annual Report* October 2013–October 2014: Glasgow: Interfaith Scotland.

Interfaith Scotland *Newsletter* Spring 2015: Issue 27: Glasgow: Interfaith Scotland.

Interfaith Scotland *Draft Report*: October 2014–October 2015 Glasgow: Interfaith Scotland.

Interfaith Scotland *Newsletter* 2016: Issue 28: Glasgow: Interfaith Scotland.

Interfaith Scotland *Newsletter* 2017: Issue 29: Glasgow: Interfaith Scotland.

Interfaith Scotland *Newsletter* 2018: Issue 30: Glasgow: Interfaith Scotland.

Interfaith Scotland *Newsletter* Spring 2019: Issue 31: Glasgow: Interfaith Scotland.

Interfaith Scotland *Newsletter* Summer 2019: Issue 32: Glasgow: Interfaith Scotland.

Interfaith Scotland *Newsletter* Spring 2020: Issue 33: Glasgow: Interfaith Scotland.

Interfaith Scotland *Newsletter* Summer 2020: Issue 34: Glasgow: Interfaith Scotland.

Interfaith Scotland *Newsletter* Spring 2021: Issue 35: Glasgow: Interfaith Scotland.

Interfaith Scotland *Newsletter* Summer 2021: Issue 36: Glasgow: Interfaith Scotland.

Interfaith Scotland *Newsletter* Spring 2022: Issue 37: Glasgow: Interfaith Scotland.

Interfaith Scotland *Newsletter* Autumn 2022: Issue 38: Glasgow: Interfaith Scotland.

Interfaith Scotland *Newsletter* Spring 2023: Issue 39: Glasgow: Interfaith Scotland.

Interfaith Scotland *Newsletter* Autumn 2023: Issue 40: Glasgow: Interfaith Scotland.

Jaffrelot, C. (2011). 'Religion and Nationalism', in P. B. Clarke (ed.), *The Oxford Handbook of the Sociology of Religion*, 406–17. Oxford: Oxford University Press.

Jakelić, S. (2014). 'Beyond Critique: Beyond Religious Nationalism', *Immanent Frame : Religion, Secularism and the Public Sphere* http://blogs.ssrc.org/tif/2014/03/04/beyond-religious-nationalism/

Jensen, J. S. (1993). 'Is a Phenomenology of Religion Possible? On Ideas of a Human and Social Science of Religion', *Theory and Method in the Study of Religion* 5 (2): 109–34.

Jerryson, M. (2017). 'Buddhism Can Be as Violent as Any Other Religion', *Aeon* at https://aeon.co/essays/buddhism-can-be-as-violent-as-any-other-religion

Kaviraj, S. (2007). 'The Making of a Language of Patriotism in Modern Bengal', in A. S. Leoussi and S. Grosby (eds), *Nationalism and Ethnosymbolism: History, Culture and Ethnicity in the Formation of Nations*, 248–66. Edinburgh: Edinburgh University Press.

Keating, M. (2005). *The Government of Scotland: Public Policy Making After Devolution*. Edinburgh: Edinburgh University Press.

Kedourie, E. (1960). *Nationalism*. London: Hutchinson.

Kesting, M. S. (2014). 'Ecumenicism in Scotland', *International Journal for the Study of the Christian Church* 14 (2): 175–92.

Kidd, S., and Jamieson, L. (2011). 'Experiences of Muslims Living in Scotland' Edinburgh: Crown Copyright 2011.

Kim, H., and Singh, G. (2016). 'The Challenges of Managing Religious Diversity in India: Between Hegemonic Domination and the Quest for Equality', in A. Dawson (ed.), *The Politics and Practice of Religious Diversity: National Contexts, Global Issues*, 49–66. Abingdon: Routledge.

King, R. (1999). *Orientalism and Religion: Post-Colonial Power, India and the Mystic East*. London: Routledge.

King, U. (1998). 'Feminism: The Missing Dimension in the Dialogue of Religions', in J. D'Arcy May (ed.), *Pluralism and the Religions: The Theological and Political Dimensions*, 40–59. London: Cassell.

Kingdom, J. (1991). *Government and Politics in Britain: An Introduction*. Cambridge: Polity Press.

Koenig, M., and Knöbl, W. (2015a). 'Religion, Nationalism and European Integration', in W. Spohn, M. Koenig and W. Knöbl (eds), *Religion and National Identities in an Enlarged Europe*, 1–16. Basingstoke: Palgrave MacMillan.

Koenig, M., and Knöbl, W. (2015b). 'Varieties of Religious Nationalism', in W. Spohn, M. Koenig and W. Knöbl (eds), *Religion and National Identities in an Enlarged Europe*, 146–62. Basingstoke: Palgrave Macmillan.

Kohn, H. (1994). 'Western and Eastern Nationalism', in J. Hutchinson and A. D. Smith (eds), *Nationalism*, 162–4. Oxford: Oxford University Press.

Knott, K., Poole, E., and Taira, T. (2013). *Media Portrayals of Religion and the Secular Sacred*. Farnham: Ashgate.

Kujawa-Holbrock, S. A. (2022). 'Confronting White Supremacy: Critical Pedagogies for Interreligious Engagement', in L. Mosher (ed.), *The Georgetown Companion to Interreligious Studies*, 176–85. Washington DC: Georgetown University Press.

Larson, M. H., and Shady, S. L. H. (2018). 'The Possibility of Solidarity: Evangelicals and the Field of Interfaith Studies', in E. Patel, J. H. Peace and N. J. Silverman (eds), *Interreligious/Interfaith Studies: Defining A New Field*, 147–59. Boston: Beacon Press.

Law, S. (2013). 'Humanism', in S. Bullivant and M. Ruse (eds), *The Oxford Handbook of Atheism*, 263–77. Oxford: Oxford University Press.

LeDrew, S. (2012). 'The Evolution of Atheism Scientific and Humanistic Approaches', *History of the Human Sciences* 25 (3): 70–87.

Leirvik, O. (2005). 'Christianity and Islam in Norway: Politics of Religion and Interfaith Dialogue', *Canadian Diversity* 4 (3): 10–17.

Leirvik, O. (2014a). *Interreligious Studies: A Relational Approach to Religious Activism and the Study of Religion*. London: Bloomsbury.

Leirvik, O. (2014b). 'Muslims in Norway: Value Discourses and Interreligious Dialogue', *Scandinavian Journal of Islamic Studies* 8 (1): 142–54.

Leirvik, O. (2020). 'Area, Field, Discipline', in H. Gustafson (ed.), *Interreligious Studies: Dispatches from an Emerging Field*, 17–23. Waco: Baylor University Press.

Levine, A. J. (2022). 'Anti-Jewish Bigotry's Causes, Symptoms, and Treatment: Recommendations for Interreligious Studies', in L. Mosher (ed.), *The Georgetown Companion to Interreligious Studies*, 186–96. Washington DC: Georgetown University Press.

Lewis, E., and Cantor, N. (2018). 'Introduction', in E. Patel *Out of Many Faiths: Religious Diversity and the American Promise*, xi–xxi. Princeton: Princeton.

Lincoln, B. (1996). 'Theses on Method', *Method and Theory in the Study of Religion* 8: 225–7.

Long, A. J. (2000). 'Unitarianism', *The Expository Times* 112 (2): 46–51.

Lynch, M. (1998). 'A Nation Born Again?: Scottish Identity in the Sixteenth and Seventeenth Centuries', in D. Broun, R. J. Finlay, M. Lynch (eds), *Image and Identity: The Making and Re-Making of Scotland Through the Ages*, 82–104. Edinburgh: John Donald Publishers.

Maan, B. (2008). *The Thistle and the Crescent*. Glendaruel: Argylle Publishing.

Maan, B. (2014). *Muslims in Scotland*. Glendaruel: Argylle Publishing.

McCall, C. (2016). 'First Official Jewish Tartan Unveiled', *The Scotsman*, 29 March.

McCarthy, K. (2007). *Interfaith Encounters in America*. New Jersey: Rutgers University Press.

McCarthy, K. (2018). '(Inter)Religious Studies: Making a Home in the Secular Academy', in E. Patel, J. H. Peace and N. J. Silverman (eds), *Interreligious/Interfaith Studies: Defining A New Field*, 2–15. Boston: Beacon Press.

McCarthy, K. (2020). 'Secular Imperatives', in H. Gustafson (ed.), *Interreligious Studies: Dispatches from an Emerging Field*, 171–7. Waco: Baylor University Press.

Macaulay, J. (2018). 'Celebrating Life with no Need for Church' 17 July www.bbc.co.uk/news/uk-scotland-edinburgh-east-fife-44844043 (last accessed 14 August 2024).

McCrone, D. (1992). *Understanding Scotland: The Sociology of a Stateless Nation*. London: Routledge.

McCrone, D., Morris, A., and Kiely, R. (1995). *Scotland – the Brand: The Making of the Scottish Heritage*. Edinburgh: Edinburgh University Press.

McCutcheon, R. T. (ed.) (1999). *The Insider/Outsider Problem in the Study of Religion: A Reader*. London: Cassell.

McCutcheon, R. T. (2001). *Critics not Caretakers: Redescribing the Public Study of Religion*. Albany: State University of New York Press.

McCutcheon, R. T. (2003). *Manufacturing Religion: The Discourse of Sui Generis Religion and the Politics of Nostalgia*. Oxford: Oxford University Press.

Mackenzie, J. S. (2011). 'Keeping It Real!: Constructing and Maintaining Traditional Authenticity in a Tibetan Buddhist Organisation in Scotland', *Sociological Research Online* 16 (3): 7, http://www.socresonline.org.uk/16/3/7.html (last accessed 14 August 2024).

McLean, I., and McMillan, A. (eds) (2003). *The Concise Oxford Dictionary of Politics*. Oxford: Oxford University Press.

McLelland, G. (2013). 'Time for Atheists, Secularists and Humanists to Engage in Interfaith Dialogue?', in Xaverian Missionaries of the United Kingdom and United States (eds), *Common Ground: Conversations among Humanists and Religious Believers*, 48–50. Coatbridge: Xaverian Missionaries of the United Kingdom and United States.

Mandair, A. P. S., and Dressler, M. (2011). 'Introduction: Modernity, Religion-Making and the Postsecular', in A. P. S. Mandair and M. Dressler (eds), *Secularism and Religion-Making*, 3–36. Oxford: Oxford University Press.

Marshall, C. (2014). 'Religious Education "Can Halt Violent Extremism"', *The Scotsman*, 30 December.

Martin, C. (2014). *A Critical Introduction to the Study of Religion*. London: Routledge.

Martin, C. (2016). 'Religion as an Ideology: Recycled Culture vs. Religion', in C. R. Cotter and D. G. Robertson (eds), *After World Religions: Reconstructing Religious Studies*, 63–74. London: Routledge.

Masuzawa, T. (2005). *The Invention of the World Religions: or How European Universalism was Preserved in the Language of Pluralism*. Chicago: Chicago University Press.

Mendietta, E., and Vanantwerpen, J. (eds) (2011). *The Power of Religion in the Public Sphere*. New York: Colombia University Press.

Mikva, R. S. (2023). *Interreligious Studies: An Introduction*. Cambridge: Cambridge University Press.

Minister, K. (2018). 'Transforming Introductory Courses in Religion: From World Religions to Interreligious Studies', in E. Patel, J. H. Peace and N. J. Silverman (eds), *Interreligious/Interfaith Studies: Defining A New Field*, 2–15. Boston: Beacon Press.

Mitchell, J. (2005). 'Scotland: Devolution is not Just for Christmas', in A. Trench (ed.), *The Dynamics of Devolution: The State of the Nations*, 23–42. Exeter: Imprint Academic.

Mitchell, K. A. (2011). 'The Politics of Spirituality: Liberalizing the Definition of Religion', in A. P. S. Mandair and M. Dressler (eds), *Secularism and Religion-Making*, 125–40. Oxford: Oxford University Press.

Mombo, E., and Iminza, F. (2022). 'Kenya's 'Triple Heritage' Context: Implications for Interreligious Studies', in L. Mosher (ed.), *The Georgetown Companion to Interreligious Studies*, 370–8. Washington DC: Georgetown University Press.

Morgan, D. (2008). 'Introduction: Religion, Media, Culture: The Shape of the Field', in D. Morgan (ed.), *Key Words in Religion, Media and Culture*, 1–19. London: Routledge.

Morgan, P. (1995). 'The Study of Religion and Interfaith Encounters', *Numen* 42: 156–71.

Morris, B. (1987). *Anthropological Studies of Religion: An Introduction*. Cambridge: Cambridge University Press.

Mortimer, T., and Prideaux, M. (2018). 'Exploring Identities between Religious and the Secular through the Attendees of an Ostensibly "Atheist Church"', *Religion* 48 (1): 64–82.

Morton, G. (1998). 'What If?: The Significance of Scotland's Missing Nationalism in the Nineteenth Century', in D. Broun, R. J. Finlay and M. Lynch (eds), *Image and Identity: The Making and Re-Making of Scotland Through the Ages*, 157–76. Edinburgh: John Donald Publishers.

Mosher, L. (2022). 'What Is Interfaith Studies? Considering from the Between', in L. Mosher (ed.), *The Georgetown Companion to Interreligious Studies*, 3–14. Washington DC: Georgetown University Press.

Moyaert, M. (2020). 'The Scholar, the Theologian and the Activist', in H. Gustafson (ed.), *Interreligious Studies: Dispatches from an Emerging Field*, 34–42. Waco: Baylor University Press.

Munro, A. (2013). 'Bid to Remove Religious Voice from Education', *The Scotsman*, 6 November.

Nairn, T. (1977). *The Break-up of Britain: Crisis and Neo-Nationalism*. Edinburgh: New Left Books.

Nash, D. (2013). 'The (Long) Nineteenth Century', in S. Bullivant and M. Ruse (ed.), *The Oxford Handbook of Atheism*, 212–28. Oxford: Oxford University Press.

NHS Scotland. (n.d.) *A Celebration of New Life* Edinburgh: NHS Scotland.

NHS Scotland. (n.d.). *Spiritual Care: A Multi-Faith Resource for Healthcare Staff*. Edinburgh: NHS Scotland.

NHS Scotland (n.d.) *Religion and Belief Matter: An Information Resource for Healthcare Staff*. Edinburgh: NHS Scotland.

NHS Scotland (2009). *Spiritual Care Matters: An Introductory Resource for all NHS Scotland Staff*: Edinburgh: NHS Scotland.

NHS Scotland. (2011). *Reflections of Life*. Glasgow: NHS Scotland.

National Records of Scotland. (2013). *2011 Census: Key results on Population, Ethnicity, Identity, Language, Religion, Health, Housing and Accommodation in Scotland – Release 2A*. Edinburgh: Crown Copyright

National Records of Scotland. (2024). *Scotland's Census 2022 – Ethnic group, national identity, language and religion* Edinburgh: Crown Copyright 2024. https://www.scotlandscensus.gov.uk/2022-results/scotland-s-census-2022-ethnic-group-national-identity-language-and-religion/ (last accessed 28 May 2024).

Nicolson, C. (2023). 'Why Was Nicola Sturgeon Arrested and What Happens Next?' BBC News https://www.bbc.co.uk/news/uk-scotland-65323861 (last accessed 27 May 2024).

Northern Ireland Statistics Research Agency (NISRA). (2012). *Census 2011: Key Statistics for Northern Ireland*. Belfast: Crown Copyright.

Office for National Statistics (ONS). (2022a). *Population Estimates for the UK, England, Wales, Scotland and Northern Ireland: mid-2021* https://www.ons.gov.uk/peoplepop

ulationandcommunity/populationandmigration/populationestimates/bulletins/
annualmidyearpopulationestimates/mid2021. (last accessed 14 August 2024).

Office for National Statistics (ONS). (2022b). *Religion, England and Wales: 2021 Census* https://www.ons.gov.uk/peoplepopulationandcommunity/culturalidentity/religion/ bulletins/religionenglandandwales/census2021. (last accessed 14 August 2024).

Outside In. (2018). *Transforming Hate in Youth Settings: An Educational Tool and Practice Manual for Working with Young People.* https://transforminghate.net (last accessed 14 August 2024).

Owen, S. (2011). 'The World Religions Paradigm Time for a Change', *Arts and Humanities in Higher Education* 10 (3): 253–68.

Özkirimli, U. (2005). *Contemporary Debates on Nationalism: A Critical Engagement.* Basingstoke: Palgrave MacMillan.

Özkirimli, U. (2010). *Theories of Nationalism: A Critical Introduction*, 2nd edn. Basingstoke: Palgrave MacMillan.

Pals, D. (1986). 'Reductionism and Belief: An Appraisal of Recent Attacks on the Doctrine of Irreducible Religion', *The Journal of Religion* 66 (1): 18–36.

Pals, D. (1987). 'Is Religion a Sui Generis Phenomenon?', *Journal of the American Academy of Religion* 55 (2): 259–82.

Pals, D. (2006). *Eight Theories of Religion.* Oxford: Oxford University Press.

Parsons, G. (1993). 'Contrasts and Continuities: The Traditional Christian Churches in Britain Since 1945', in G. Parsons (ed.), *The Growth of Religious Diversity: Britain from 1945 Volume I: Traditions*, 23–94. London: Routledge.

Patel, E. (2018). *Out of Many Faiths: Religious Diversity and the American Promise.* Princeton: Princeton University Press.

Patel, E., Peace, J. H., and Silverman, N. J. (2018). 'Introduction', in E. Patel, J. H. Peace and N. J. Silverman (eds) *Interreligious/Interfaith Studies: Defining A New Field*, xi–xxi. Boston: Beacon Press.

Paton, D. M. M. (2002) 'The Myth and Reality of the 'Men:' Leadership and Spirituality in the Northern Highlands, 1800–1850', *Scottish Church History Society*, 31(1): 97–144.

Peace, J.H. (2022). 'Foundational Contributions and Next Steps: The Development of Interreligious/Interfaith Studies,' in L. Mosher (ed), *The Georgetown Companion to Interreligious Studies*, 471–81.Washington, D.C: Georgetown University Press.

Pearce, B. (2012). 'Case Study 2: The Inter Faith Network and the Development of Inter Faith Relations in Britain', in L. Woodhead and R. Catto (eds), *Religion and Change in Modern Britain*, 150–5. London: Routledge.

Pederson, K. J. (2004). 'The Interfaith Movement: An Incomplete Assessment', *Journal of Ecumenical Studies* 41 (1): 74–94.

Pennington, B. K. (2022). 'The Interreligious Studies Agenda: Three Dilemmas', in L. Mosher (ed.), *The Georgetown Companion to Interreligious Studies*, 15–23. Washington DC: Georgetown University Press.

Piacentini, T. (2018). 'African Migrants, Asylum Seekers and Refugees: Tales of Settling in Scotland, 2000–15', in T. M. Devine and A. McCarthy (eds), *New Scots: Scotland's Immigrant Communities Since 1945*, 176–204. Edinburgh: Edinburgh University Press.

Piętka-Nykaza, E. (2018). 'Polish Diaspora or Polish Migrant Communities? Polish Migrants in Scotland, 1945–2015', in T. M. Devine and A. McCarthy (eds), *New Scots: Scotland's Immigrant Communities Since 1945*, 126–49. Edinburgh: Edinburgh University Press.

Platvoet, J. G. (1999). 'To Define or Not to Define', in J. G. Platvoet and A. L. Molendijk (eds), *The Pragmatics of Defining Religion: Contexts, Concepts, Contents*, 245–65. Leiden: Brill.

Prideaux, M. (2019). 'Understanding Neighbourhoods as Multifaith Spaces', *Religions* 10 (9): 500.

Quack, J. (2014). 'Outline of a Relation Approach to 'Nonreligion'', *Method and Theory in the Study of Religion* 26 (4–5): 439–69.

Ramaswamy, S. (2010). *The Goddess and the Nation: Mapping Mother India*. London: Duke University Press.

Ramey, S. (2016). 'The Critical Embrace: Teaching the World Religions Paradigm as Data', in C. R. Cotter and D. G. Robertson (eds), *After World Religions: Reconstructing Religious Studies*, 48–60. London: Routledge.

Rieffer, B. A. J. (2003). 'Religion and Nationalism: Understanding the Consequences of a Complex Relationship', *Ethnicities* 3 (2): 215–42.

Ritchie, M. (2009). 'Comment', *The Herald*, 9 October.

Robertson, D. (2016).'Moderator: Time for Church Leaders to Stop Living in Denial', 25 March https//freechurch.org/news/moderator-time-for-church-leaders-to-stop-living-in-denial (accessed 29 March 2016).

Rodell, J. (2013). 'Common Ground: A Humanist Perspective', in Xaverian Missionaries of the United Kingdom and United States (eds), *Common Ground: Conversations among Humanists and Religious Believers*, 44–7. Coatbridge: Xaverian Missionaries of the United Kingdom and United States.

Rodger, H. (2015). 'Vandals Target Muslim Graveyard in Glasgow', *The Herald*, 26 March.

Rosie, M. (2004). *The Sectarian Myth in Scotland*. Basingstoke: Palgrave MacMillan.

Rosie, M. (2014). 'Tall Tales: Understanding Religion and Scottish Independence', *Scottish Affairs* 23 (3): 332–41.

Saeed, A., Blair, N., and Forbes, D. (1999). 'New Ethnic and National Questions in Scotland: Post- British Identities among Glasgow Pakistani Teenagers', *Ethnic and Racial Studies* 22 (51): 821–44.

Scottish Inter Faith Council. (n.d.). *A Celebration of New Life*. Glasgow: Scottish Inter Faith Council.

Scottish Inter Faith Council. (2003). *Report on the Pagan Federation*, 26 October. Glasgow: Scottish Inter Faith Council.

Scottish Inter Faith Council *Newsletter* January 2009: Issue 15: Glasgow: Scottish Inter Faith Council.

Scottish Inter Faith Council *Newsletter* August 2009: Issue 16: Glasgow: Scottish Inter Faith Council.

Scottish Inter Faith Council *Newsletter* March 2010: Issue 17: Glasgow: Scottish Inter Faith Council.

Scottish Inter Faith Council *Newsletter* September 2010: Issue 18: Glasgow: Scottish Inter Faith Council.

Scottish Inter Faith Council *Newsletter* February 2011: Issue 19: Glasgow: Scottish Inter Faith Council.

Scottish Inter Faith Council *Newsletter* August 2011: Issue 20: Glasgow: Scottish Inter Faith Council.

Scottish Inter Faith Council *Values in Harmony* (2011) Glasgow: Scottish Inter Faith Council.

Scottish Inter Faith Council *Newsletter* March 2012: Issue 21: Glasgow: Scottish Inter Faith Council.

Scottish Inter Faith Council Youth Committee. (n.d.). *Our Sacred Earth: A Guide for Becoming More Eco-Friendly in Your Faith Community*. Glasgow: Scottish Inter Faith Council.

Segal, R. (2005). 'Theories of Religion', in J. R. Hinnels (ed.), *Routledge Companion to the Study of Religion*, 75–92. New York: Routledge.

Settle, M., and Braiden, G. (2015). 'Police: Scots Jihadi Bride Will Be Prosecuted If She Returns to Britain', *The Herald*, 11 March.

Seymour, M., and Gagnon, A. G. (eds) (2012). *Multinational Federalism: Problems and Prospects*. Basingstoke: Palgrave MacMillan.

Sharpe, E. J. (1986). *Comparative Religion: A History*. London: Duckworth.

Sherwood, H. (2024). 'Inter Faith Network Headed for Closure as Gove "Minded to Withdraw" Funding', *The Guardian*, 16 February.

Shipps, J. (1987). *Mormonism: The Story of a New Religious Tradition*. Chicago: University of Illinois Press.

Siddiqui, U. (2016). 'Muslim Minorities in Peril: The Rise of Buddhist Violence in Asia' 8 September. *Al Jazeera Centre for Studies*, http://studies.aljazeera.net/en/reports/2016/09/muslim-minorities-peril-rise-buddhist- violence-asia-160908090547506.html (accessed 27 September 2017).

Sier, M. (2013). 'Religious and Non-Religious Engagement: Common Ground Rules', in Xaverian Missionaries of the United Kingdom and United States (eds), *Common Ground: Conversations among Humanists and Religious Believers*, 31–4. Coatbridge: Xaverian Missionaries of the United Kingdom and United States.

Smith, A. D. (1986). *The Ethnic Origin of Nations*. Oxford: Blackwell Publishing.

Smith, A. D. (2010). *Nationalism* (2nd Edition). Cambridge: Polity Press.

Smith, J. Z. (1982). *Imagining Religion: From Babylon to Jonestown*. Chicago: University of Chicago Press.

Smith, J. Z. (1993). *Map Is Not Territory: Studies in the History of Religions*. Chicago: Chicago University Press.

Smith, J. Z. (1998). 'Religion, Religions, Religious', in M. Taylor (ed.), *Critical Terms for Religious Studies*, 269–84. Chicago: Chicago University Press.

Smith, J. Z. (2000). 'Classification', in W. Braun and R. T. McCutcheon (eds), *Guide to the Study of Religion*, 35–44. London: Continuum.

Smyth , Sr. I. (2013). 'Reflecting on Our Common Ground', in Xaverian Missionaries of the United Kingdom and United States (eds), *Common Ground: Conversations among Humanists and Religious Believers*, 41–3. Coatbridge: Xaverian Missionaries of the United Kingdom and United States.

Soysal, L., Özçürümez, S., and Diner, C. (2015). 'Turkey in Europe, Europe in Turkey: History, Elites and the Media', in W. Spohn, M. Koenig and W. Knöbl (eds), *Religion and National Identities in an Enlarged Europe*, 96–123. Basingstoke: Palgrave Macmillan.

Spohn, W. (2015). 'The (Fragile) Normalization of German Identity within Europe', in W. Spohn, M. Koenig and W. Knöbl (eds), *Religion and National Identities in an Enlarged Europe*, 17–38. Basingstoke: Palgrave Macmillan.

Stanley, B. (2012). 'Scotland and the World Missionary Conference, Edinburgh 1910', *Scottish Church History Society* 41(1): 113–32.

Stedman, C. (2013). 'Six Tips for Christians on Talking to Non-Christians', in Xaverian Missionaries of the United Kingdom and United States (eds), *Common Ground: Conversations among Humanists and Religious Believers*, 7–10. Coatbridge: Xaverian Missionaries of the United Kingdom and United States.

Stephen, J. (2002). 'The Kirk and the Union, 1706–07: A Reappraisal', *Scottish Church History Society* 31(1): 68–96.

Sutcliffe, S. (2000). 'A Colony of Seekers: Findhorn in the 1990s', *Journal of Contemporary Religion* 15 (2): 215–31.

Sutcliffe, S. (2002). *Children of the New Age: A History of Spiritual Practice*. London: Routledge.

Sutcliffe, S. (2004). 'Unfinished Business – Devolving Scotland/Devolving Religion', in S. Coleman and P. Collins (eds), *Religion, Identity and Change: Perspectives on Religion in Global Transformations*, 96–118. London: Routledge.

Sutcliffe, S. (2010). 'After "the Religion of My Father's: The Quest for Composure in the Post- Presbyterian" Self', in L. Abrams and C. G. Brown (eds), *A History of Everyday Life in Twentieth Century Scotland*, 181–205. Edinburgh: Edinburgh University Press.

Sutcliffe, S. (2016). 'The Problem of "Religions": Teaching against the Grain with New Age Stuff', in C. R. Cotter and D. G. Robertson (eds), *After World Religions: Reconstructing Religious Studies*, 23–36. London: Routledge.

Sutherland, L. T. (2012). 'Tylor and Neo-Tylorian Approaches to the Study of Religion: Re- evaluating an Important Legacy in the Theorisation of Religion'.

Paranthropology: Journal of Anthropological Approaches to the Paranormal 3 (3): 47–57.

Sutherland, L. T. (2017a). 'Theorizing Religion and Nationalism: The Need for Critical Reflexivity in the Analysis of Overlapping Areas of Research', *Implicit Religion* 20 (1): 1–21.

Sutherland, L. T. (2017b). 'One Nation, Many Faiths: Civic-Cultural Nationalism and Religious Pluralism in the Scottish Interfaith Literature', *Implicit Religion* 20 (1): 68–88.

Sutherland, L. T. (2017c). 'Tylor and Debates about the Definition of 'Religion': Then and Now', in P. F. Tremlett, L. T. Sutherland and G. Harvey (eds), *Edward Burnett Tylor, Religion and Culture*, 87–104. Oxford: Bloomsbury.

Sutherland, L. T. (2018a). 'One Nation, Many Faiths: Representations of Religious Pluralism and National Identity in the Scottish Interfaith Literature'. Unpublished PhD thesis. Edinburgh: University of Edinburgh.

Sutherland, L. T. (2018b). 'Unity in Diversity: Representations of Religious Minorities in the Scottish Interfaith Literature', *The Journal of the British Association for the Study of Religion* 20: 145–68.

Sutherland, L. T. (2019). 'Religion and National Identity in Contemporary Scotland: A Theoretical Analysis of Categorisation in the Scholarly and Popular Imagination', *Journal of the Sydney Society for Scottish History* 18: 49–60.

Swamy, M. (2016). *The Problem with Interreligious Dialogue: Plurality, Conflict and Elitism in Hindu-Christian-Muslim Religions*. London: Bloomsbury.

Swindon, P. (2016). 'Hundreds of Floral Tributes Laid Near Spot Where Glasgow Shopkeeper Asad Shah Was Killed', *The Herald*, 28 March.

Taylor, C. (2011a). 'Western Secularity', in C. Calhoun, M. Juergensmeyer and J. van Antwerpen (eds), *Rethinking Secularism*, 31–53. Oxford: Oxford University Press.

Taylor, C. (2011b). 'Why We Need a Radical Redefinition of Secularism', in E. Mendietta and J. Vanantwerpen (eds), *The Power of Religion in the Public Sphere*, 34–59. New York: Colombia University Press.

The University of Edinburgh. (2014). *Faith and Belief in Scotland: A Contemporary Mapping of Attitudes and Provisions in Scotland*. Edinburgh: Crown Copyright 2014.

The Scottish Government. (2011). *Belief in Dialogue: Religion and Belief Relations Good Practice Guide*. Edinburgh: Crown Copyright.

The Scotsman (2011). 'Losing Our Religion to Make Humanist Vows', *The Scotsman* 19 February.

Thomas, T. (1993a). 'Old Allies, New Neighbours: Sikhs in Britain', in G. Parsons (ed.), *The Growth of Religious Diversity: Britain from 1945 Volume I: Traditions*, 205–42. London: Routledge.

Thomas, T. (1993b). 'Hindu Dharma in Dispersion', in G. Parsons (ed.), *The Growth of Religious Diversity: Britain from 1945 Volume I: Traditions*, 173–204. London: Routledge.

Trevor-Roper, H. (1983). 'The Invention of Tradition: The Highland Tradition of Scotland', in E. J. Hobsbawm and T. Ranger (eds), *The Invention of Tradition*, 15–42. Cambridge: Cambridge University Press.

Tweed, T. (2006). *Crossing and Dwelling: A Theory of Religion*. Cambridge: Harvard University Press.

Van den Berghe, P. (1981). *The Ethnic Phenomenon*. New York: Praeger.

Van der Veer, P. (2013). 'Nationalism and Religion', in J. Breuilly (ed.), *The Oxford Handbook of the History of Nationalism*, 655–71. Oxford: Oxford University Press.

Vernon-Yorke, S. (2022). 'Is Interfaith Inclusive of Women? Or in Other Words 'Why Don't You Just Go Get Us Some Tea', Paper Presented at the Annual Conference of the British Association for the Study of Religion, Milton Keynes, 30 August.

Watson, F. (1998). 'The Enigmatic Lion: Scotland, Kingship and National Identity in the Wars of Independence', in D. Broun, R. J. Finlay, M. Lynch (eds), *Image and Identity: The Making and Re-Making of Scotland through the Ages*, 18–37. Edinburgh: John Donald Publishers.

Weber, M. (2002 [1904]). *The Protestant Ethic and the Spirit of Capitalism*. London: Penguin.

Widiyanto, A. (2020). 'Nation Building', in H. Gustafson (ed.), *Interreligious Studies: Dispatches from an Emerging Field*, 242–8. Waco: Baylor University Press.

Wiebe, D. (1999). *The Politics of Religious Studies*. New York: Palgrave.

Wolf, G. (2006). 'The Church of the Non-Believers', in *Wired* https://www.wired.com/2006/11/atheism/ (last accessed 14 August 2024).

Wolffe, J. (1993). 'Fragmented Universality: Islam and Muslims', in G. Parsons (ed.), *The Growth of Religious Diversity: Britain from 1945 Volume I: Traditions*, 133–72. London: Routledge.

Womack, D. F. (2018). 'From the History of Religions to Interfaith Studies: A Theological Educator's Exercise in Adaptation', in E. Patel, J. H. Peace and N. J. Silverman (eds), *Interreligious/Interfaith Studies: Defining A New Field*, 16–25. Boston: Beacon Press.

Womack, D. F. (2020). 'Gender and Christian-Muslim Relations', in H. Gustafson (ed.), *Interreligious Studies: Dispatches from an Emerging Field*, 263–8. Waco: Baylor University Press.

Xaverian Missionaries of the United Kingdom and the United States. (2013). 'Introduction', in Xaverian Missionaries of the United Kingdom and United States (eds), *Common Ground: Conversations among Humanists and Religious Believers*, 3–6. Coatbridge: Xaverian Missionaries of the United Kingdom and United States.

Young, J. R. (1998). 'The Scottish Parliament and National Identity from Union of the Crowns to the Union of Parliaments, 1603–1707', in D. Broun, R. J. Finlay, M. Lynch (eds), *Image and Identity: The Making and Re-Making of Scotland Through the Ages*, 105–42. Edinburgh: John Donald Publishers.

Zenk, T. (2013). 'New Atheism', in S. Bullivant and M. Ruse (eds), *The Oxford Handbook of Atheism*, 245–60. Oxford: Oxford University Press.

Web links

Action of Churches Together Scotland (ACTS) – http://www.acts-scotland.org/about-us/about-acts. (last accessed 31 January 2024).

BBC News on Religious Leaders Forum meeting – https://www.bbc.co.uk/news/uk-scotland-scotland-politics-26903855. (last accessed 15 August 2024).

BBC News on 2011 Scottish Parliamentary election – https://www.bbc.co.uk/news/special/election2011/overview/html/scotland.stm. (last accessed 24 January 2024).

BBC News on 2014 Scottish independence referendum results – https://www.bbc.co.uk/news/events/scotland-decides/results. (last accessed 24 January 2024).

BBC News on 2015 UK General Election results – http://www.bbc.co.uk/news/election/2015/results. (last accessed 24 January 2024).

BBC News on 2016 UK EU membership referendum – https://www.bbc.com/news/politics/eu_referendum/results. (last accessed 31 January 2024).

Census information on Wales – https://www.gov.wales/ethnic-group-national-identity-language-and-religion-wales-census-2021-html. (last accessed 27 January 2024).

Edinburgh Inter Faith Association (EIFA) – https://www.edinburghinterfaith.com/about. (last accessed 31 January 2024).

Hindu Temple of Scotland (Rutherglen) – https://hindutempleofscotland.org/about-temple. (last accessed 31 January 2024).

Indian Census – https://www.census2011.co.in/religion.php. (last accessed 26 January 2024).

Interfaith America – https://www.interfaithamerica.org/. (last accessed 15 August 2024).

Interfaith Network for the United Kingdom - https://www.interfaith.org.uk. (last accessed 23 January 2024).

Interfaith Scotland (IFS) – https://interfaithscotland.org. (last accessed 24 May 2024)

IFS YouTube channel – https://www.youtube.com/@InterfaithScotland/videos. (last accessed 23 January 2024).

Interfaith Wales – https://interfaithwales.co.uk/. (last accessed 27 January 2024).

Islamic Tartan – https://islamictartan.com/. (last accessed 01 January 2024).

Muslim Council of Scotland – https://mcscotland.org/. (last accessed 31 January 2024).

Northern Ireland Interfaith Forum – http://interfaithni.org/. (last accessed 27 January 2024).

Office for National Statistics (ONS) for England and Wales – (https://www.ons.gov.uk/peoplepopulationandcommunity/culturalidentity/religion/bulletins/religionenglandandwales/census2021#religion-in-england-and-wales. (last accessed 14 August 2024).

Pew Research on religious affiliation in the USA – https://www.pewresearch.org/religion/religious-landscape-study. (last accessed 28 January 2024).

Scottish 2022 Census releases on religion, ethnic groups, language and national identity – https://www.scotlandscensus.gov.uk/news-and-events/scotland-s-cen

sus-religion-ethnic-group-language-and-national-identity-results/. (last accessed 15 August 2024).

Scottish Inter Faith Week (SIFW) – https://scottishinterfaithweek.org/. (last accessed 23 January 2024).

Scottish Pagan Federation (SPF) – https://scottishpf.org. (last accessed 31 January 2024).

Scottish Register of Tartans – https://www.tartanregister.gov.uk/index. (last accessed 31 January 2024).

UN Interfaith Harmony Week – https://www.un.org/en/observances/interfaith-harmony-week. (last accessed 08 May 2024).

World Council of Churches (WCC) – https://www.oikoumene.org/about-the-wcc. (last accessed 31 January 2024).

Index

www.ingramcontent.com/pod-product-compliance
Ingram Content Group UK Ltd.
Pitfield, Milton Keynes, MK11 3LW, UK
UKHW020928220625

459955UK00001B/13